Superstitions

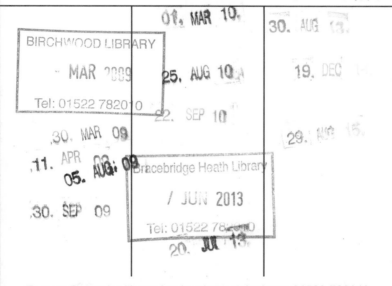

Superstitions

beliefs, rituals and magic

Xavier Waterkeyn

NH
NEW
HOLLAND

First published in Australia in 2008 by
New Holland Publishers (Australia) Pty Ltd
Sydney • Auckland • London • Cape Town
www.newholland.com.au

1/66 Gibbes Street Chatswood NSW 2067 Australia
218 Lake Road Northcote Auckland New Zealand
86 Edgware Road London W2 2EA United Kingdom
80 McKenzie Street Cape Town 8001 South Africa

National Library of Australia Cataloguing-in-Publication Data:

Author: Waterkeyn, Xavier.
Title: Superstitions : beliefs, rituals and myth / Xavier Waterkeyn.

ISBN: 9781741106619 (hbk.)
Subjects: Superstition.
          Rites and ceremonies.
          Magic.
          Divination.
Dewey Number: 001.96

Publisher: Fiona Schultz
Publishing manager: Lliane Clarke
Project editor: Diane Jardine
Editor: Kirsten Chapman
Designer: Tania Gomes
Production manager: Linda Bottari
Printer: Imago

Disclaimer

The techniques and methods described within this book are for entertainment and information purposes only.
The author and publisher make no claims about the validity of the various signs and portents or the efficacy or
non-efficacy of the sundry treatments, methods, charms, hexes or spells described herein.

Readers are advised that they use magic at their own risk and that forms of witchcraft, sorcery and folk
magic should only be employed by qualified or licensed shamans, sorcerers, sorceresses, warlocks, witches and
thaumaturges.

Picture credits

Getty Images: Pages 12–13, 18, 20, 22, 28, 31, 33, 35, 37, 41, 42, 44 background, 49, 56, 58, 60, 62, 64, 69, 71,
73, 74, 76–7, 95 (left), 100, 105, 107, 108, 120, 124–25, 142, 144, 150, 168, 173, 176, 180, 192, 194–95, 198, 202,
203, 205, 206, 213, 214, 216, 218, 219, 222, 230, 232, 258
iStock: Pages 8, 9, 11, 24, 25, 26, 27, 29, 45, 46, 47, 50, 55, 59, 66–7, 68, 75, 81, 82, 83, 84, 85, 89, 91, 95 (right),
97, 102, 103, 104, 109, 111, 115, 116, 117, 122-123, 132, 133, 134, 135, 139, 140, 143, 146, 147, 148, 149, 151, 152,
154, 159, 160, 161, 162, 163, 164, 165, 166, 167, 169, 174, 179, 182, 183, 185, 189, 190–91, 193, 199, 200, 204, 211,
217, 220, 221, 227, 228, 230, 232, 235, 236, 237, 238, 244, 247, 252, 256, 257, 258, 263, 264, 267

contents

introduction

Before the modern age of science, the world was slightly more confusing and mysterious. People then, as now, were interested in health, relationships, safety and money—not necessarily in that order—and they wanted life to be as easy, or at least as stress-free, as possible. Consider, for example, sickness and disease, which even today take up a lot of people's attention and time.

In the absence of germ theory or scientific explanations as to why people become sick, the business of medicine was largely a matter of guesswork and leeches. Then, as now, the secret—which some doctors are still reluctant to tell you—is that most things get better on their own. However, in the lag-time between falling sick and recovering, people will often try anything to get better. If you do something, *anything*, and you recover you're likely to think that this was because you tied a frog to your wart or whatever else the 'cure' was. There is one documented case from England, for example, in which the Black Death wiped out almost an entire village. Only one old lady survived. She attributed it to drinking a large quantity of pig fat, so for a time, lard was at a premium.

In more recent centuries, science has given us a lot of things, but what it has given us most is a whole new set of explanations as to how and why things happen. However, long before science there was organised religion, and long, long before organised religion, there was disorganised religion—highly disorganised. Without a scientific explanation for why things happen in the world, it was natural for our ancestors to make up explanations, and the most reasonable explanation often seemed to be that the world was inhabited or controlled by potent beings, who caused events by working through a mysterious power called magic.

These beings were all different. They could be easily offended, they had tempers, they were moody and they were frequently inconsistent, unpredictable and irrational. In fact, they were just like people, only more so. Like people they'd occasionally give off signs that they were displeased or about to lose their temper—and, just like people, you could learn to read these signs. You could get on their good side if you made the right noises and gestures or, if all else failed, you could bribe them. It was important to know the ways of these beings, because they were powerful enough to move the ocean and the sky, to make crops grow or wither, to make your life heavenly if they liked you, hellish if they didn't—or at the very least a purgatory of petty irritations.

It must have been marvellous living in the world when almost everyone thought that it was full of gods and goddesses, devas and dervishes, faeries, genies, naiads, dryads, nymphs, satyrs, ghosts and spirits of every size, shape, colour and mood. It must have been horrible too. It must have been like living with giant, petulant toddlers, demanding your attention with their obsessions and compulsions, and throwing tantrums left, right and centre that rocked, heaven, earth and the underworld.

These spirits would have been seen as the cause of the 'good luck' and 'bad luck' in the world. You would have to be careful to perform the right rituals or act in a way that pleased benevolent spirits in order to receive good luck. However, if you invited the attention of a bad spirit or offended an ordinarily benign superbeing, bad luck is how they would let you know about it. It's easy to understand superstitions and superstitious thinking in this light. It may be irrational, but it's all very logical.

Types of superstitions

Signs, portents and prophecies: all those little clues that the gods are about to have a hissy fit or, on a more positive note, that they want to tell you or give you something for your benefit.

Protection: the magical armour that can keep you safe from bad magic—according to whatever rules the local spirits operate under—often in the form of a spell, charm or talisman.

Contagion: the magical contamination that happens when you acquire an object that gives you some of the spirit's power, through association, connection or reflected glory.

Seduction: certain rituals will earn you the favour of the spirits.

Evasion: magical gestures will help you avoid offending the gods in the first place.

Appeasement: folklore has discovered a wide range of bribes to placate the spirits if you—foolish and ignorant mortal that you are—clumsily commit a breach of etiquette or transgression. The appeasement may take the form of a sacrifice, ritual, spell or whatever else might settle a frayed supernatural temper. As you'll soon find out, there are innumerable beliefs about what works and what doesn't.

Nullification: when all else fails you could try a magical formula that would defuse a situation or render the spirit powerless.

superstition and religion

Depending on how you look at things, it's not a great leap from superstition and magic to religion. Depending on your level of cynicism, you could see religion as what happens to folk beliefs when the accountants become involved. As religions are formed, then compete for believers, some succeed and some fail. It's a historical fact that many of the superstitions we hold today are the remnants of otherwise dead religions and myths. In fact the word 'superstition' comes from the Latin word *superstites*, meaning 'the warriors who survived a battle'.

'Old wives' kept many of these beliefs alive whether they were accurate or not—and some beliefs do indeed still work. In the meantime we can suppose that, at the other end of the scale, young husbands tended to concentrate on mainstream religion—as well as raping, pillaging and conquering.

Often, the only thing that survives of a religion and its beliefs is the 'operating manual'. Most ancient religion was handed down orally or—if it was ever written at all—it was in books so secret that only the most initiated were allowed to look at them. In those cases—even if the books later became public—they could be destroyed by followers of rival religions or even of the same religion, but with slight variations. Over the ages the message could become mixed up or lost, until all we are left with is the 'what to do' or 'what not to do'. So whenever you hear a superstition that begins, 'Never do …' and you ask why, most of the time you won't receive a real explanation. The original rationale is long forgotten and all you're ever told is that doing whatever it is will bring you bad luck or, worse, eternal punishment.

superstition today

We're now living in the so-called age of science and are supposed to be past believing in such nonsense, yet superstition and old wives' tales continue to surround us and affect the way we behave and live. Why?

Well, for starters, a lot of people don't understand science, so psychologically speaking it might as well be magic.

And science, even by its own admission, doesn't know everything.

Furthermore, science has demonstrated that there is some truth to many superstitions. Putting mouldy bread on a sore can work, if the mould is penicillium.

Our ancestors may have been ignorant in many ways, but they had skills and knowledge that we've now forgotten. They survived long enough, under what were often horrible conditions, to produce us, and their half-truths have often been more enduring than some of the raw facts.

It's also a good idea not to underestimate the power of belief and ritual. The young Irish woman who writes her prospective lover's name on a potato and buries it during a full moon may feel more positive about her chances. Her attitude might change; she might become more bold and daring. Suddenly the young man she's interested in might become more interested in her. Next thing you know, they're married and there's a baby on the way—although it doesn't have to be in that order.

As you can see, the lines between superstition, religion and magic aren't well defined, nor can they be. Exploring beliefs, rituals and practices through the ages provides us with fascinating insights into the cultures and societies that gave birth to them, and they tell us a lot about ourselves too. You can also have a bit of fun trying out the spells that ward off sickness, lovelessness, danger and poverty. In most cases this sort of stuff is perfectly harmless—and who knows, they *might* work. We shouldn't be so arrogant as to think that we know everything about how the universe functions or about which actions lead to which outcomes. If Chaos Theory, which is scientifically accepted, can suggest that a butterfly flapping its wings in the Amazon could create an atmospheric disturbance that leads to a hurricane, or if equally respected Quantum theory can tell us with a straight face that Schrödinger's cat may live or die—not only depending on the random decay of an atom but also on the expectations of the scientists conducting the experiment—then science is hardly in a position to make fun of people who make strange signs to ward off the evil eye or who carry around a rabbit's foot for good luck.

Unfortunately, for many superstitions, as I've said, the reasons behind them are lost to history and only in a very few cases do we know from where or from when a superstition came. Even if our ancestors didn't know why some things worked, they reasoned that if they did work, that was good enough. I believe that if it works for you too, then do it. You can always explore the 'why' later or invent a story to help explain it.

And that's maybe the most important reason that superstition has survived and will continue to survive.

Superstition is glamorous. Magic is fun. Human beings love telling stories, and for many people the stories that magic, superstition and folk beliefs give us are more valuable than the dry-as-dust explanations of scientists. I'm a big fan of science, but perhaps if scientists spoke more to our hearts with the poetry of magic than just to our minds with the cold tongue of rationality, then superstition wouldn't have the hold it has. Our ancestors understood the value of a good story, even if it wasn't true—and there's still a part of us that wants them to be true.

Important note:

Cynics among you may see little difference between religion and superstition. Since it's impossible to talk about superstition in any really engaging way without mentioning religion, I'm not even going to try to separate the two.

I've written this book from a neutral, humanistic point of view and have no intention of deliberately offending the sensitive or politically correct, nor am I interested in attacking anyone's strongly held beliefs or convictions.

Whether you live in a high-tech society and go to a church, mosque, temple or synagogue, or whether you live in a jungle and kneel before a wooden statue that you smear with chicken blood— for the purposes of this book and, to be honest, all purposes really—it's all the same to me. For me, and I suspect for you, it's much more interesting to look at 'superstitions' in comparison to 'mainstream beliefs' of all denominations, in all their richness and diversity and to examine them from as many different points of view as possible, than just to give you a list of 'good' and 'bad' luck signs and rituals without some ethnic or historical context.

One person's 'superstition' may be another person's 'fact', and to make this book a lot more entertaining and fun to read, I've assumed—perhaps with the occasional lapse—that all the superstitions or beliefs I've mentioned in this book are, or were at one point, real and true to somebody—although of course both reality and truth, as always, are up for grabs.

Xavier Waterkeyn

part one: People

In the fifth century BCE the Greek philosopher Protagoras wrote that 'Man is the measure of all things: of things which are, that they are and of things which are not, that they are not.' Protagoras had a point. People in general tend to use themselves as a benchmark for understanding reality. Since superstitious thinking is one way of understanding reality, it's hardly surprising that the vast majority of superstitions are about people—what they do and how they interact with the world. As people are first and formost interested in other people—which is why gossip magazines outsell science magazines—it stands to reason that that there are a lot of superstitions about relationships too.

the human body

The Human Body

The human body is an amazing thing and, unless something goes wrong, we tend to take it for granted. Even though life is still a sexually transmitted disease with 100 per cent mortality, in the days before sewerage—or even the rule of law—disease and death were much more serious and common than they are today.

In the days when most medicine consisted of was herbs, incantations and the judicious application of leeches, treatment was a pretty hit-and-miss affair. Surgery was little short of butchery with heavy doses of alcohol or, if you were lucky, opium as an anaesthetic. So it made sense to employ whatever magic you could to help things along a little.

Even when healthy, the body was rich with meaning. Unless you were a slave, for much of history the body was one of the few possessions that was truly yours. You are in intimate contact with your body every moment of your life. No wonder then that it could be both a target for magic as well as being magical in itself, and the subject of so much superstition.

Folklorically any part of the body that was a hole, or at least hole-like, was a potential entry point for evil spirits or for bad luck. Gemstones set in jewellery were common devices to protect the orifices.

Bones

The superstition that men have one less rib than women comes from the biblical myth that God fashioned Eve out of Adam's rib. This is in itself a mistranslation. The original Hebrew word more accurately translates as 'side', the implication being that men and women are two sides of the same original conception. Nevertheless the legend stuck and for centuries the fear of being accused of practicing necromancy prevented people from doing basic anatomical dissections which eventually determined that men and women have indeed the same number of ribs—twelve.

Brain

For thousands of years, from the time of the ancient Egyptians, the brain was supposed to be nothing more than the site of sperm production. The Egyptians removed the brains of the dead through their noses and filled the cavity with resin, as they didn't believe the brain had any important use in the afterlife. Even in the Renaissance, Leonardo da Vinci, who'd done a lot of anatomical dissections and perhaps should have known better, drew mythical tubes connecting the brain to the penis—tubes through which the sperm was meant to travel. However, some cultures did associate the brain with consciousness. There were ancient surgical operations called trepanations, which involved cutting out circular pieces from the skull to let out demons who were possessing the bodies of patients.

clitoris

Female sexuality is, for reasons unknown, incredibly threatening to some men, and superstitions about it abound. The general response is to control women as much as possible.

The Kikuyu of Mathare Valley, Kenya—among other peoples—still practice female circumcision which, in its extreme form, leads to the excision of the labia and the clitoris. This is to satisfy the myth that sex for women is for reproduction and not for pleasure. The operation severely limits the pleasure that women can derive from sex, although it's difficult to gauge whether the procedure really does what it's intended to do—limit the female's sex drive.

Sigmund Freud was responsible for the modern superstition that 'clitoral orgasms'—which are in fact the principle ones that women can have—were the result of 'infantile sexuality'. In his mind, the only proper ones to have were vaginal. Pity then, that vaginal orgasms don't actually exist.

Ears (and cheeks)

Itching ears mean that someone is talking about you. If it is your left ear or cheek that itches, someone is telling lies about you; if the itch is on the right, someone is singing your praises.

People with thin, angular ears have bad tempers. People with long or prominent ears have a gift for music and the bigger the earlobes, the smarter you are. In the East in particular, having large earlobes is a sign of wisdom—statues of the Buddha and other sages are always depicted with huge earlobes.

On a related note, there is a tradition that ear-piercing began (at least among the gypsies) out of a belief that it would improve the eyesight, although the Bible associates the practice with slavery.

Eyebrows and eyelashes

One tradition has it that you should:
Trust not the man whose eyebrows meet,
For in his heart you'll find deceit.

Eyebrows that meet in the middle were also supposed to be one of the marks of a vampire or a werewolf.

Eyelashes tend to be more innocent. You can make wishes on eyelashes. If you find one on your cheek, you should put it on the back of your right hand, make a wish, then shake your hand over your left shoulder. Alternatively, you can put it on the tip of your finger or the end of your nose, then make a wish and blow. If the eyelash flies off, your wish will come true. You are allowed a maximum of three blows or three attempts.

Eyes

The 'windows to the soul' are rich with meaning. This is unsurprising, given that human beings—like other primates—have allocated a great deal of brainpower to processing visual data. If we were bats, perhaps ears would have the same level of importance to us. Ask anyone which sense they'd rather do without and, almost universally, they would sacrifice hearing, touch, smell and taste before losing their vision. Given the great natural power of eyes, we ascribe even more power to them through magic.

There is a common superstition in many cultures that giving a statue eyes brings it to life, and some Hindus prick the eyes of a statue with a golden needle to consecrate it. The Theravada Buddhists of Ceylon have the *netra pinkama*, an eye ceremony that takes the belief even further. The ceremony takes place in a closed temple and only after a considerable amount of ritual purification. The craftsman who paints the eyes cannot look at a statue directly and has to paint the eyes in with his back turned. He looks into a mirror and holds the brush over his shoulder. Once he completes the painting, the craftsman's gaze becomes dangerous. He's blindfolded, let out of the temple and led to another object. The blindfold is removed and the craftsman gazes upon the object, thus transferring the magic to it. Then the craftsman destroys the object with a sword. This apparently finally releases whatever dangerous energy the craftsman was holding in his eyes.

One old wives' tale we are told as children is that if we cross our eyes, they'll stay that way. The more developed version of this is that you shouldn't pull faces, because if the wind changes, your features will freeze in that position forever.

Evil eye

It doesn't take much of a stretch from the idea that eyes have power to the idea that some might use that power malevolently. People from all times and places have blamed witches, witchdoctors, sorcerers and other magical individuals for all sorts of misfortunes. The magician has only to look at you the 'wrong way' to give you no end of grief.

A magical person may not even know that they possess black magic. So you're immediately under suspicion if you have: cross eyes, a squint, a nervous tick, eyes that are different colours or have a rare condition that make your pupils oddly shaped.

Here's just a small list of nasties attributed to the evil eye:

- death of farm animals or crops
- birth defects in animals or human
- cows unable to give milk
- souring of milk or milk that can't be churned into butter
- sickness and disease
- unusual, premature death
- any run of bad luck, really.

Many methods of avoiding the evil eye involve reducing the chances that anyone might become jealous of you. So people would deliberately stain clothes or mark possession with minor defects. Sometimes objects would be deliberately made with magical signs or incantations to protect them.

It also stands to reason then that there are whole cottage industries in magic dedicated to warding off the evil eye and its effects. The most common device is a magical talisman, operating as a sort of continuous shield. These talismans are often themselves in the shape of an eye, the principle of fighting fire with fire. Fishing boats often have eyes painted on their bows and, all through the Middle East, it's easy to buy lucky charms in the form of blue beads or blue eyes to avert the evil eye. Various plants were efficacious against the evil eye, including holly, mistletoe, rue and oaks and their acorns. Amber was supposedly good too, as were red threads knotted nine times.

Horns were weapons you could use against the evil eye, whether they were real, depicted in drawings and paintings, or even purely symbolic, as when people make the sign of the horn with their hand to protect themselves from bad magic. To make the sign of the horn, hold your middle two fingers down, while extending the index and little fingers in the direction that you think the witchcraft is coming from, or even pointing upwards to heaven. In Mediterranean countries you should always use this gesture with care. In the wrong context it's really rude, and in Italy you can use it to imply that the man that you use it towards is a *corunuto* (a cuckold), which is generally considered insulting no matter where you're from.

In case you think that only the ignorant and superstitious have a problem with the evil eye, remember that even 'educated' and 'sophisticated' people think that it's rude to stare. This may be a remnant of the evil eye superstition or it may go back to our primate origins. If you ever want to upset a chimpanzee in a zoo, just stare into its eyes for long enough. Among the great apes, staring is universally understood as a challenge to dominance.

Witnessing things inappropriately can also get you into trouble, as happened to the hunter Actaeon. The goddess Artemis found he was peeping at her while she was bathing. She turned him into a stag. As he tried to escape, his own hounds hunted him down, tore him apart and devoured him. Even innocent gazing has its dangers—God told Moses that no one could look upon His face and live. Justice is blind so that she not be distracted when she lays down her judgement.

Itching eyes are signs that you're going to see something important. An itching left eye is a bad omen, an itching right eye means you're in for something pleasant.

Although eyes usually accurately reflect emotion, the most common superstition is that you can 'tell someone is lying' by looking into their eyes. To some extent this is true, but it probably works best with amateur liars—more experienced liars learn how to withstand the confrontation of somebody staring at them.

Hair

S amson was a Nazirite, a member of a particular Jewish sect. He'd made a vow to God not to cut his hair, and God bestowed on him great strength. When the treacherous Delilah cut Samson's hair while he slept, God deserted him. So strictly speaking, Samson's strength came from God, and the loss of strength was God's reaction to Sampson's breach of contract. Nevertheless, in Judeo-Christian tradition, the biblical story of Samson and Delilah demonstrates an ancient belief that power resides in hair. This belief ranges far and wide, from

Aztec priests to the Masai clan of the El Kiboron in Uganda. The penalties for cutting hair are the usual—drought, floods and impotence, to name a few.

Traditional Muslim women never cut their hair, nor do Sikh men, who wear their long hair under their distinctive turbans. Under British law, Sikh men don't have to wear motorcycle helmets, because they can't fit them over their turbans.

Hindu men may sport long dreadlocks as a sign of holiness, and Rastafarians aren't known to visit barbers often either. There's a Jewish injunction against shaving the 'four corners of the head', which is why Jewish boys don't have their hair cut until their third birthday and orthodox Jews have beards and those long, tasselled sideburns called *peyes*. Some Muslim men grow a single lock of hair, because they believe that, at the hour of their death, they'll be drawn up to heaven by their hair.

Hindu men sport dreadlocks as a sign of holiness.

Even today many athletes don't cut their hair while they're on a winning streak because they don't want to risk their luck. And it's supposed to be bad luck to comb your hair after dark.

Long hair isn't only a sign of holiness or piety or success. The power of witches was also said to reside in the hair, which is why witches' heads would be shaved before they were executed.

People who actually did cut their hair—and nails—would dispose of it carefully, so that no witch, sorcerer or witchdoctor could steal it and use it in a spell against them. This was widely practiced, from medieval Europeans to the Maori of New Zealand. Some people even burn their hair and nail clippings to stop them falling into the wrong hands.

Cutting hair on Good Friday or on any Sunday is considered bad luck: 'Best never be born than on Sunday shorn.' If you do, the Devil will be with you all week.

There are lots of theories about the hair equals power equation. The ancient Greeks and the Punjabis of India alike believe that semen originated and was stored in the head, and that hair was potent by association. There's also a European superstition that a man with hairy legs will always find a bride.

In spite of the almost universal belief that hair means something, there's considerable inconsistency as to what it does mean. The Punjabi demand that men shave their heads in times of mourning to 'purify themselves', but that women shouldn't cut their hair. Women should stay polluted to add to the purity of the men. (Contrast this with Catholic nuns, who often had their hair cut prior to taking the veil.)

Again, among the Punjabi it's considered bad luck for women to wash their hair on Thursday or a Sunday. Doing so would cause the household to lose money. Tuesdays were particularly bad, if a woman washed her hair and allowed the wet hair to drip on a child, because she would kill it, and the child would be reborn in her womb. If she washed her hair on the day of a dead man's funeral, she'd be fated to marry the man in a future incarnation.

The hairline often grows to a point in the centre of the upper forehead. Although this pattern is more common in men, it does occur in women too. In women, having such hair means that the woman will live to be a widow, hence the term 'widow's peak', which is used nowadays whether or not the possessor is a woman or a man.

Curly hair is considered lucky. If you're not naturally endowed, one theory is that you can make it curly by eating bread crusts, or, as one author has remarked, carrots, spinach, prunes or anything else that your mother wants you to eat.

Rain, brushing your hair one hundred times a day, and cutting your hair frequently is all supposed to encourage your hair to grow. Sage tea has also been recommended to treat baldness.

If a hairpin falls from your face, a friend is thinking of you, and if you find a fallen hairpin, you should pick it up and hang it from a hook for good luck.

Eating a raven's egg will make your hair go black, but if you have a fright or shock, your hair will turn white overnight.

Hands and fingers

There's a whole esoteric practice called palmistry devoted to the art of determining a person's fate through the features of the hands. Palmistry's origins go back at least to the ancient Greeks. According to legend, at the same time that the goddess Rhea gave birth to Zeus, she gave rise to finger spirits, and fingers were then assigned to certain gods. The index finger belonged to Zeus (Jupiter in Roman mythology), the middle finger to Chronos (Saturn), the ring finger to Aphrodite (Venus) and the little finger to Hermes (Mercury).

The Romans described the index finger as *salutaris* (healthy and useful) and the middle finger as *impudicus* or *infamis* (shameful or disgraceful)—and this is the origin of the rude sign of 'giving someone the finger'.

The traditions of the ring finger are particularly interesting, considering that this is anatomically the weakest finger. It's supposed to be a healing finger, and if you stroke an injury with it, the pain will go away and the wound will heal more rapidly. Because the Romans continued the Greek tradition of linking the third finger to the heart, they called it the *anularis* (the ring finger). Wedding rings go on this finger as a symbolic bondage of the heart with love, using the most durable and warm of all the metals, gold.

A crooked little finger denotes that the person who has it will die rich.

An itchy right palm means money's on the way in, an itchy left palm and money is on its way out, but you can rub your left palm on some wood to take the charm away and keep your money.

Moist hands are said to be a sign of an amorous nature. People who have cold hands are said to be affectionate and have warm hearts, but it doesn't follow that people with warm hands are cold and unemotional.

The habit of shaking hands arose in more violent times as a short-handed way of saying, 'See how much I trust you?

Handshaking, originally a sign of trust between potential combatants, has evolved into a sign of agreement. US President George W. Bush and Iraqi President Jalal Talabani.

I'm unarmed.' The right hand was the hand that held the weapon, the 'strong hand', the 'right' hand to use. Because of the myriad superstitions about the left, many people still think that it's bad luck to shake hands with the left or 'sinister hand', although some more charitable people view the left hand as the 'hand of the heart' and that a left hand shake is emotionally warmer.

Crossing hands can be risky. If two people are reaching for the same thing and their arms cross, there'll be a quarrel, but if four people stand in a circle and all shake hands with arms crossed at the same time, there'll be a wedding.

From the Middle Ages, and well into the nineteenth century, people would cut off the left hand of a hanged man and pickle and dry it. The right hand was also good if the man had been hanged for murder and the right hand was the one that had done the deed. The pickled dried hand was called a 'Hand of Glory', and it was highly prized. A candle would be made from the body fat of the dead man, combined with new, unused or 'virgin' beeswax and sesame oil. The candle would then be placed in the severed hand, as if the hand were a candlestick, then lit. Thieves prized such hands, because they were of particular use in their profession. The hands were said to give light only to their holder and keep the thief in darkness to other observers. The hand was said to unlock any door it came across, and if by chance someone were to find you in the middle of the job, the hand would render them motionless for a time, allowing you to escape.

Left hand

Left hands and left-handedness have received a lot of bad press over the centuries. Priests bless with the right hand and offer sacrifices to the gods with the right hand. The left hand is the bad hand, the wrong hand, the hand of the Devil. The word sinister is Latin for 'left'.

Many cultures require that you wipe yourself with the left hand after defecating and religious law certainly requires this of Muslims. Thus, under Shariah law, when a thief has his right hand cut off he is not only mutilated, he now has to use the same hand for both toilet and table. The convicted thief is therefore forever denied the pleasure of eating.

Women in many cultures dare not use the left hand in cooking for fear that they risk accusations of sorcery. Among the Nuer of the southern Sudan and western Ethiopia, only the right half of a sacrificial fruit or animal could be eaten. In some cases the Nuer would immobilise their left hand until it atrophied. The Toradja of central Celebes (Sulawesi), Indonesia, use only their left hand when making gardens for the dead.

Spells cast with the left hand are often evil, and leftward omens, like the flight of birds from the right to the left, are similarly nasty.

Fortunately, the Chinese have a more equal view of things. To them, the left is the side of yang, heat, light, summer and sky. The right is yin, cold, dark, winter and earth. It's only through the correct dynamic balance of yang and yin that the universe is whole and complete.

Equally fortunate, in baseball, it's considered very lucky for a team to have a left-handed pitcher.

Heart

Before the modern discovery that human consciousness was more associated with the brain, most people believed that the heart was the seat of the human soul. As such the ancient Egyptians took special care over the preservation of the heart and routinely removed it from corpses for mummification. The heart would be stored separately in a canopic jar.

The human heart played an important role in the religious lives of the Central American civilisations. Over the centuries perhaps millions of prisoners of war died on altars at the tops of pyramids dedicated to the gods. The most famous examples are the Mexica (Aztec) sacrifices to Huitzilopochtli (Hummingbird of the South), the sun god, who demanded to be fed human hearts so that he'd keep the sun rising and setting in the sky. It was important that the priests would cut open the sacrificial victims' chests with knives made of black volcanic glass (obsidian), and that the hearts should be removed from the bodies while they were still beating. One probably inflated Aztec account of the reconsecration of the Great Pyramid of Tenochtitlan in 1487 states that the Aztecs tore out the hearts of 80,400 prisoners over four days.

As to other 'matters of the heart' it may come as a surprise to many, but the idea of romantic love is not universal and until relatively recent times it was a foreign concept to many cultures. Western civilisation derives its ideas about love from the Greeks, through the Romans and then to the cultures that sprang from them. The modern phenomenon of romantic love as an ideal of emotional fulfilment came out of the middle ages. The heart was central to the imagery of this idea, probably because of the way that the heart races in the presence of the beloved. It follows then, that love's magic involves heart imagery

Temple of Eagle and Jaguar Warriors, Malinalco, Mexico.
The Aztec are famous for tearing out the hearts of their sacrificial victims.

and the colour red or pink. By extension then, red roses become a symbol for love. Passion too, is in the blood although the connection between blood and the heart as its pump wasn't formally recognised in the West until William Harvey published his findings in 1628, but the Arabs had known this since the mid 1200s and the Chinese had discovered this at least as early as the second century BCE. The Chinese character for love has the symbol for 'heart' or 'spirit' right at its centre. Without the heart element, the character's meaning is 'friendship'.

The Akan of Ghana and the Gyaman of Cote d'Ivoire in West Africa have a completely different symbol for love. The *Osram Ne Nsoroma* Adinkra symbol depicts a star representing a woman, next to a crescent moon that represents the man.

joints

There is a widely held belief among arthritis sufferers that their joints will flare up at the sign of bad weather or an approaching storm. The only things that could account for this are an increase in humidity and a drop in barometric pressure. However, arthritis suffers take showers, catch planes and are constantly exposed to all sorts of other fluctuations in humidity and air pressure without any ill effects, suggesting that this belief is more in people's heads than in their joints. Temperature is a greater comfort factor, but even people without arthritis have trouble moving their limbs in the cold, especially if they've been immobile.

mouths (and yawning)

Many have perceived yawning as risky, because evil spirits might take the opportunity to enter the body through a wide-open mouth. Even Satan himself could enter. To shield yourself, cover your mouth with the back of your hand. A more prosaic explanation for covering your mouth while you yawn is that when city streets were a lot dirtier than they are today, there were a lot more flies about and covering your mouth stopped them flying in. Some Amerindians have the tradition that the yawn is a sign of death, and to avoid it you had to snap your fingers for luck.

The mouth is a favourite part of the body for judging character, and many people believe to some extent that the set of the mouth determines basic personality traits. Traditionally, pouting

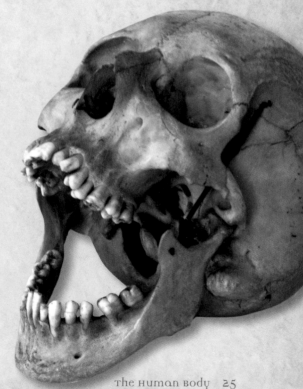

mouths indicate petulance; down-turned mouths = bad-tempers; thin mouths = pettiness and overly thick lips = too great an attachment to sensuality. Tradition aside, it's not too great an effort for the 'magical thinking gland' in your head to derive any number of similar beliefs for yourself.

Inside your mouth, having widely-spaced teeth is a sign of good luck. This makes sense as it comes from a time when dental hygiene wasn't what it is now and gaps between teeth made them easier to clean. It's especially good luck to have a space between your front teeth. It means you'll be rich. It certainly seems to have worked for model and actress Lauren Hutton and for the singer Madonna.

On a final oral note, it's said that if you lie, blisters will form on your tongue.

The tooth fairy

The charming myth of the tooth fairy is an almost textbook example of how a superstition comes into being and sticks around because it appeals to people's imaginations.

The ancient tradition was to bury baby teeth so that witches, sorcerers and the usual assortment of black magicians couldn't use the tooth to perform evil on the child. Then, sometime in the seventeenth century, there arose in France the tradition of the tooth mouse, who transformed itself into a fairy to help torment an evil king by knocking out all his teeth. This became the fairy tale of **'La Bonne Petite Souris'** (The Good Little Girl Mouse).

This story caught on in the early history of Anglo/French North America, and by 1949 author Lee Rothgow had written **The Tooth Fairy**. Subsequently, the custom arose of telling children to put their teeth under their pillow at night. In the morning the tooth fairy would exchange the tooth for a coin. The custom caught on because it was fun. The custom now in some cultures is to put the tooth in a glass of water next to the bed, thus saving the parents the trouble of fishing around under a pillow while trying not to disturb their son or daughter.

In the Spanish-speaking world, they've retained the tradition of the **raton de los dientes** (the tooth mouse), which is called Ratoncito Perez after the character described in the work of the Priest Luis Coloma, who wrote a Spanish version of the story in 1894 for the eight-year-old prince who would eventually become King Alfonso XIII.

In parts of lowland Scotland, the tooth mouse is a tooth rat.

Nails

As with hair, certain times are better for cutting nails than others. The Chinese believe that if you clip your nails at night, you may draw the attention of a ghost. Use this poem for guidance:

Cut them on Monday, cut them for wealth;
Cut them on Tuesday, cut them for health;
Cut them on Wednesday, cut them for news;
Cut them on Thursday, a new pair of shoes;
Cut them on Friday, cut them for woe;
Cut them on Saturday, a journey to go;
Cut them on Sunday, cut them for evil;
And all of the week be as cross as the Devil.

Bad poetry aside, never cut the nails of a sick person on any day, or they'll never recover.

Of course, there are other myths associated with nails. Broad fingernails mean that you're generous, long nails that you spend money too easily. Specks on nails—now generally and falsely attributed to a calcium deficiency—mean that you are a liar, the number of specks indicating the number of lies.

Nose (and sneezing)

Along with the heart, the nose was a contender for the anatomical seat of the soul. Ever wonder why so many old statues have their noses broken? It's because people believed that part of the spirit of a person resided in their paintings and statues, especially in the nose, and that if you wanted to kill the spirit in the statue, you had to break off the nose.

Nose superstitions also include judgements about character: thin noses denote jealous natures; receding noses stubbornness and bad temper; noses that

tilt at the tip, liveliness. Napoleon believed that men with large, prominent noses had strength, courage, intelligence and determination, and he would select his generals on the basis of their noses—among other attributes. It's poetic justice that the Duke of Wellington, the man who defeated Napoleon at Waterloo, had a prominent, but well-formed, aquiline nose.

Not only might orifices let in bad luck, they could also let out good luck. When someone sneezes we say 'God bless you' or 'Gesundheit' because in the Middle Ages people believed that such a violent and sudden body function—the speed of sneeze is approximately 240 kilometres (150 miles) per hour—was enough to expel the soul from the body. 'God bless you' puts the soul back in.

In Peru when the chief sneezed, the courtiers would cry, 'save you!'. Across the world in South Africa, the Zulus think that sneezes summon the spirits they call *makosi*, while in Calabar in Nigeria the natives say, 'far from you', and make shooing away gestures to drive away the evil you have involuntarily invoked with your sneeze.

However, many other people consider sneezing to be a good omen. In Monomotapa in Zimbabwe, when the king sneezed, he was blessing everyone in the world. Some European sneezing lore can be quite elaborate. If you sneeze in the morning before breakfast, you'll receive a gift before the end of the week. Sneezing three times in a row is a sign of good luck; money is on the way. A popular English rhyme had it that:

Sneeze on a Monday, sneeze for danger,
Sneeze on a Tuesday, kiss a stranger,
Sneeze on a Wednesday, get a letter,
Sneeze on a Thursday, something better,
Sneeze on a Friday, sneeze for sorrow,
Sneeze on a Saturday, see your sweetheart tomorrow,
Sneeze on a Sunday, your safety seek,
Or the Devil will have you all through the week.

And along the same lines: 'Sneeze on a Sunday morning fasting, Enjoy your true love everlasting.'

Although some people consider it polite to hold back a sneeze, the old wives' tale that it is unhealthy is actually true. According to T.J Craughwell's *Old Wives Tales*, holding back a sneeze can result in: 'fractures in the nasal cartilage, major nosebleeds, burst eardrums, broken blood vessels in the eye, detached retinas and even fatal strokes', and suppressing a sneeze can: 'drive millions of tiny pathogenic particles deep into the sinus tissues, which can lead to serious infections … it can force air under the skin causing a condition known as facial emphysema.' So don't hold back, and never put your finger under someone's nose to stop them sneezing.

penis

No book on superstitions and old wives' tales would be complete without mentioning the foot size–penis size equation. Unfortunately for those interested in such things, in 2002 urologists at St Mary's Hospital, London, teamed up with researchers at University College London and after studying the anatomies of 104 men they concluded that there was *no correlation* between the length of the foot and the length of the penis. The results were published in the October 2002 *British Journal of Urology International* (Vol. 90, Issue 6; p. 586).

Furthermore there is no way to predict the erect size of a man's penis from his flaccid measurement. Some penises simply don't gain much, others might look small, but turn out to be concertinas.

toes and feet

Webbed toes are lucky, as is having an extra toe, and you should always put on your right shoe on before your left. However, take care of your footprints, as someone with evil intent can make you lame by placing a sharp object on them or by driving a nail into them.

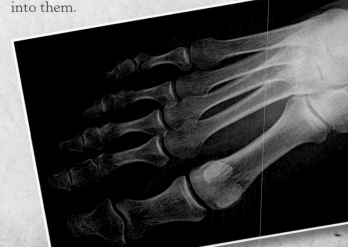

Body fluids (and solids)

Magical in the extreme, the fluids of the body have so many meanings that there are several careers in anthropology, psychology and folklore studies that you could build just from these liquids alone.

Blood

Blood has always been one of the most important offerings that you can give to a god or spirit, and blood sacrifices are usually the most powerful. It isn't always necessary to kill the blood donor, but it helps. The superstition that blood is a good bribe endures even today. In the fishing villages of north Scotland the first fisherman to reach the fishing grounds on New Year's Day and shed blood will be guaranteed good luck for the rest of the year. It was also good luck if a girl child shed blood the first time she reaped the harvest. It's also been said that whichever side in a battle draws first blood will be the victor.

Cauls

Back in the days before hygiene concerns, or middle-class sensibilities relegated births and deaths to hospitals, people were a little bit closer to the realities of life. Paradoxically, they were also more superstitious and not averse to using some of the more unusual and disposable body parts for magical purposes.

Although few people in the West outside the world of obstetrics have seen one, the caul is an especially powerful object. Technically the caul is the amnion, the thin membrane that constitutes the inner lining of the womb and separates the foetus from the rest of the uterus. Before birth the baby swims in amniotic fluid, which is mostly made up of foetal urine— let's not go there—like a doll floating in a large water balloon. When the baby is born, the water breaks, the amniotic fluid gushes out and the baby emerges. The skin of the water balloon, the caul, may break or it may remain more or less intact. The baby may emerge still inside the caul, or with remnants of the caul adhering to the body, especially the head. Such a child 'born in the caul' is called a caul bearer. In ancient Egypt a caul bearer was consecrated to the goddess Isis. Later, in Europe, beliefs arose that a child born in the caul could travel widely throughout his life without tiring, or that he could look into the future. However, the most common belief was that the caul bearer was supposed to be very lucky or destined for greatness—which isn't necessarily the same thing. Lord Byron and the writer Kahlil Gibran were both born with a caul, and both died young. It seemed to work both ways for American actress Lillian Gish though, who lived to be 99.

Among those who could afford it, it was traditional to rub a piece of paper onto the caul until the membrane stuck to the paper. The midwife would then present the caul to the mother as a much-valued heirloom. Keeping the *hallihoo* (fortunate hood) was important. If it was lost, the child could pine away and die.

The value was always more than just sentimental. A superstition arose that the luck of the caul would transfer to the person who possessed it, and this turned cauls into commodities. In particular it was supposed to make sailors drown-proof. Carrying a caul on board a ship was supposed to prevent shipwrecks, and some shipmasters were prepared to pay handsomely for this sort of insurance. There is a record of a caul in a classified advertisement in the *Morning Post* of London going for the sum of twenty guineas in 1779. Depending on how you do your sums, in 2008 terms, this is equivalent to about $5000 for what was essentially a thin piece of dried meat with good press. Even as late as 1919 you could sell a good caul for three guineas, or about $900, the price having gone up from a pre-war cost of just one shilling and six pence, or only $20, because German U-boats had made life at sea a lot more dangerous.

ear wax

In South America one old wives' tale has it that ear wax is an effective treatment for acne when you apply it to a stubborn pimple.

faeces

Most superstitions regarding faeces relate to animal dung. However, in Jharkhand state, in India, women accused of witchcraft are forced to eat human faeces in order to diminish their power. Some burglars of old believed that pooing in front of a house that they'd robbed would save them from being caught.

menstruation

Although biologists haven't studied menstruation in other animals all that much it seems that only some mammals menstruate, only primates have a true menstrual cycle and only human beings have quite noticeable blood loss during this phase of the cycle. Humans are also unique in that the blood lost denotes a period when the female is at her *least* fertile. Human beings also don't go 'into heat'; they have concealed ovulation, so human males don't know when the females are fertile. In a sense, humans are ready for sex all the time—a fact of which they are all too aware.

Given that menstrual cycles are unique to human females, and that the average 28-day cycle approximates that of the waxing and waning of the moon, menstruation was bound to develop a lot of mystical baggage over the millennia. Menstruation is one of the great female 'mysteries' and has been the subject of both reverence and fear throughout the ages.

The Hua people of the Eastern Highlands of Papua New Guinea have a rather complicated relationship between foods and menstrual blood. Hua males may not partake of: red pandanus oil, because it looks like menstrual blood; zokoni mushrooms, because they smell like menstrual blood; or snails, because their slime resembles vaginal secretions. In fact all foods that are dark in their interiors—just as women are dark in their interiors—are a threat to Hua masculinity because they contain too much female *nu* (life force).

Nevertheless, by the same reasoning, the Hua consider certain things as edible because they contain the *nu* of people they can trust. Thus the blood, body oils, fingernails, flesh, saliva, semen and sweat of particular individuals, or food that they've prepared, are all suitable for consumption as food if they've come from a trusted person with compatible *nu*.

The Mae Enga of New Guinea's Central Highlands are even more cautious about women who are having their periods. They believe that without magical protection a man who comes into contact with a menstruating woman will vomit, his blood will 'die' and turn black, his vital juices will corrupt, his skin will darken and hang in folds from his rapidly emaciated flesh, his mind will dull and his death will be slow but inevitable. The Mae Enga believe that if a man is fed menstrual blood, it will kill him quickly and that Mae Enga women have been known to do this as a revenge against infidelity.

The tribes of Papua New Guinea are as many and varied as their beliefs and practices.

The general mistrust of the menstruating woman is widespread. Other common beliefs throughout the world prevent menstruating women from touching tools or weapons, handling hunted animals or cooking their meat. They shouldn't go near curing hams, as the hams will go off. Nor should they milk cows or churn butter, as they make milk curdle. Menstruating women also 'defile' mirrors by looking into them.

The Roman scholar Pliny the Elder mentioned the following superstitions as facts in his book *Historia Naturalis*:

A menstruating woman, if she approached a vessel of wine, would turn it sour; she would cause wheat to wither, buds to shrivel, fruit to fall from trees, bees to die in the hive and iron and steel to rust.

However, like many superstitions, those relating to menstruation are contradictory, and Pliny is no exception. He also cites menstrual blood as a treatment for: bleeding, goitre, gout, headache, hydrophobia (presumably as a symptom of rabies) and inflammation of the salivary glands. Moroccans use menstrual blood in dressings for sores and eye diseases in infants. The Asante of Ghana shower a girl with gifts and celebrate with singing and dancing when she experiences her first period. Though they consider menstrual blood a dangerous pollutant, their priest can make powerful *kunkuma* (protective charms) from brooms smeared with menstrual blood.

The common thread through these beliefs seems to be that women are more filled with female energy at this time than at any other, and that this female energy corrupts male energy, so there are numerous taboos about menstruating women having sexual contact with men.

In Judaism menstruating women must observe the *Tahrat HaMishpacha* (laws of separation). From the first sign of blood, *niddah*, which lasts from five to seven days, until a woman's seventh 'clean' day (so for a total of 12 to 14 days) a husband and wife are forbidden sexual intercourse or even to share the same bed on account of her ritual impurity. On her final day of separation, the woman must wash and clean herself thoroughly, then take a *mikvah*, a further, purely ritual, bath in rainwater, melted snow or flowing spring water, after which the husband and wife must engage in sex. This also happens to be the time when a woman is at her most fertile.

However, among the animist Hazda of Tanzania, it's the men who are segregated from the women at this time.

Menstruating women are often forbidden to enter temples or other sacred places. In Orthodox Christianity they cannot partake of the Eucharist. In some cultures they even have to spend time in hammocks or in suspended cages, so they don't defile the earth—or even the sun.

There are lots of theories about the complexity of beliefs about menstruation. The most provocative link it to some sort of envy on the part of men. The Freudians of the Western world think that the bleeding woman echoes a castrated male, and in some cultures the link is a little more overt. There's an indigenous Australian creation myth of a half-human bird called the Jurijurili who threw a boomerang. As the boomerang returned, it circumcised the bird and cut the vulvas of its wives.

We shouldn't see these beliefs as necessarily 'anti-female'. The Yurok of California believe that, at the time of her period, a woman's magic is at its strongest. This view is widely held, but some cultural rationalisations insist that her power is so strong that without some ritual or magical protection, a woman would have no defence from spirits that would be trying to attack her. Attentive folklorists might ask themselves, 'If she's so strong, why doesn't she have any defence.' You can explain this paradox by realising that in so many superstitious traditions, magic often comes in two forms: wild and disciplined. Raw, wild magic is uncontrolled and often unconscious—it has to be tamed. If it isn't, as would often be the case with a Yurok woman, her community too would have no defence against any wild magic that might leak out. Perhaps the most powerful magic is the superstition that menstrual blood is a potent love potion—one taste alone guarantees eternal faithfulness.

Regardless of the superstitions surrounding menstruation, even in the developed West there's something extraordinary about the fact that, after a short period of time, any group of young women who spend a lot of time together will find that their cycles all synchronise.

milk

Whereas the ancient Greeks attributed the formation of the stars to a scattering of breast milk, some Muslims believe that Allah created the sun, moon and stars from the sweat from the face of Muhammad before his earthly incarnation.

semen

The earliest superstition concerning semen was that it—and it alone—contained the new human in the same way that a seed contains a plant. The female womb was seen as simply the pot in which one put the seed to let it grow. Early investigators, working on this assumption, even imagined that they could see a small person, conveniently packed up in a foetal position, in the head of every sperm cell that they looked at under a microscope. These 'homunculi' were of course no more real than Percival Lowell's imagined canals of Mars when he looked at the red planet through a telescope.

The belief that semen was 'it' inspired some medieval alchemists to try to propagate themselves without women, by putting their semen into clay pots with the appropriate spells. This leads to some interesting images.

In many cultures, semen has to be protected. In Jewish folklore any spare semen not used expressly for the breeding of children would be stolen by the demon Lilith. Lilith wasn't always a demon. She started life as the first female and the first wife of Adam. Importantly, God didn't produce her out of Adam's rib, but from the same clay. The story goes that, because they were thus equal, Lilith refused to 'lie below' Adam, so she pronounced God's name and flew away. To cut a long story short, she changed careers and became a demon to make life difficult for young children, and she was held to be responsible for their deaths. She also acquired an insatiable desire for semen to breed more demons and would visit men who slept alone at night for their nocturnal emissions. Lilith's seduction became the accepted explanation for wet dreams.

Masturbation has long been seen as truly suspect. The biblical character Onan became famous for it, although strictly speaking his was a story of withdrawal, coitus interruptus and 'spilling his seed on the ground' rather than masturbation *per se*. Still, the results offended God so much that he killed Onan outright, one of the examples in the *Bible* of God doing the dirty work himself, rather than having a middle-man—or middle-angel—do it.

Considerable superstitions about masturbation have continued to emerge. The Anti-Onananism camp continues to quote from William Actons tract on 'self-pollution':

The health soon becomes noticeably impaired; there will be general debility, a slowness of growth, weakness in the lower limbs, nervousness and unsteadiness of the hand, loss of memory, forgetfulness and inability to study and learn, a restless disposition, weak eyes and loss of sight, headaches and inability to sleep or wakefulness. Next comes sore eyes, blindness, stupidity, consumption, spinal affection, emaciation, involuntary seminal emissions, loss of all energy or spirit, insanity or idiocy—a hopeless ruin of both body and mind.

In short, with a few exceptions, the debilitating symptoms of the sin of Onan sound a lot like a normal case of puberty.

There have also been a number of bizarre superstitions linking food and masturbation. Dr Sylvester Graham believed that 'mild foods' inhibited sexual appetites and invented the Graham Cracker as a treatment. Dr John Harvey Kellogg created Corn Flakes for much the same purpose.

In the East, Taoists share the idea that semen is a 'vital' fluid, and they have developed all manner of disciplined sexual practices designed to give men orgasms without ejaculation. Ultimately a man who never gives up his semen is promised immortality for having preserved his 'yang essence'. It evidently works for Lilith too, as her immortality comes from draining the 'strength' from men.

Even non-demonic human females can benefit from semen. There is a common belief that when smeared on the face, it's good for the complexion—all those enzymes!

smegma

This combination of oils, dead skin cells, moisture and bacteria that mammals secret around their genitals is most commonly seen in non-circumcised males. There's a widely held belief that smegma is carcinogenic, and mainstream medical literature repeats this story time and time again. However, there's no scientific basis for this belief, so you can consider the equation 'smegma = penile, cervical or prostate cancer' to be an example of a modern superstition. This myth-making happens inevitably when people who ought to know better report on 'facts' that they can't be bothered checking first. It's difficult to know how many men have been circumcised unnecessarily because doctors thought they were saving them from cancer.

spit

The emphasis on the fluids of the mouth tends to be more on their expulsion than on the fluids themselves. Spitting at someone is one of the great signs of contempt and is generally considered rude or vulgar in the West. Westerners of delicate sensibilities are often shocked when they visit South East Asia, where spitting seems to be a national pastime in certain areas. Spitting is certainly a risky activity in the south-eastern states of America. When a shaman of the Cherokee wants to destroy someone, he'll gather his enemy's spittle on a stick and mix it into a paste along with seven earthworms and splinters of a tree struck by lightning. Then he puts the mash into a joint of wild parsnip and buries the parsnip in a hole in a forest. One assumes that the enemy then dies painfully from causes 'unknown'.

Various people spit for luck, in particular gamblers as they are about to throw dice. People would often put money in their mouths if they suspected that it could be 'spirited away', or if they were given coins they might spit on them for luck, especially if the coins were won in gambling. Eventually sanitation or taste began to prevail and the custom evolved among the Germans of putting coins near your mouth as if to spit on them, but not actually doing so. Businessmen in Germany made sure that their *Handsel*, the first money taken on the day, would be well wet with spit, to ensure big takings.

Despite hygiene concerns, craftspeople of various ages have spit on their hands before working, not, as many commonly think, to improve the grip, but because the spit was magic and would make the work of the hands more effective. Dancers spit in their shoes to ensure a flawless performance.

A deal that people shake hands on becomes even more magically protected if the dealers spit into their hands before shaking. Among the Wajagga of East Africa sealing a deal was even less

An Andean shaman holding cocoa leaves. Spitting the chewed leaves out is considered disrespectful.

sanitary. The parties to an agreement would sit down with a bowl of milk or beer between them. In turn each would say some magic words, take some of the liquid into their own mouth, then spit it into the mouth of the other.

Spitting has, since ancient times, been a simple spell to avert evil. In Greece you should spit whenever you give someone a compliment, in order to avoid the powers of any spirit that might have overheard you and become jealous. In other traditions, if two people inadvertently washed from the same water, especially if they washed their hands at the same time, this was bad luck and the people would soon quarrel and part. However, the water could be 'purified' of bad luck if you spat in it. Other spells include: spit on your 'breast' three times to avoid the evil eye; spit on a child to deter evil spirits; spit when passing a house with sickness in it in order to avoid infection; if you have a bad dream, spit three times over your left shoulder; or, if you meet the Devil in the West Counties of England, you can get rid of him by spitting between his horns.

However, if you want to give someone bad luck, spit behind their back.

Spittle could also be a cure. According to *Mark* (7:32–35) Jesus cured a deaf and mute man by spitting. Throughout the Middle Ages people used spitting as a cure for everything from swellings to open wounds and people would spit into poultices or herbal mixtures to 'activate' them or increase their potency.

Pliny held that the spittle of a woman who had been fasting was good for curing eye complaints. This belief persisted well into the twentieth century. By extension, dabbing a newborn baby's eyes with a finger wet with spittle would ensure good eyesight. Women could also prevent their children's wounds from scarring if they spat on the wound before they ate breakfast. There was also a belief that you could eliminate unwanted birthmarks by licking them away. On the other hand, a fasting man's saliva was said to be poisonous to snakes, especially if he could spit in the snake's mouth.

sweat

Many cultures believe that inducing perspiration will bring out disease along with the sweat. The inhabitants of western Ireland would construct 'sweating houses' to cure diseases, especially ones that 'cling to the bones'. This 'purging yourself of evil' idea is common throughout the world, and many Amerindians take this one step further and create ritual saunas—sweat lodges—in which the participants chant, sing or perform other rituals in a clockwise direction, while enduring a very hot steam bath. This can create an altered state of consciousness and bring the participants closer to the spirits. The sweat lodge can also represent a womb, so sweat lodges are often used in naming ceremonies. On leaving the sweat lodge, the person is ritually reborn.

In Europe there is a belief that a woman's perspiration will always be found on her apron. As such, if a man wipes his hands on a woman's apron, their perspiration will mix and the man will soon fall in love with her.

urine

Considered dirty in the West, objectively and rationally urine is actually one of the cleanest of bodily fluids, and, unless you have a kidney or bladder infection, your urine, in particular your mid-stream urine (the urine after you've flushed out your urethra) is sterile—germ free. Psychologically it's another story. Other mammals use urine to mark territory, but for social animals like humans, who live in areas of high population density, negligent toilet habits are at the very least antisocial or inconsiderate.

In the non-West urine gets mixed press. The Hindu Laws of Manu state that if a man urinates on a fire, on a cow or into the wind, he will 'lose his wits'. Surely there are easier ways to put out a fire, and one obvious observation is that if a man chooses to urinate on a cow or into the wind, his wits would have to be pretty compromised in the first place. If you doubt this, look into the numerous reports of men who have died from electrocution while urinating on electrified railroad tracks in subways. Perhaps in centuries to come we'll hear of a superstition against urinating on iron, long after railroads have become obsolete.

On the positive side, urine is also used in many purification rituals. The Zoroastrians of India, the Parsi, drink small quantities of ritually consecrated bull's urine, a sort of 'holy piss', mixed with the ashes of a temple fire. They also take ritual 'baths' in the urine, called *nirangdin*, by rubbing small quantities all over their bodies three times, followed by three rinses of sand, and three of water. *Nirangdin* is used in many rituals, including initiation, holy days, marriage ceremonies and in elaborate exorcism rites that last for nine days.

The Hindu laws of Manu state that if a man urinates on a cow he will lose his wits.

magical
medicine

magical medicine

Sickness is never easy to deal with, but most cures throughout history have been worse than the diseases themselves. Below are some complaints and their 'cures' that are firmly rooted in superstition. They have no connection to the efficacy of herbal extracts or the few medicines that are derived from animal sources. Minerals and crystals also warrant a separate treatment. Many of the names of these complaints are charmingly archaic and only approximately refer to any diseases, conditions or syndromes that modern medicine classifies or recognises.

Some cures were all-purpose, like putting a chalk mark symbolising the disease on a kettle, then putting the kettle on the fire. As the fire burns the mark off, the disease would disappear too. Similarly, Tibetan physicians would write the prescription for a treatment down on a piece of paper. If you were too poor to have the prescription filled, or if the ingredients were not available, you could swallow the prescription as

this was thought to be almost, if not as good as taking the prescribed medicine itself. Other treatments were much more specific.

Ague and fevers

Ague is any fever that is marked by accompanying chills, uncontrollable trembling and sweating. It's more a symptom than a condition and it's characteristic of many infectious diseases like malaria.

If there's an ague going around, tie a red ribbon to a neighbour's gate, preferably a neighbour you don't like, because the fever will then attack him instead of you. If you like your neighbours, you can cut a lock off your hair, wrap it around a pin and stick the pin in an aspen tree. Incant:

Aspen tree, aspen tree,
I pray thee shake instead of me.

There are a variety of cures for more ordinary fevers. Herbs are popular, but a more magical treatments is to make three knots in a long thread, with two knots close together at one end and one knot at the other end. Rub the patient with the thread, then cut off the part of the thread with two knots and throw it into a fire. Incant: 'I put the sickness on top of the fire'. Then tie the thread with the last knot around the patient's neck.

Alternatively cut the patient's nails, take the parings and insert them into a ball of virgin beeswax. Stick the ball to the door of a neighbour you don't like. This will transfer the sickness to him.

In South America, there was a specific practice to draw out a fever. First, put a towel on your head. Then, take a glass full of water, tilt the top of your head and press your towelled scalp to the top of the glass. Then sit straight up. In this position the glass is now upside down and the towel stops the water leaking out. Eventually a stream of bubbles starts rising in the water. The bubbles rise, taking the fever with it.

Bleeding

To stop bleeding, wear a shoelace from a shoe belonging to a member of the opposite sex.

However, more often than not a common treatment for practically any disorder was to bleed the patient deliberately. Physicians could do this by making wounds or by applying leeches and waiting until the parasites had gorged themselves and dropped off.

People believed that bleeding removed 'poisons' from the blood, but no doubt many people—who might otherwise have lived if nature had been left alone to do her job—have died either directly or indirectly from iatrogenic (physician-caused) blood loss.

The practice of physician-induced blood-letting, was called 'phlebotamy' a term still used to describe taking small samples of blood for diagnosis.

In Tibet, swallowing the paper that a treatment is written on is considered almost as good as taking the prescribed medicine.

Boils

These painful, swollen areas of skin filled with pus are still quite common. If there aren't any antibiotics around, try placing herbal poultices over the boils for three days and nights, then put the poultices in a coffin of someone who will soon be buried, so that they're buried with the corpse. Or convince a friend to go to a cemetery on your behalf and walk six times, anticlockwise, around the grave of a recently interred corpse.

Burns

The English recommend that you touch a burn with a piece of church linen—the corner of an altar cloth or a chalice napkin. The Irish say lay your hand over the burn, blow on it three times and incant: 'Old cloth beneath the clay, burn away, burn away. In the name of God, thou be healed.'

And here's a charm from the Shetland Islands:

Here come I to cure a burnt sore.
If the dead knew what the living endure,
The burnt sore would burn no more.

And from west England:

Three Angels came, from north, east and west.
One brought fire, another brought frost,
And the third brought the Holy Ghost.
So out fire and in frost,
In the Name of the Father, Son and Holy Ghost.

colds

There are plenty of common myths about colds and how you catch them. In spite of extensive research on the subject and considerable investment in educating the public, millions of people still believe that:

- cold or being exposed to cold causes you to catch a cold.
- going outside with wet hair will give you a cold.
- wearing wet shoes or wet socks will give you a cold.

So let me add my voice to the chorus: cold does not increase susceptibility to catching colds, nor does it make a cold worse if you already have one. Being wet doesn't cause a cold, and if you sneeze after swimming in cold water, it's because water probably went up your nose and your mucous membranes are irritated.

The current mainstream medical consensus is that colds are caused by a family of pathogens called rhinoviruses, and if more people catch them in the winter, it's because people spend more time indoors in cold weather. Indoors they're in closer contact with each other, so that any sickness that's around has more of an opportunity to spread by direct or indirect contact.

However, you'll no doubt continue to find people convinced that cold temperatures cause colds. I can only say that if people are convinced of something like this, then they may actually be affecting their immune systems subconsciously, making themselves more vulnerable to any disease-causing agents in the air, or even giving themselves symptoms when they're otherwise healthy. Their belief that cold causes colds becomes a self-fulfilling prophecy—just like so many other superstitions. However, if you are still superstitious enough to believe that cold causes cold, to cure it, catch a falling oak leaf before it touches the ground, or cover yourself in bear fat.

consumption

Swallowing baby frogs before breakfast, or smearing yourself all over with dog's fat, should cure you of tuberculosis.

cramp

To relieve cramp in your leg, try any of the following: tie a cotton string around your ankle; wrap a moleskin or an eel's skin around your leg; lay your shoes over your leg; wear cork garters; or lay pieces of cork between the sheet and mattress on your bed.

Alternatively stand on your affected leg, suck your left thumb, cross yourself with your right hand and incant:

Foot, foot, foot is fast asleep;
Thumb, thumb, thumb in spittle we steep;
Crosses three we make to ease us;
Two for thieves and one for Jesus.

If you have cramp in your stomach, ask a blacksmith or jeweller to make a ring using the metal from the nails, hinges and handles of a coffin, bent horseshoe nails or—like the Tudor kings of England—from pieces of gold and silver consecrated by a priest on Good Friday.

To prevent cramps, as well as nightmares, and to have good luck, place your shoes at the foot of your bed at night, soles uppermost and arranged in a 'T' shape.

Drunkenness

Not so much an illness as a temporary incapacity, unless it turns into alcoholism, drunkenness is usually more inconvenient to the sober, than to the drunk. To cure drunkenness, or at least shock the drunk out of his complacency, put a live eel, or the eggs of an owl, into the drunk's drink. Women who don't want to risk marrying a drunk should avoid getting wet when doing the laundry.

Fits

Seizures occur in a variety of conditions, such as hypoglycaemia or even panic attacks, but mostly they are associated with grand mal epilepsy. Historically epilepsy was considered to be a sign that the gods were favouring you and wanted to communicate with you. Many prophets and seers could be 'seized' by ecstatic visions.

The ancient Greeks believed that you could tell what the gods were trying to say by the pattern of an epileptic's convulsions. There's even a name for foretelling the future this way— spasmatomancy.

For those who found fits to be inconvenient, embarrassing or crippling they could resort to grating a small piece of human skull and sprinkling it on your food. A less disgusting prescription is to carry twigs from an ash tree in silk bags about your person. For centuries peony root, hung around the neck was also a popular cure for the 'falling sickness'.

If you're a woman, collect nine silver

coins and nine sets of three halfpennies from nine bachelors. If you're a man, collect the same from nine maidens. Then have someone make the silver coins into a ring, and pay the maker of the ring with the 27 halfpennies. You might find it easier though to wear a ring made from a half-crown that's been put in a collection plate for a church, or wear a necklace made from nine pieces of elder wood, or drive a nail into the ground where you fell if you'd had a fit.

A more active treatment is to go to the parish church near midnight on 23 June, just as Midsummer Day is about to clock in. Walk three times up and down each aisle, then crawl three times under the communion table from north to south, timing this so that you complete the last crawl just as the clock strikes midnight.

If your case is really serious, you'll need to resort to more desperate measures:

- Take the heart of a jackass, cook it and eat it on toast.
- Take the heart of a crow, mash it up and mix it with the crow's blood and eat the result for nine consecutive days.
- Drink an infusion of mistletoe—if you're not worried about being poisoned, as mistletoe is highly toxic.
- Or, for industrial-strength magic, cut your nails and hair and bury the cuttings with a live cock in a hole dug in the ground where you last had a fit.

The mashed heart of a crow mixed with its blood is a more unusual treatment for fits.

Goitre

This unpleasant swelling of the thyroid gland in the neck is due to an absence of iodine in the diet. Goitres can grow to the size of a large grapefruit and beyond, making you look as if your neck is pregnant. Fortunately, because iodised salt is cheap and easily available, it's now rather rare. However, in times past one treatment was to catch a live snake and pass it nine times across the neck, then put the snake, alive, in a bottle.

Headaches

There are a couple of magical options for this one. You could nail a lock of hair from the head of the headache sufferer to an aspen or ash tree. Alternatively, around your neck wear the noose from a rope with which a man has been hanged. Some Australian Aborigines treated headaches and fevers by binding the head with a cord. This makes sense, as headaches often come with a pounding sensation of increased blood flow and restricting blood flow at least alleviates this symptom.

Picking up luck

Many people have heard the phrase: 'See a penny, pick it up and all day you'll have good luck.' There's an almost identical saying involving pins, but it's not always that simple. If the point of the pin is towards you, don't pick it up. If the head is towards you, pick it up by the head. A New England superstition maintains that when you pick up a pin you'll soon be offered a lift somewhere. If a pin falls and sticks upright this means that a stranger is coming.

When the saying about pennies first came into currency (no pun intended) a penny was worth something—up to about $20 in today's equivalent money. Anyone finding $20 in the street today would count themselves lucky. Even though inflation has taken the wind out of the value of a penny, the superstition still exists. Pennies, though, are now confined to the United Kingdom and many people in America still refer to one-cent coins as pennies. In fact, the most expensive penny in the world is the Sheldon 1793 NC-1 chain cent, the first regularly minted coins in circulation in America. Only four are known to exist, so if you were to pick one up in the street, or anywhere else for that matter, you could expect to make yourself $275 000—very lucky indeed.

itching

Mild itching is often more a sign than a condition. An itchy right hand means that someone will pay you a visit soon, and you'll be shaking hands. An itchy thumb on either hand is a bad sign, hence the famous line from the second witch in Macbeth: 'By the pricking of my thumbs, something wicked this way comes.'

An itchy nose means that you will suffer injury from the hand of a fool who will soon visit you. An itchy right eye heralds laughter; an itchy left eye heralds tears. Itchy lips mean that you'll soon be kissed. If your upper lip itches more, the kisser will be tall, if the lower lip, the kisser will be short.

Itchy knees mean you'll be kneeling on strange ground; itchy feet, that you'll be walking on strange ground, and itchy elbows that you'll be sleeping with a stranger.

Rheumatism

Even today the word 'rheumatism' can mean up to 200 different conditions, from arthritis to fibromyalgia to tenosynovitis. Rheumatic conditions could have any or all of the following signs and symptoms: inflammation, soreness

William Shakespeare's birthplace, Stratford-upon-Avon. The witches from Shakespeare's play, Macbeth, *speak of many superstitions that were commonly believed as literal truths at the time.*

or tenderness in the joints, tendons or muscles and some degree of immobility. Folk cures include:

- wearing an eel skin around your waist
- carrying the bone from the foot of an animal—preferably a hare—or carrying buckshot in your pocket
- carrying a potato that you've begged or stolen from someone else, or a horse chestnut, or a piece of mountain ash
- wearing a ring from a silver coffin handle, or tying a brass wire to your wrist. Many people swear by the efficacy of wearing a bracelet or anklet made of copper
- in Java, rubbing pepper into the fingernails and toenails
- in Japan, burying yourself neck-deep in soil, gravel or mud in places that have geothermal heat; in places that don't have hot springs, you can put warm stones on your back, bury yourself in a churchyard, or simply take a hot mud bath
- carrying a haddock bone, because the haddock is sacred to St Peter
- crawling under bramble bushes to 'scrape off' the rheumatism—and some skin besides
- or, even more invasively, allowing bees to sting your afflicted area. There is some modern scientific evidence to support the efficacy of bee venom.

'Knuckle cracking causes arthritis' is yet another old wives' tale. There's no connection between them. However, this doesn't mean that you can crack your knuckles with complete impunity. There is evidence to suggest that if you do so habitually, you could tear the ligaments in your fingers and lose some hand strength. So if you have this habit, it might be a good idea to stop, or at least do it less often.

Treatments for rheumatism are said to be more effective if applied by a woman who has given birth to a child feet first.

sore eyes

Bathe the eyes in tea made in rainwater that fell on Holy Thursday (the day before Good Friday/Easter). If you prefer an ointment, make one from salt, human milk and crushed bed bugs.

toothache

Many cultures have concluded that a 'worm' causes dental caries, because the world's most common human affliction leaves holes in the teeth very much in the same way that worms leave holes in apples.

Some Australian Aborigines used spells to encourage the worm to leave the tooth. The European attitude was more to kill it with drastic measures, like fumigations of smoking henbane seeds. Even though no one had ever actually seen the 'toothworm', this didn't stop the English believing that it looked like an eel, or the Germans from believing that it looked like a red, blue and grey maggot.

If fumigations of poisonous seeds didn't work you could, in increasing order of disgustingness:

- put on your trousers or stockings right leg first
- carry a double nut in your pocket

- drive a nail into an oak tree that has been struck by lightning
- bite off at ground level, the first fern that appears in spring. (Traditionally and astrologically this means 23 March)
- take clay from the grave of a dead priest and say one 'Our Father' and one 'Hail Mary' prayer.
- apply gunpowder and sulphur to the tooth
- wear a small bag around your neck containing the forelegs and one hind leg of a mole
- wear a small bag around your head containing a tooth taken from a corpse
- apply a splinter from a gallows from which a murderer has been hung
- drink from a human skull
- touch your mouth, or the tooth, with the finger of a dead child.

Australian Aborigines use spells to encourage the 'worm' that causes toothache to leave the tooth.

warts

Because warts go away all on their own after about a year or two, anything that you do to them will 'work' if you persist long enough, so there's a huge number of wart 'cures'. Here are some that don't involve frogs. They can be broadly divided into variations on three themes: magical dissolution, magical stealing and magical mimicry.

Dissolution cures involve applying something to somehow dissolve the wart. You could:

- Touch a nail to your warts, then using the nail, carve a cross into a pecan tree.
- Say your prayers backwards over the warts.
- Steal a dishrag, rub it on the wart, then hide it in a tree stump.
- Steal a piece of meat and bury it where three roads meet.
- Bury a rooster's comb.
- Wash the warts with water in which you've boiled eggs.

Magical stealing usually involves a substance acquiring the wart energy through contagion:

- Rub the wart with beans, peas, seeds or stones then throw them away.
- Rub your warts with a large, black snail then hang the snail on a thorn. Do this on nine consecutive nights, presumably changing the snails on each night.
- Rub the wart with a piece of corn.
- Bore a hole in a tree and plug it with the piece of corn.
- Fill your mouth with corn, dig a hole and spit out all the corn into the hole and cover it up.
- Rub the wart with oil of sassafras, damper (soda bread) or a piece of onion and throw it away.

Finally, mimicry cures involve connecting two substances magically. As one disappears so does the other. For example:

- Rub the wart with a piece of stolen raw meat. Wrap the meat in paper and throw it somewhere that your dog will find.

- Pierce the wart, take a drop of blood from the wart and put it into a hollowed-out corn kernel, then feed the kernel to a chicken.
- Rub the warts with a peeled apple and feed the apple to a pig.
- Cut notches in a twig, one for each wart, then burn the twig.
- Tie knots in a piece of string, one for each wart, then bury the string. As the string rots, the warts vanish.
- Put vinegar on a wart and on a penny at the same time. As the penny dissolves, so does the wart.
- As a funerary procession passes, rub your warts and say: 'May these warts and corpse pass away, never to return.'

wens

Wens are sebaceous cysts that form when oil glands block up. They can be annoying, disfiguring and painful. If hot compresses don't help, and you don't want to resort to minor surgery, touch the hand of a dead man.

a word about pus

Pus, that unpleasant looking, yellow, viscous fluid that comes out of pimples, pustules, abscesses and other pyogenic bacterial infections is actually composed of a body fluid called liquor puris and dead immune cells.

Nowadays, if you find pus in large quantities, physicians consider it a really bad sign and treat the infection with antibiotics. But back in the bad old days of bubonic plague it was considered a good sign. A principle symptom of the bubonic plague was the presence of 'buboes', lymph nodes in the groin and under the armpits swollen with pus. If the buboes burst, it was taken as evidence that the body was 'purging itself of ill humors' and physicians actually encouraged it to happen. In reality, bursting buboes just made things worse by spreading the infection.

Superstitions are not always cute or good for you.

the ages of man and woman

The ages of man and woman

The word 'liminal' means, more or less, 'in-between'. Transitional places and times don't fall into larger categories easily. They are neither here nor there—neither then nor now. They are therefore inherently suspicious and vulnerable. Are either dawn and dusk night or day? Is a threshold inside or outside? Liminal places and times are like chinks in the armour of reality, through which unseen and probably negative forces might enter. The superstitious are wary of liminality, which explains perhaps why there are so many ceremonies to ease the transition from one state to another, like births, deaths and marriages. Each ceremony, to some extent, had its connection to an ancient belief or superstition.

Birth

It's a time of great excitement but before the development of anaesthetics and simple hygiene childbirth could also be a time of great concern. Numerous superstitions have attached themselves to the birth process. Among people as far flung as the Lapps of northern Scandinavia and the tribes of northern Borneo, there is a belief that all knots in the vicinity of the birth should be untied. Knots were symbols of binding and impediment and had to go, lest they halt the safe and smooth passage of the child into the world. The belief extends itself even to knots in the hair of anyone in the vicinity. These 'witches' knots' may well have been caused by black magic, but regardless of how they got there they'd have to be combed out to ensure the safety of the baby and the mother.

There's an old poem about the supposed fate of a child depending on what day of the week it's born:

Monday's child is fair of face,
Tuesday's child is full of grace,
Wednesday's child is full of woe,
Thursday's child has far to go,
Friday's child is loving and giving,
Saturday's child works hard for a living,
But the child born on the Sabbath day, is
lucky, bonny, wise and gay.

Other superstitions say that children born on Good Friday will be unlucky and sad all their lives, and that babies born in May are sickly and never do well.

Breach births (children born feet first) will have magical healing powers, and children born by Caesarean section will be strong throughout their lives, have the power to see spirits and to find hidden treasure. Nevertheless, there is a superstition that if the baby is born feet first, you must rub bay leaves on its feet within the first few hours of its life, or it will grow up lame, or become lame after an accident.

To bring luck to any newborn, spit on it or rub it all over with lard.

Blowing out the birthday candles

The charming ritual of making a wish come true when you blow out the birthday candles is an amalgam of many beliefs. Bees were supposed to come directly from heaven and their wax was sacred, which is why church candles for solemn rites are always made of beeswax. Candles drove away not only physical darkness, but spiritual darkness as well. Blowing is a common way of invoking good luck, and is more polite than spitting. Cakes were just as much of a luxury item in ancient times as they are today, and they were usually baked only on sacred days and consecrated to the gods. Whichever way you look at it, making a wish when you blow out the candles on your birthday is very lucky, a custom with very deep meanings indeed.

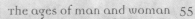

twins

Since twin or multiple births are much rarer among humans than among other animals, twins are spooky in many cultures. One tradition is that the birth of twins uses up more than the usual ration of soul and that they might suck up the entirety of the father's soul. Many cultures associate twins with evil. In some cases magical purification will cleanse the evil, in other cases the mother could find herself exiled from the group or one or both twins might be killed.

However, the Kpelle of Liberia consider twins to be shamans, practitioners of holy magic and they revere them accordingly. In fact, many African tribes consider the birth of twins to be the result of direct intervention by the gods, and they are therefore lucky, especially if born to royalty. One exception is the Ashanti, who would smother royal twins to prevent dissent about succession. The whole 'twins are bad luck' idea may stem from concerns about this sort of high-level sibling rivalry. Romulus and Remus, the founders of Rome, are a pair of famous twins who ended badly. There are also many folk legends about the 'good' twin and the 'evil' twin.

There's concern about the rivalry of twins even in the *Bible*. Jacob and Esau are said to have wrestled in the womb of their mother. Intriguingly, there is an increasing body of scientific evidence for such a battle. The vanishing twin phenomena records that of the total number of twins who are actually conceived, few actually make it to full term. Often one twin fails to develop fully, and the mother, and by extension the twin, partially or

completely reabsorbs the failed foetus. One estimate is that as many as seven per cent of all pregnancies are vanishing twin pregnancies.

There is a widespread superstition that twins are somehow mystically connected all their lives, that they feel each other's pain and that one twin always knows when the other twin dies. Real life twins vary tremendously in reporting how much, if any, of this superstition is true.

names

The naming of a child is considered one of the most important rites in many cultures and has profound implications.

In harsher times or in harsher climates, where people live life on the edge of survival, it is often common to practice infanticide, especially of female infants. The medieval Japanese did not consider a child to be fully human until it had been out of the womb for 40 days. During this time, if the child was considered deformed or defective in any way, it could be killed with impunity. The ancient Greeks commonly practiced infanticide by leaving unwanted babies out and exposed to the elements, and until comparatively recent times, the Inuit would control their population in this way too. All this would change once the baby was named. Naming gave the baby full status as a human being. Killing a named child was killing a person.

Names are sacred and magical. The true name of the god in Hebrew tradition—YHWH—is too sacred to be pronounced and the Jews typically refer to God as Hashem, which means literally, 'the name'. Among the indigenous people of south-eastern Australia, only certain highly initiated men could learn the true name of the supreme deity.

The power of names is that they provide the key to the person. If somebody who knows the right magic also knows your name, he or she can cast a spell for good or ill specifically created for you, like a disease linked to your DNA. Typically, sorcerers can control demons once they know the demons' names.

There exist, therefore, many traditions in which one has both a common-use name and a true name. Many cultures hold two naming ceremonies. The first gives you your use name, in the second a shaman, witch doctor or similar gives you your true name.

It's considered very unlucky to reveal the intended name of a child before their baptism as without the protection of the sacrament, the child is vulnerable to being taken by faeries or pixies or any other supernatural being that enjoys kidnapping infants.

It's considered a good sign if a baby cries at its baptism. In some cases it's inevitable. Greek Orthodox baptisms require that the child be almost fully immersed in the baptismal font, and the water is usually cold. In other traditions if the baby doesn't cry, it's considered a sign that the baby has been born without original sin.

Sharing your true name with others is a gesture of ultimate trust. It's also assumed that those who use their true name as a common name are so powerful that they are invulnerable and no magic can touch them.

For those of us who are not impervious to magic, many traditions forbid the mentioning of personal names, the names of spirits, the names of the dead or the name of anything really that you didn't want to deliberately bring into your life.

Naturally, the sacred true name given to you at an initiation would be protected even after you were dead. During Confucian ancestral rites the name of the deceased would be written down on a special spirit tablet, but never actually said aloud. In some groups you might have to abandon your name if it was the same as, or even if it sounded like, the name of someone who had died. This can become complicated and some people have to change their names as much as half-a-dozen times if the wrong relatives die. As usual this superstition is an extension of the rather schizoid attitude most cultures have toward the dead. The dead could be benevolent and loving, but also malicious and nasty, and we're all better off not disturbing them even with the innocent necromancy of saying their names aloud.

In the 'modern' West it is still considered unlucky—or perhaps just bad taste—to give a child the same name as a dead sibling. Less common is the superstition that if you name a son after his father, the son will die before the father.

Even today we do a lot to protect names for economic reasons, thus all the laws about trademarks. But it's not all about money. Typically the numbers of famous players in team sports—their game name if you like—is permanently retired after the player retires as a gesture of respect. This is usually team specific, for example, no other NFL (gridiron) player for the New York Jets will ever wear Joe Namath's 12. In football no one will ever wear Diego Maradona's 10 for Argentina. Also in football many teams reserve the number 12 for their fans—the 'twelfth' man—but Reading reserves the number 13 for this purpose. Baseball's New York Yankees hold the record for the most retired numbers (16 to date) including Lou Gherig's 4, Babe Ruth's 3 and Joe DiMaggio's 5.

On a lighter note, names are an important part of spells to learn the truth about a situation, especially a romantic one. Write the names of anyone that you're interested in romantically on a piece of paper. Wrap them up in separate balls of clay and put them in a bowl of water. The first ball to float to the top will give you the name of your true valentine.

The New York Yankees hold the record for the most retired numbers.

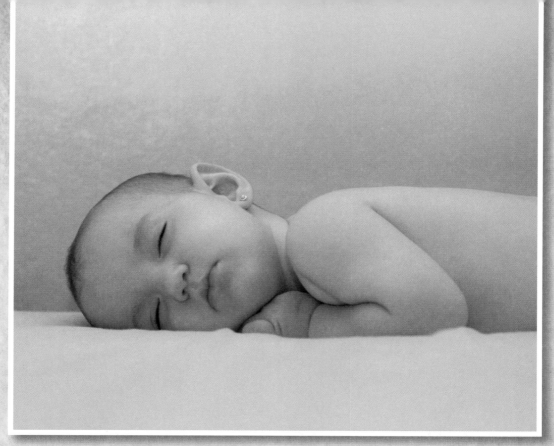

If clay is hard to come by, a variation is to wrap the names in balls of bread. You could also burn the papers, gather the ashes, wrap them up in more paper, put the paper on a mirror marked with a cross, then put the whole arrangement under your pillow to dream of the lover that night. In a similar vein, you could also write the letters of the alphabet on separate pieces of paper. Put them face down in a bowl of water overnight. The one that floats will reveal the initial of your future spouse.

Names can create magic in unexpected ways. You could cure a child of whooping cough if you fed it a cake baked by a woman whose maiden name was the same as her married name. A similar cure came from feeding the child bread given by a woman who'd been married twice to different men with the same surname—as long as the men came from different families.

If three women with the same initial sit down at the same table, it's a sure sign that that one of them will be married within a year. The same applies if three unmarried people with the same first name sit down at a table together.

Babyhood

Babies are vulnerable to faeries until their first sneeze, so midwives would drive pins and nails into bedposts of the birth bed to keep away evil spirits. In Scotland midwives would carry around snuff to hurry things up a bit.

Mothers should not cut a baby's nails, but nibble them and eat the parings until the child is 12 months old. If she doesn't, the child will grow up to be a thief.

To ensure the good health of your baby, put a rabbit's foot in its crib. Sulphur is a powerful charm against evil and you can put a bag of it around the baby's neck or in its shoes. You can also put the baby out and let it get wet in the first shower of April. If the baby has colic, a bout of incessant crying for no apparent reason, you can cure the baby by giving it hot water that has been poured into a shoe.

In Britain, if the baby's first tooth emerges on the lower jaw, the child will have a long life, but if first tooth emerges from the upper jaw, the child will supposedly die in infancy. Among the Azande of central Africa such a child is called *irakorinde*—he who has bad teeth—and they believe such a child will bring bad luck to the crops. If the child survives, his tribesmen ask that he never eats the first crops, especially peanuts and corn, or the rest will be ruined. Central Asians shared the superstition and went so far as to expose such infants to the elements as a form of infanticide, an even crueller practice than you might think when you consider that the first tooth emerges when the child is anything from three months to twelve months old. Some traditions have it that a baby born with teeth may be a vampire.

The belief that external events could affect a child's future appearance was quite common. The Aztecs believed that a woman who saw an eclipse would have a baby with a harelip. Certain Native Americans believed that if the mother ate certain foods, certain results would follow.

The Dalai Lama was recognised as the 49th incarnation when as a child he identified objects belonging to him from his previous incarnation.

Berries caused birthmarks and steelhead salmon would give the baby weak ankles. Infants should avoid mirrors. If they see their own reflections before they are six months old, the child will die within a year.

Parents, family and other stakeholders in the destiny of the baby are naturally curious to see if they can predict character or the child's future talents or career. It's said that a baby with large ears will be generous; small ears indicate stinginess. A big mouth bodes a talent for public speaking or singing; a small mouth is a sign of meanness. A large gap between the teeth means the baby will be lucky in life; large teeth mean the child will be physically strong, and small regular teeth belong to children who will be even-tempered, cautious and methodical.

If you offer a coin to a baby and the baby refuses to take it, it will grow up to be a spendthrift.

In northern England it's very important that the first time you take a newborn out of the house, you should give it some salt, an egg, some bread and some money, so that the baby will never lack for any of the essentials in its life.

If you present a baby with several objects belonging to various members of the baby's family at the same time, and the baby picks one up, the choice will tell you which person the baby will most take after. High-ranking Tibetan Buddhist priests use this method for confirming the reincarnation of their spiritual leaders. The Dalai Lama himself was chosen when as a baby he picked up and held on to objects belonging to his previous incarnation in preference to all the others he was presented with.

friendship

In Greece when someone gives you a gift of perfume or cologne, give them a coin to ritually pay for it, or else you'll soon be separated.

There are similar superstitions elsewhere. You should never give gloves as a gift, or soon you'll be shaking hands goodbye. Scissors and knives in general should never be given as a gift, because they will 'sever the friendship'. By extension, never give a knife as a housewarming present, or your neighbour will become an enemy. And never give knives as a wedding gift, as they may 'cut the ties that bind': 'For woe is me! Such a present luckless prove, For knives, they tell me, always sever love.' The gift of a knife from a lover is especially unlucky. The cure for this is easy enough. Give the giver a coin so that you symbolically 'buy' the scissors or knives. This maintains the relationship.

Friends taking a walk together should never allow anything to come between them—telegraph poles, street lamps, post boxes, trees, etc.—as this is bad luck for the relationship. If the friends are holding hands and they have to part because of the obstacle they should say 'bread and butter' to invoke a union and maintain their relationship until they've passed the obstacle and can rejoin hands.

In India, serving a weak cup of tea to a friend is a bad sign. Presumably it can be fixed by serving a strong cup instead.

The best stones to ensure the fidelity of friends are amethyst, garnet and topaz.

Hubris, compliments and envy

A common theme among superstitions is the warning against positive thinking. This arises particularly in societies that are paranoid or under stress, which is nearly all at some time or another. It's the ancient belief that if you feel too good about yourself, you're bound to get into trouble: 'pride goeth before a fall' and all that. This may have some basis in fact. After all, pride is only a short step to overconfidence and recklessness.

However, many also believe that even saying something positive about others may bring them trouble. This is a little harder to fathom. One folk explanation is that the gods are powerful, but jealous. If they hear you complimenting somebody in too loud a voice, they may decide to bring that person down to size. And it's not only the gods. You should also avoid the envy of magical humans—and this could be anybody at all. There's even a theory that the custom of tipping waiters originated so that they wouldn't feel jealous of the diners.

Sometimes it's not enough to refrain from being positive, you actually have to do something negative to fool the evil spirits into ignoring the favoured person. Rabbis in Palestine used to customarily insult their sons. Turks and Russians used to spit on a handsome, bright or charming child, and the Greeks believe that you should spit after paying someone a compliment.

Why incredibly powerful beings should feel threatened by frail humans, or why an all-powerful God would fail to protect followers from 'lesser gods', is something that few people ever explore properly or with any sense of logic.

Rabbi's would insult their sons to fool evil spirits into ignoring the favoured one.

marriage and weddings

Something old, something new,
Something borrowed, something blue
With a sixpence in her shoe.

A wedding dress should be new for good luck—a superstition that insures that wedding dressmakers will stay in employment, creating clothing that, hopefully, is only ever used once in a lifetime. Thrift doesn't help here either, as it's supposedly unlucky for a bride to make her own dress. If you're following the 'something borrowed' tradition, then borrowing a veil is very lucky, especially if it's come from someone who's had a happy marriage.

In the final preparation, it's lucky if the bride leaves one item off or one stitch undone until the very last moment, then not to look at herself in the mirror once she's 'complete'. However, once the wedding ceremony is over, it's lucky for the bride and groom to stand side by side as they look at themselves in a mirror.

The wedding veil was the original symbol of virginity, which is why the bride lifting the veil to kiss the groom was a signal of the loss of virginity. In the West the wedding dress traditionally is white, originally to symbolise a pure heart and only later in the Victorian era to denote virginity, with off-white and veilless attire for second marriages or otherwise to send an obvious signal. However, in some parts it's still acceptable to wear white and a veil if the bride is no longer a virgin but is marrying the only man she's ever had sex with. Another traditional and less sexist colour for a wedding dress was blue—the colour of love. Even today a bride is supposed to wear 'something blue' in reverence to the colour. Blue garters are especially lucky.

In the East white is often considered the colour of funerals and death. Brides in China traditionally wear more varied colours, red and gold being very auspicious. However, in traditional Shinto Japanese weddings, both the bride and groom wear white.

Some days are considered unlucky for a wedding date:

- 11 February
- any day in Lent, which usually rules out all of March or most of April
- any day in May, as a May marriage will bring poverty
- 2 June
- 2 November, All Souls' Day
- 1 December
- 28 December, Holy Innocents' Day
- during a thunderstorm.

Once you decide upon a date, stick to it, postponement is bad luck. On the day of the wedding the bride must leave her parent's house by the front door, right foot first. If the sun shines on her it's lucky and especially so if she sees a rainbow.

A horse and carriage in which the horses refuse to move or a car that refuses to start are obviously bad signs, and, although unlikely for many these days, it's bad luck to see a pig on the way to the church. More likely and also unlucky, is to see a funeral procession.

In Anglo countries it's bad luck for the bride and groom to see each other on the day of the wedding until they meet in church, but in France the groom traditionally fetches his bride and escorts her to the chapel.

It's bad luck for the bride or groom to sneeze during the wedding ceremony—although it's good luck if a cat sneezes in the bride's house on the eve of the wedding. It's good luck if the bride cries a lot on the wedding day, but if the bride tears her gown or bursts a seam, her husband will mistreat her. The wedding ring should fit, because if it falls off, it's an ill omen. The worst luck of all is if it falls off the bride's hand and rolls away from the altar steps.

Even after the wedding ceremony itself, the newlyweds are vulnerable. If a stone rolls across the path of the newlyweds this is very unlucky.

Once the newlyweds leave the church, it's traditional to throw rice or some other grain at the couple to symbolise fertility and the hope that the marriage

Chinese brides wear red and gold, which are considered very auspcious colours.

will produce children. Somehow an urban myth has developed that says that this is a bad thing, because if birds come to eat the rice, it swells up in their stomachs, which then burst and kill the birds. This idea is patently ludicrous, because the whole digestive system of birds is specifically designed to deal with grass seeds, which is what rice actually is. So feel free to throw rice at weddings and give the birds a carbohydrate kick. With their metabolism they need all the calories they can eat and it's much better for the environment than paper confetti.

On a multicultural note, not everyone throws rice. Here's a sample of what people throw in various places:

- Czech Republic: dried peas
- France: wheat
- Greece: candied almonds (also a traditional gift at christenings)
- India: puffed rice and flower petals
- Italy: coins, candy and dried fruit
- Korea: nuts and dates
- Mexico: red beads
- North Africa: figs and dates
- Turkey: candy

In Switzerland, however, it's traditional for the bride and groom to throw sweets at children in the churchyard.

The bride should always cut the first slice of a wedding cake, or the couple will be childless, although another superstition insists that that bride and groom should hold the knife or spatula to cut the cake together. To satisfy both superstitions the bride and groom should hold the knife together with the groom's hand over the bride's hand. Because the bride's hand is on the bottom she is the 'first' to cut the cake. The potential parents should keep the top tier of their wedding cake for the christening celebration of their first child.

In ancient traditions the cake wasn't eaten but thrown at the couple, as cakes were consecrated to the gods and the good fortune would stick to the couple, along with the crumbs. Today, however, all the guests should eat some of the cake, even if it's only a crumb. To refuse to taste the cake is unlucky for the person who doesn't eat *and* for the bride and groom. Traditionally a wedding cake had a ring baked inside it, so guests would eat their cake carefully. Whoever found the ring would have good luck for the rest of the year. Any leftover wedding cake should be saved for the spinsters. If an unmarried woman places a piece of wedding cake under her pillow at night, she will dream of her future husband. Whatever she actually dreams, it is the dream of the third night that will come true.

In olden days the bridesmaids would undress the bride for the bedchamber of the honeymoon. Bridesmaids would lay the bride's stockings on the nuptial bed in the shape of a cross, for luck. In the days when a wedding dress was secured with pins, the bridesmaid who got a pin first would be the first to marry. And yet there are other contradictory superstitions— that a bride should not have a pin as part of her dress at all, and if one is, it has to be thrown away—If a pin is instead given to a bridesmaid, she won't be married until Whitsuntide.

Being a bridesmaid can be a tricky business. If a bridesmaid trips in the aisle during the ceremony it's bad luck, and being one three times is a sure path to perpetual spinsterhood, unless you become a bridesmaid seven times to break the curse. For really hard cases the bride should give her bridesmaid her shoes, suggesting that the bridesmaid will follow the bride in her footsteps. Ideally the shoes should always be something old for this reason, especially if the bride has been happy.

The first newlywed to buy something after the marriage will be the dominant partner. This often meant that the bride would ceremonially buy something from her bridesmaids on the first night of the honeymoon. The Hindus hold a similar belief.

At Hindu weddings the bride and groom are barefoot on the wedding altar, and if the bridesmaids are doing their job right, they'll steal the groom's shoes and hide them so that he'll have to pay to get them back. In the Middle Ages if the man stamped on his wife's shoes, he'd wear the pants (or the breeches) in the marriage, and some German couples still compete to see which one can step on the other's feet first. In some parts of Britain, once the ceremony is over, the first who steps over the threshold of the church or the new house will call the shots in the marriage.

The tradition of the groom carrying the bride over the threshold when they first enter their new home came from the superstition that if the bride tripped while entering the house for the first time, it would be very bad luck. There was even a fear that witches with evil intent would cast a spell on the threshold so that the bride would trip deliberately. To avoid this the groom would do his duty, but should the groom trip it's especially unlucky as now both members of the pair will have bad luck.

The word honeymoon comes from an old Celtic tradition that for good luck the newlyweds should spend the first month of their marriage drinking lots of mead, a wine made from fermented honey—hence honey for the phase of a moon. Throw an old shoe at a bride and groom to ward off evil and jealousy, or tie old shoes to the back of a wedding car or coach to ensure a happy honeymoon. In some parts of Mexico those-in-the-know insist that the couple's bed be made with blue sheets, as blue will make the groom more virile.

Wedding rings are full of magic. A wife should never remove her ring except in an emergency. The risk is that if a wife lost her ring, she would lose her husband, and if the ring should ever break, she and her husband would die. The ring is useful for other reasons besides preserving the marriage or signalling 'hands off' to other men. If you find someone brave enough to take off their wedding ring, you can use it in spells. One of the seemingly infinite number of cures for warts involved pricking a wart with a gooseberry thorn, then passing the thorn through a wedding ring. Turn a wedding ring around three times in you hand, and your wish will come true. An unmarried woman can take a wedding ring and tie a strand of her own hair to it. Then she takes a glass, half filled with water from a south running stream. The woman then suspends the ring in the glass, like a pendulum. If the ring hits the rim of the glass, she will not marry. If the ring turns quickly, she will be married, if it turns slowly, she will be married twice.

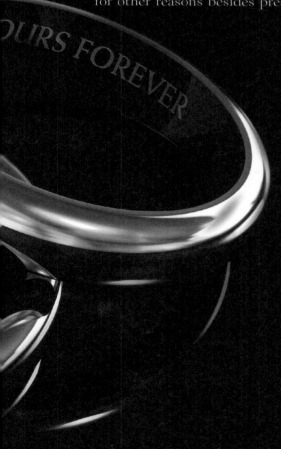

Travel

Take care that a hare, a black cat, a shrew or a person with flat feet don't cross your path as you commence a journey, or the journey is doomed to bad luck. Cancel the bad luck by returning to your starting point. Then count to nine, ten or twenty and eat or drink something. This has the effect of 'rebooting' the journey, so you can start again and hope that you don't come across a parade of flat-footed people marching down the street.

That wonderful, general purpose good-luck liquid, saliva, could come in handy, and it was good luck to spit on someone before they set out, especially if they had to travel on Friday the 13th. Sneezing and turning your head to the right at the beginning of a trip was also a good omen. And if you find a black snail, grab it quickly by its eye stalks, or 'horns', and throw it over your left shoulder for luck.

It's bad luck for a family member or friend to watch out for you once you disappear from their sight, and you should never look back. That's bad luck too.

And never start a journey with your left foot, that would be setting out on the 'wrong' foot.

pregnancy

Back in the days before overpopulation and low infant mortality rates, society encouraged couples to have children fast and frequently. With this much social pressure a number of superstitions arose around getting pregnant as quickly as possible.

If your apron falls off, you will be pregnant within the year. A woman who wants to become pregnant should rock an empty cradle, as long as the cradle has never held a child. If you rock the empty cradle of an existing child, the baby will die an early death.

A pregnant woman should avoid hares or rabbits lest her child be born with a harelip. Birth defects were frequently attributed to women becoming frightened by a particular animal during her pregnancy. This was the explanation offered for the famous gross deformities of John Merrick, The Elephant Man.

Pregnant women should avoid cyclamens, as they encourage miscarriages —another enduring superstition.

Determining the gender of the unborn baby, in the days before amniocentesis and ultrasound, was a fun activity. One old wives' tale has it that you can suspend a chain over a woman's belly and that if it swings back and forth, it's a boy, if it swings in a circle, then it's a girl.

Another famous sign is that if the shape of a woman's pregnant belly is round and high on her body, then she is carrying a girl. If the belly is more pointed and she is carrying low, then the baby is a boy. Another superstition contradicts this, saying that if the belly is almost spherical, like a beach ball, then the woman is carrying a boy, if she looks as if she's carrying a melon across her belly, then the child is a girl.

Another gender-determining method fixates on breasts. If the woman's left breast is larger, she's having a girl, if the right breast is larger, then she's carrying a boy. This smacks of sexism if you consider the ancient superstitious prejudice that left equals 'bad' and right equals 'good'. Also sexist is the superstition that if a woman is craving sweets she's carrying a girl, and if she's craving spicy or sour foods she's carrying a boy. This smacks of the 'sugar and spice' business. Needless to say, none of the signs outlined above have any truth in them at all. Similar thinking happens in the superstition that if y o u put a knife

It was thought that pregnant women should avoid cyclamens.

under your mattress you'll conceive a boy, but if you put a skillet you'll have a girl. In the region of the Ozark Mountains in Missouri, a father who wants a boy has to sit on his roof, near the chimney, for seven hours.

In South America there's another dubious way of determining gender, if not actually selecting the gender. If you have a child already, look at the back of his or her neck. If the neck seems to follow a straight ridgeline, then the next child should be a girl. If the back of the neck is more 'V' shaped, then the next child should be a boy.

There are a few old wives' tales that may have some truth in them. One is that if the mother is having a difficult labour, the child will be a boy. Statistics seem to back this one up. Boys are also more likely to experience foetal distress syndrome than girls.

Another superstition is that a girl will sap more strength from her mother, leaving mum with lifeless, stringy hair, a puffy face and more weight on her hips. In fact, when carrying a girl the mother produces more oestrogen, so is likely to put on more fat—as yet there's no explanation for what happens to her face and hair.

Many people believe that the mother can accurately dream of the gender of the child and one study has confirmed that women who have such dreams are right about 75 per cent of the time, but only if the expected mother has had twelve or more years of schooling. Why educated mothers should be better predictors of the gender of their children remains unexplained.

crossroads

Crossroads don't only work on the horizontal plane, they also work vertically. They're the places that gods descend from the heavens, and devils rise from the hells.

The Greeks had a goddess for crossroads—Hekate. Crossroads are significant because they are the places where demons and ghosts gather, so mortals traversing crossroads needed all the help they could find. Fortunately, Hekate was relatively easy to please. Just have a meal at one of her crossroad temples at the time of the new moon— another liminal point—and she'd use her powers to keep the evil ones away. For similar reasons in Haiti, Voodoo adepts appease Legba-Carrefour, the Master of the Crossroads, who is also the guardian of fences, gates, thresholds, boundaries and other places of transition.

Crossroads are also great dumping grounds, places where you could take spiritual garbage, like the remains of purification rituals or other unclean things. People who had murdered their parents were typically buried at crossroads, as were suicides. You could also bury sickness and disease at crossroads. If you have a stye in your eye, simply cross the crossroads and say 'Stye, stye, go out of my eye—and go to the stranger who next passes by!'

The Japanese believe that reaching the age of 42—the *yaku-doshi*—is extremely important and potentially inauspicious and unlucky.

In Haiti, voodoo practioners appease the god Legba-Carrefour, the Master of the Crossroads.

You could disperse the bad luck by using the following spell:

- Gather one bean for every year (42).
- Take a coin and rub it all over your body.
- Wrap the coin and beans in some paper.
- Place the paper parcel in a bamboo tube.
- Throw the bamboo tube away at a crossroads.

Of course, even in the modern world, for purely logistical reasons, crossroads are still the most frequent sites of automobile accidents. Perhaps we should recall Hekate from her long retirement.

Death

The transition from life to whatever afterlife we believe in is replete with superstition. No other single phenomenon attracts more fear and speculation, not even sex.

There are many traditions about the treatment of the dead, and the existence of funeral rites and customs are virtually universal across all cultures. Even the ancient Neanderthals buried their dead with some ceremony at least 70,000 years ago.

Superstitions regarding the recently departed are usually variations on the theme of 'uncleanliness' or 'pollution', but they surpass the practical and tangible concerns about decomposition. In Jewish culture *Cohenim* (the priests) cannot touch a corpse. In the area around Lake Titicaca in Bolivia, the locals strangle the corpse 'to prevent the stench escaping'.

The Zoroastrians (the Parsi of Iran and India) consider the corpse so unclean that it cannot be allowed to touch the earth. So they build *dakhmas*, so-called 'Towers of Silence', and place the dead on the tops of the towers, where vultures are allowed to pick the bones clean. The bones are then thrown into a central pit in the tower, covered with quicklime and allowed to crumble to dust.

In many cultures the corpse must always be carried out feet first through the front door. If the corpse can look back on the family, it might beckon another to join them in the afterlife. Feng shui practice avoids putting beds in bedrooms in such a way as that when a person is lying down their feet are pointing at the door. This is considered the 'corpse position', and it's very unhealthy for the living. However, when a corpse is being laid to rest within a house, it's considered good luck for the feet to be pointing to the east, as this is the direction of the rising sun and dawn has an ancient association with rebirth. Also the corpse has to be carried to the cemetery with the sun behind it, even if this meant taking a longer detour.

Other no-nos to do with funerals include:
- Pregnant women should not attend funerals.
- Never wear anything new to a funeral, especially new shoes.
- Never count the cars in a funeral procession.
- Never hold a funeral on a Friday or there will be another death in the family within the year.
- Never bury a woman in black or she'll return to haunt the family.
- Delaying the actual funeral is unlucky, because it may invite death to hang around, waiting for more souls to take from the same household.

The ancient Greek character Charon was the ferryman who carried the souls of the dead across the River Styx and into the underworld. Charon demanded payment for passage and would refuse to ferry souls too cheap to pay—or perhaps more tragically, too poor. Those who did not pay the fare would be condemned to stay on this side of the Styx and become ghosts. This belief led to the widespread practice of placing a coin for payment with the body, often in the corpse's mouth.

Another belief was that the corpse's eyes should always be shut, because the dead would be looking for someone to accompany them into the afterlife and could steal a soul. This led to the practice of holding down the shut eyelids with two coins, thus killing two birds with one stone. If you could steal back the coins that had lain on a corpse's eyes, and replace them with other coins to pay the ferryman, you could place the coins on your own eyes and look into the souls of men, or into the future.

In Greece, a recently widowed person must smash a plate in front of their house before going to the funeral.

Funeral processions, being liminal experiences, are fraught with danger. It's considered unlucky to walk or drive in front of a funeral procession, and in England undertakers would stick metal pins in every gate on the route of a funeral procession. The iron in the pins would protect the living and the dead from evil spirits.

Rain, while inconvenient for the mourners, is good for the soul of the dead during a funeral:

Happy is the bride the sun shines on,
Happy is the corpse that the rain rains on.

Because fire seems to consume objects and make them disappear, many traditions have assumed that fire transports material objects into the spirit world. Often personal possessions would be burned with a body. The Chinese burn paper money from the 'Bank of Hell' to send fortune to their departed friends and relatives.

In Korea it's believed that if the dead die far from home, their spirits will get lost and be cursed to wander the earth forever, so, whenever possible, the dying are brought home to end their lives.

An enduring superstition of death from the United Kingdom concerns flowers. Never combine red and white flowers in an arrangement, to do so invites death.

The transition from life to whatever afterlife we believe in is replete with superstition.

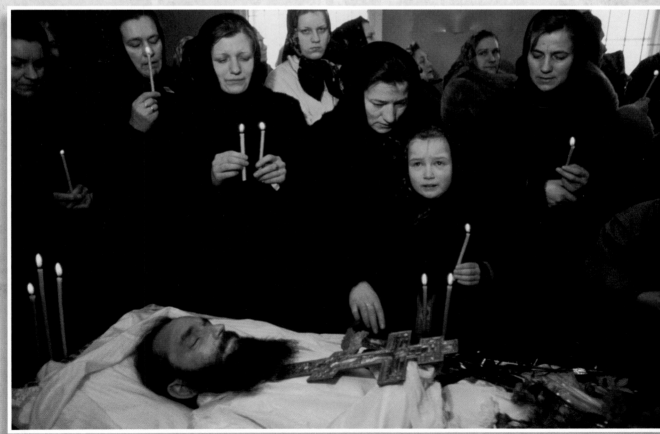

Executions

Back in the days when hangings and beheadings were more common, a number of beliefs grew up about executions. One was that if the rope broke on a hanging, the criminal was innocent. It was simply inconceivable that the gods would allow an innocent man to die or even be injured. To find the correct perpetrator of murder, people once believed that the corpse of a murder victim would bleed if touched by the murderer.

A Hindu cremation in India. Many traditions use fire to transport the dead into the spirit world.

suicide

The ancient Greeks and Romans thought suicide to be an honourable way to die and a condemned criminal could be assured that if he killed himself, his family could still inherit his estate.

Orthodox Hindu widows were called upon to throw themselves upon the funeral pyres of their husbands in a practice known as suttee. The Japanese have always thought that suicide was a perfectly reasonable way to go. Famous examples, of course, are the Kamikaze suicide pilots of World War II and the practice of *seppuku* (literally, belly cutting), ritual disembowelment and beheading for samurai men. Samurai women, in contrast, would cut their jugular veins in a practice simply known as *jigai*.

In contrast, Judaism and Christianity have generally condemned the practice. Christianity taught that self-murderers had committed a mortal sin. Corpses of suicides were, for centuries, buried just outside the consecrated ground of the church or cemetery. If a suicide was buried inside a church ground, the body would be laid lengthwise against a wall so that no one could step over it. If a pregnant woman stepped over the grave of a suicide, she was certain to miscarry and nothing was said to grow on ground where a suicide had been buried.

Since the soul would not be admitted to heaven, there was a danger that the dead would return to life as vampires or other undead creatures, so people were known to pour acid on the body to dissolve it. There was also a belief that spirits could lift the corpse of a suicide from the grave, carry it to its old house and lean it against the front door. The body would fall to the floor when the first person in the household opened the door in the morning.

Much of Islam has also always frowned on suicide, in spite of the propensity among some contemporary Muslims to kill themselves in acts of terrorism, with the promise that they will be rewarded by—among other things—sex in paradise with a hundred virgins in one day. It has, however, been suggested that you can discourage some acts of this type by threatening to cover the corpse of a suicide bomber—or what's left of it—in pig's blood and to bury the body inside a pig's carcass. No self-respecting *houri* in paradise would be game to touch a Muslim buried in a pig's corpse.

Islam has always frowned on suicide.

cemetery, tomb and grave

A well-known superstition is that you shudder or suddenly have goose pimples when someone is 'walking on your grave'. Considering that you are probably still alive and well when you shudder, we must assume that it is the site of your future grave that someone is walking over.

In the days when many women and their children died in childbirth, it was a comfort to know that to be buried with a stillborn infant was a certain entry to heaven.

In Christian tradition corpses should be laid so that the dead will face east, to face the Archangel Gabriel when he blows his horn on the day of resurrection. Ideally the grave should be on the south side of the church, if you are in the northern hemisphere and vice versa in the southern hemisphere.

If rain falls on the coffin during a funeral, or if there is a clap of thunder and a flash of lightning at the end of the services, this is a sign that the soul of the departed has reached heaven.

Islam tends not to put too great an emphasis on the remains of the dead. Nevertheless in some cases the tombs of holy men have a hole in them so that the prayers of the faithful may reach them.

In the traditions of many cultures of Africa, people are buried with the dried remains of their umbilical cords. It's believed that these remnants retain the protective spirit of the afterbirth, the spiritual double that protected the person through life, and who will now rejoin them in the afterlife.

Some Christians believe that the first person buried in a new churchyard would be claimed by the Devil. If possible then, it should be a condemned criminal. Once land has been used as a graveyard, it should never be used to grow things,

even if the remains were all moved and the ground deconsecrated. Flowers will grow on the grave of someone who was good in life, weeds on the tomb of someone who was bad.

Urinating on the graves was a sure way to annoy the dead, and if you wanted to raise their spirits, pour blood on the graves and call them by name.

When passing a cemetery, hold your breath or risk breathing in the spirit of a recently dead person who has not yet found their way to heaven.

Heavy tombstones are lucky because of the common fear that the dead will rise again if they're not held down. So the heavier the tombstone, the better. If you find a lily growing on a grave and wish to remove it, cut it, but don't uproot it, otherwise the corpse will rise at the next full moon. Never make a headstone out of red stone, or the dead will seek out more red – it's a sure way of creating a vampire.

If you pass through a graveyard at night and you're getting a little nervous, feel free to whistle to stay safe but on no account must you sing or demons will join you in song then take you away with them to hell.

lucky in love

lucky in love

The lore of magic, superstitions and love is so vast that you would need a book the size of an encyclopaedia to cover it all. Romantic relationships in particular have always been both important and potentially dangerous, especially in the West, which tends to have a more dewy-eyed view of the world than many other cultures.

Midsummer's Day

Some of these superstitions and spells are said to work only on Midsummer's Day. This is traditionally 24 June in the Northern Hemisphere and 24 December in the Southern Hemisphere.

Although if you really want to be precise, it varies slightly from year to year so you may want to consult an astronomer for the right date.

For Midwinter's Day reverse these dates.

aphrodisiacs

Few superstitions have done quite as much harm to nature as the belief that certain parts of animals will give men a better sex life. Although the developed world now has access to genuine aphrodisiacs, such as Viagra, millions throughout the world still swear by more traditional substances.

Rhinoceroses and elephants have died by the thousands simply to provide tusks and horns. The symbolism is obvious. If these animals have these long, thick, hard protuberances, then by ingesting these things you too will have long, thick, hard … you get the picture. Unfortunately, powdered rhinoceros horn and elephant tusk still fetch high prices in some markets, even though rhino horn is mostly keratin, and elephant tusk is mostly dentine. The fools who buy them are forking out big money for what is essentially pulverised fingernail and powdered teeth.

Tigers' penises are also highly prized for their supposed aphrodisiac properties. Ingesting those sounds far worse.

Spanish Fly is actually a beautiful green beetle that produces a chemical called cantharidin. This substance is a powerful irritant that stimulates the nervous system, a little like cayenne pepper on steroids. Crushed Spanish Fly contains about five per cent cantharidin, and the powder is nasty smelling and bitter, but that doesn't stop men from taking it, or even putting it directly on their penises. Cantharidin actually works, if you find irritation stimulating, but it is also highly toxic. The amount you need is tiny, and the difference between an effective dose and a harmful dose isn't much at all. Many who have used it have done themselves permanent damage.

Being creatures that are thought to be almost entirely stomach and genitals, oysters have a reputation as an aphrodisiac—at least in the West. They do, after all, bear a passing resemblance to human female genitalia. The Chinese, however, prescribe oysters specifically to inhibit sex—in particular nocturnal emissions, also known as 'copulation with ghosts'. Whether you eat oysters to increase or decrease your sexual activity, at least oysters haven't been hunted to near extinction.

Men have also looked to plants for help with their sex lives. Some Chinese swear by ginseng for a variety of ills and it helps that the plant resembles a human being in its shape. The very name means 'man root', but no study has show that it is an effective aphrodisiac.

The extract of the bark of the yohimbine tree, an evergreen which grows in Africa, is a much better candidate for legitimate use as an aphrodisiac. The active ingredient, yohimbine chloride, is now a prescription medicine to treat erectile dysfunction, although there's no indication that it increases libido, or the sex urge itself.

Nature, however, may have come up with a real aphrodisiac. It's called tangkat ali. This flowering plant is native to Indonesia and Malaysia and has traditionally been used also for the treatment of malaria. Some studies have now found it to be effective against certain types of cancer cells. Significantly, there are indications that it increases testosterone levels in animals and humans, and that it might actually improve erectile function and increase human libido.

Opposites attract

The theory that opposites attract makes for interesting theatre, film and literature. However, for better or worse, real life is not story land, and the theory that opposites attract is a complete myth. Here are some facts from 'Sex in America: A Definitive Survey' (Laumann et al. Little Brown 1994), which you could probably safely extrapolate to the population of the whole world.

Among sexually active unmarried people:

- 68 per cent of Catholic men pair up with Catholic women, and 67 per cent of Catholic women pair up with Catholic men.
- 61 per cent of Protestant men pair up with Protestant women, and 72 per cent of Protestant women pair up with Protestant men.
- 81 per cent of women who didn't finish high school end up with men with the same level of formal education.
- 71 per cent of women with a graduate degree end up with men with graduate degrees.
- Only two per cent of men with graduate degrees reported even having a romantic relationship with a woman who hadn't finished high school.
- Most striking of all, in spite of all the rhetoric about racial harmony, 94 per cent of white men pair up with a white woman, while 89.5 per cent of white women pair up with a white man.
- And 82 per cent of black men pair up with black women, while 97 per cent of black women pair up with a black man.

It seems that equality and mutual respect is not the same as affinity.

Birds of a feather continue to flock together.

encouraging love

If your love is taking a while to find, you can even help things along a bit. Take an ivy leaf and put it against your heart. Say the following:

Ivy, Ivy, I love you,
In my bosom I put you,
The first young man / woman who
speaks to me,
My future husband / wife s/he shall be.

Boys wishing to gain the love of a girl should take an orange and prick all the pits of the skin with a needle. He should then sleep with the fully pricked orange under the armpit of his choice (for once the left or right doesn't matter from a magical point of view). The next day he should offer the girl the orange. If she eats it, she'll return his love.

To attract love, carry around the 'beard' of a wild turkey.

finding love

There are hundreds of ways to find out the name of your future love, or even if you'll marry at all. Many are connected with particular days.

On a Friday go out in complete silence and gather nine holly leaves. Tie the nine leaves into a three-cornered handkerchief, using nine knots. Put the handkerchief under your pillow, and you will dream of your future lover, but only if you stay silent from the moment you set out to gather the leaves until the moment you wake the following day.

Run three times around a church on the eve of St Valentine's Day (13 February) at midnight and you'll dream of your future lover when you sleep.

Take a flowering Haw-thorn branch and hang it on a signpost at a crossroads on 30 April, the evening before May Day. Let it hang all night. Your future lover will come from the direction that the wind has blown the branch. If the branch blows away altogether, you will never marry.

Pluck a rose on Mid-summer's Day. Take the plucked rose and wrap it in white paper. Put it away for two days. If it's still fresh and sweet then you'll marry. If the rose has turned brown it's a bad sign.

In the early morning of Saint John's Eve (23 June), before you've eaten anything, gather some St John's Wort while it is still covered in dew. Sleep with it under your pillow that night, and you will dream of the person you marry. Alternatively the herb can keep away any demons on St John's Eve and could promote fertility for childless women.

On the eve of All Saints' Day or Halloween (31 October) go to your bedroom. Light two candles on your dressing table. Stand in silence in front of your mirror, brush your hair and eat an apple. You'll see the spirit of your future lover looking over your shoulder, reflected in the mirror glass.

At the first full moon of winter, if the moon is shining strongly enough to cast a shadow then take a silver bowl and fill it with water. Catch the moon's reflection in the bowl. Take a new silk handkerchief and look at the moon's reflection through the cloth. The number of moons you can see through the handkerchief will be the same as the number of months before your wedding day.

During any other full moon, stand on a stone that you've never stood on before. With your back to the moon, hold up a mirror so that you can see the moon's image in the glass. The number of moons you see will reflect the number of years before your wedding.

There are several other ways to find out about your love prospects. Take two acorns. Give one acorn your name and the other the name of a prospective love. Drop them together into a bowl of water. If they float together, you will be lovers. If they float apart, tough luck.

If a girl finds nine peas in a pod, she should put the pod on the lintel of the front door. The first man to cross the threshold will be her future love. Alternatively, gather your friends around a table. Fill a bowl with peas. Take turns eating the peas one at a time. The person who eats the last pea will be the last to marry.

If you live near any ash trees, find an ash leaf that has an equal number of divisions on either side of its central vein. Say the following: 'Even, even Ash, I pluck from this tree, for this night my true love I'll see.' Now sleep with the leaf under your pillow and your future love will appear in a dream.

If you're so popular, or so indecisive, that you have a variety of potential lovers to choose from then do the following. Mark a number of onions with the names of your candidates. The one that sprouts first will have the name of your true love.

Finding two teaspoons on your saucer is a sign that you'll soon be married. If you're in China, if you see a magpie, you are about to marry.

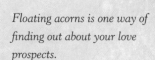

Floating acorns is one way of finding out about your love prospects.

gifts of love

Roses come with codes. To send the right message when you give them to someone here is a guide.

- Red rose: the giver is pure of heart.
- White rose: the giver is a virgin or naïve of love.
- Fully bloomed rose: the love is to be kept secret.
- Yellow rose: the giver is jealous.

Giving gloves is generally bad luck, except for Valentine's day when the gift of gloves is a sign that the giver is interested in you.

Legend has it that St Valentine wore amethyst, so give some to your lover when they finally show up, for good luck.

keeping love

Fidelity is always a concern. Here are a few spells to ensure that a lover will stay true, to test your suspicions about them or to encourage them to return.

If your lover is going away, give them a sprig of rosemary and they'll stay faithful to you.

Make a tea from the leaves of the myrtle to enhance beauty. Make a tea from the flowers of the myrtle and have your lover drink it to ensure their fidelity and keep their love.

If you're suspicious about someone, throw an apple pip on a fire. If it pops, your lover is true, if it just sits there and burns, your lover is being unfaithful.

If you're unsure, wait until your lover walks on earth or soft ground. Dig up the dirt from their footprint. Plant a marigold in the soil. If it grows, your lover is being faithful and will stay that way.

If you want to know whether a lover who has strayed will return to you, arrange seven beans in a circle on a path that you know your lover has walked on. Then, the next time they walk on the path, if they step inside the circle or on any of the beans, they'll come back. If they don't, it's over.

On Midsummer's Eve gather three roses. Early on the morning of Midsummer's Day bury one rose under a yew tree, one under a newly lain grave and place the third under your pillow. If your lover has strayed, you will haunt them in your dreams until they return to you.

Throw twelve pins onto a fire at midnight and incant:

Tis not these pins I wish to burn,
But (insert lover's name here) I wish
*   to turn,*
May s/he never rest,
Till s/he has granted my request.

If your lover drinks tea from the myrtle flower, their fidelity will be assured.

the house of
superstition

The house of superstition

Until the nineteenth century most people lived outside of cities, and even those who did live in cities, mostly worked at home or close by. So for most of human history, the vast majority of people spent most of their lives in their own houses, and the line between 'family life' and 'work life' was indistinct. Anything that happened at home would affect the rest of your life, so the home became a canvas on which people would paint their superstitions, and magic was attached even to the most ordinary of objects and the most mundane of events.

Appliances

More inspired by religious law than a superstition, Orthodox Jews will not activate any electricity, or use any appliances on the Sabbath, nor can they allow anyone in their sphere of influence to do so either, unless the device was already turned on before the start of the Sabbath. Tradition states that the Sabbath commences on a Friday after sunset, as soon as you can see three stars in the sky. It ends on Saturday, at dusk with the same requirement to see three stars in the sky.

In Greece, you should never operate a washing machine on a holy day, or it will bring you bad luck. However, this only applies to Greek Orthodox holy days.

Beds

Beds should always point east to west, parallel to the sun's course. If beds point north to south the sleeper will be restless or have nightmares. Never turn your mattress on a Sunday, or you'll have bad dreams all week, and if you want to make sure that you alienate your lover, turn your mattress on a Friday.

If three people make a bed together, someone will die in it within a week.

The expression 'getting out of bed on the wrong side' comes from the superstition that you should always get out of bed in the morning on the same side as you got in. To do otherwise will 'break the circle' and leave you bad tempered for the rest of the day.

Never climb into a bed going over the footboard, and never put a hat on a bed.

Brooms

The Chinese believe that a spirit inhabits a floor broom, so it should never be played with or used in games, nor should you use it for cleaning the effigies of the household gods or the household shrine or alter. All these practices are disrespectful and will anger the house spirits.

Never lean a broom against a bed, it will bring bad luck to those who sleep in the bed.

If you sweep a room in which a guest has stayed immediately after they've left, they will never return. Also never sweep over the feet of an unmarried person, or they will never marry.

clothing and footwear

If you stick a piece of iron onto a magnet for long enough, the iron eventually becomes magnetic. Clothes and shoes are in intimate contact with the body for long stretches of time and, using the same logic, eventually become charged with the aura of the wearer. This was especially true in Europe during the Middle Ages, when people didn't change clothing as often as they do nowadays. Considering that they didn't bathe as often either, 'aura' wasn't the only thing that the clothing would become charged with.

People naturally believed that you could use samples of clothing to cast a spell on the wearer, for good or ill. On the other hand, clothing that came from particular people could weave its own magic. During the Middle Ages there arose an entire industry in the relics and personal possessions of saints, and churches—or individuals—could grow rich if they claimed to have scraps of clothing, or better still, whole garments, or best of all, the complete remains from a holy man or woman. If you could establish a reputation that the relic had remarkable curative powers or could perform other miracles, the possessing church and its coffers, could fill with the gratitude and bribery of the expectant faithful. Even today the superstition persists. At some important level acquiring an item that was used or possessed by an admired person must serve a deep psychological need for some people. How else do you explain fans buying the caps or shirts of sports stars, as if somehow you could buy someone else's glory reflected in their hand-me-downs?

More specifically, certain items of clothing and the way that people use them have acquired their own superstitions.

Putting on your clothes inside out or backwards accidentally is lucky, but only if you don't immediately take them off and put them on the right way around. If you want to keep the luck, you'll have to keep them that way. Folklorists trace the origin of this superstition to Duke William of Normandy, who inadvertently put on his chainmail back to front just before the Battle of Hastings. His courtiers noticed this and said it was bad luck, but William

declared that it was good luck, and a sign that he was about to change his status from that of duke to that of king. Although his enemy King Harold's forces greatly outnumbered his own, the Duke's army was fresh, Harold's was exhausted, and William's battle strategy worked. He killed Harold and became William the Conqueror.

Never wash new clothes before wearing them, and when you do wear clothes for the first time you should pinch yourself for good luck, or if you're putting new clothes on children, you should pinch them. Also always make a wish when you put on new clothes for the first time, and put a coin in a pocket if the item has one to ensure that you'll never run out of it.

If you drop a pair of gloves, it's bad luck to pick them up yourself. Instead, ask a friend or a friendly passer-by to pick them up for you. Then both you and the person who picked the gloves up will have good luck. If you find gloves, it's a sign that you will soon begin a new romantic relationship.

Never give socks as a present, as it's a sign that either the giver or receiver will walk away from the relationship forever. You can counteract this simply by offering the giver a small coin in 'payment' for the items. If you're knitting socks for a friend, you can keep the relationship by knitting into the fabric some of your own hair, but never stick the knitting needles in a garment that you're knitting, or in the ball of yarn, as this will make the future wearer ill.

cutlery

Cutlery was once so expensive to make that each person had his or her own set to keep. Your knife, fork and spoon were considered so personal that anything unusual happening to them was a 'sign'.

Dropped cutlery is a general sign that someone will soon pay you a visit. Dropping a fork means that you'll soon have a visit from a male. If you drop a spoon on the ground and it lands face up, something good is coming, face down and you'll lose something or face a disappointment. Dropping a spoon can also mean that you'll soon have a visit from a woman or a young person of either gender. A dropped knife cancels the magic of either a dropped fork or spoon, but of course this only works if the drop is accidental.

The line between 'superstition' and 'politeness' is often unclear. You can trace the modern rules of politeness to superstition, hygiene or even safety, so, for example, you should never hold a knife near your face or hold it by the point, and when handing a knife to another, you should always give it to them handle first. Less easy to explain is a rule like the one that says you should never cut boiled eggs with a knife; although it may have arisen out of concern that you would darken the yolk in the days before stainless steel.

Never stir anything with a fork, to do that is to stir up misfortune. And people will slander you if you cross two forks accidentally. Never cross knives on a table, or there will be quarrels.

Knock on wood

In many traditions you should always knock on wood after something good has happened, or even if you think something good has happened, so that evil spirits won't take your luck away.

In fact 'touch wood' or 'knock on wood' is the best-known superstition in the English-speaking world, but in South America, there is a special proviso—it doesn't work if the wood is part of an object that has legs. So knocking on a wooden chair, table, cabinet or bed is useless. You'll have to find some other wooden object, like a bowl or even a pencil.

fires and hearths

Making fire wasn't always as easy as striking a match or turning a switch, so once you'd started one it was a good idea to use whatever magic you could to keep it going. New Guineans make small statues to stand near fires, watch them and stop them going out.

Fires that refuse to start are a bad sign, as fires refuse to draw if the Devil is at hand, which is pretty illogical if you think about it, considering Satan's affinity for heat. Nevertheless, to scare him away, place the poker across the grate—the iron forms a series of crosses and the Devil flees.

Oblong, hollow cinders are referred to as 'coffins', and if one flies out of the fire, there will soon be a death in the family. However, if an oval cinder, a 'cradle,' flies out, this portends a birth. If any other cinder pops out then it means a guest is coming.

Fire is purifying in many cultures. In ancient Japan when a nobleman, especially an emperor, died, the residence or palace had to be burned down.

Fire can also be a bad sign. In England if a house burns down, another should not be built in the same place. If you dream of fire, you will quarrel with someone.

As difficult as fires were to start, they were often harder to put out. Since they can cause a lot of damage, it helps to have insurance. If you can't afford insurance, hang the skin of an adder in the rafters of your house, or hang seaweed on your mantle and your house will never catch fire.

Housewarming

In North Yorkshire, England, you carry one plate of bread and one plate of salt into each room of a new house for luck. In other traditions the first items brought in would be a box of coal and a plate of salt, or a loaf of bread and a new broom.

The general advice about the risks of giving knives as gifts also applies to housewarmings. If you give a knife as a housewarming gift your neighbor or friend will soon become your enemy. The Koreans believe that the best housewarming gift is laundry detergent because the bubbles represent money and good fortune.

Housework

In the days when servants were much more common than they are now, there was a whole subculture of housework superstitions:

- Never enter a house before midday to perform a job.
- Never start a new job on a Friday.
- Never let water that had been boiled stand cold in a bedroom.
- Never sweep out a bedroom within an hour of the departure of a guest.
- Never return the shell of a soft-boiled egg to the kitchen unless you'd smashed out the bottom first.

Some superstitions have survived to the present and people continue to avoid sweeping the floor before sunrise or bringing eggs into the house after sunset for fear of bad luck.

Kitchens

The superstitions of the kitchen mainly revolve about the activity of the kitchen, principally cooking, rather than the kitchen itself.

An old Jewish superstition states that you should never leave any cooking utensil in an oven when it's not in use. If you do this habitually, one day you won't have anything else to put in the oven. When you're baking or pastry-making, never leave any dough or pastry unused, or you'll ruin all your baking.

The placement of the kitchen is especially important in Feng Shui. It's considered really bad to build a bathroom over or install a water tank over the kitchen as the water element suppresses the warming fire element of the kitchen.

Mirrors

Alchemists and other magicians have often used mirrors to look into the future. The mirrors don't necessarily have to be made of polished metal or a thin layer of metal painted on to a glass background. Any still body of water would do. Nostradamus would gaze into his scrying bowl—a bowl of water balanced on a brass tripod—to see his famous visions of the future. He communicated what he'd learnt in obscure and ambiguous quatrains in order to avoid persecution by the Inquisition.

The Latin word for mirror, *speculum*, gives us our word 'speculation', which used to mean using magic to look into the future. Speculation was a form of witchcraft forbidden by The Church for centuries. If you spent too much time in front of mirrors, you could be accused of either the sin of vanity or dabbling in the dark arts. Particularly risky was looking into a mirror at night, when evil spirits might snatch your soul away through your reflection. If you saw another's face beside your own in a mirror—assuming that there was no other real person there—you would soon die. Another high-risk activity was to have a mirror reflect your image during a thunderstorm. It was thought the Devil could capture your soul in a mirror during a lightning flash.

The most well-known superstition about mirrors is that if you break one, you're in for seven years of bad luck. This is because a mirror could capture your soul, so breaking the mirror meant damaging the soul that was reflected in it. Originally the belief was that if you

Ladders

Folklorists claim that walking under ladders is perceived as bad luck because the ladder and the ground form a triangle, and to walk through a ladder is to break the sacred shape—the representation of the Holy Trinity.

If a woman walks under a ladder, she will not marry for at least a year. However, you can walk under a ladder and keep your luck if you do one of the following: cross yourself first; cross your fingers and make a wish before going under it; or cross your fingers and spit over your left shoulder. Another solution is to keep silent until you come across your first four-legged animal.

However, if you step over a ladder while making a wish, your wish will come true.

The 'ladder = bad luck' equation might not be so far-fetched as you might think. Orthopaedic Surgeons inAmerica treat about 500,000 ladder-related injuries every year. Three hundred of these accidents are fatal. In Britain there are 40,000 ladder accidents annually, of which about 50 are fatal. In Australia, in the year ending 30 June 2005 there were 3486 ladder injuries resulting in hospitalisation and 22 deaths. Most of these accidents happen because people don't use ladders often and they don't know how to do things safely. In the spirit of false economy, they'd rather do a job themselves than hire a professional with training and insurance. Since it's difficult to tell sometimes whether the person on the ladder knows what he's doing, prudence advises that you give ladders a wide birth. Ladders don't hurt people. People hurt people.

broke your 'mirror soul', you would die, but people modified the superstition to just seven years bad luck as a sort of consolation prize. In South America, the bad luck break only occurs if the mirror breaks into three pieces.

The belief in the fatal mirror is very old. The ancient Greeks believed that you would soon die if you saw your reflection, especially if you indulged in prolonged gazing at the expense of everything else, the legend of Narcissus being an extreme case. And mirrors were not only dangerous for the living, but for the dead too. In Europe, North America and parts of India, mirrors were covered in the presence of a corpse and some Orthodox Jews today still adhere to the practice. The belief was that the soul escaping the body could become trapped in the mirror. Unable to reach whatever world of the afterlife it had been destined for, the spirit would then haunt the living.

A mirror was not only a trap, but a gateway. In France and Germany on New Year's Eve or on the Eve of Epiphany (5 January), if you performed the right magic you could see the souls of the dead in a mirror—presumably untrapped.

In the East, the mirror was also thought to reveal the 'true image of things'. When you combine this idea with the belief of spiritual entrapment, you could use mirrors to your advantage. When Taoists take their meditative walks into the mountains, they carry a 23-centimetre (9-inch) mirror on their backs. No evil spirit dare attack them from behind for fear that they might see their own true reflection in the mirror. Archaeologists have uncovered tombs throughout the world, from Egypt to Madagascar and Serbo-Croatia, in which the mourners place mirrors in front of the faces of the dead. This was possibly an insurance policy to entrap the soul specifically in the mirror and stop them from leaving the tomb and haunting the living.

Water reflections work equally well as a shield. With considerable ingenuity and lateral thinking, the East Prussians would save the water from washing a corpse. Once the funeral party had left with the coffin, the householders would pour the water around the front of the house as a barrier to prevent the soul of the deceased returning.

Naturally, since the mirror is supposed to reveal the soul, beings who don't have a soul don't have a reflection—think vampires.

photography

For obvious reasons when 'the white man' first demonstrated photography to technologically primitive societies, the tribesmen thought that white men were powerful sorcerers who were able to capture their souls. Many cultures still object to the display of photographs or images of people after they are dead. Nevertheless we've still found time to develop our own superstitions about photographs. If three people are photographed together, the one in the middle will die first.

pins

Being made of iron, pins are powerful magic against evil spirits. Stick a pin into the lapel of someone's coat to guard them against evil or, if you want industrial-strength magic, stick an onion or a sheep's heart full of pins.

If you lose an item, stick a pin into a cushion and incant: 'I pin the devil,' and you'll be sure to find the object soon.

Pins are also classically used to stick into effigies if you want to give someone a pain in a particular body part. To work properly the effigy is usually made from wax or clay with a hair or nail clipping of the person you want to hex. This explains the care with which superstitious people dispose of their clippings.

tables

It's bad luck to let a cat jump on your table. It's also bad luck to put fire tongs or a fireplace poker on a table, and if you put a bellows on the table—unlikely in this day and age—you'll make the Devil dance and there will be a quarrel in the home that night. You also invite ill luck and quarrelling if you put shoes or boots on a table, especially new ones. If you have and they've left a mess, don't sweep the table with a broom, or even put a cleaning or sweeping brush on a table, as that's unlucky too. If a pigeon visits your house, it's a good sign, but if it comes indoors and settles on a table, there will be sickness in the house.

A superstition from Herefordshire, England, maintains that putting a lantern on a table can be disastrous, especially for a farmer, as it will cause calves to be born prematurely: 'lantern on the table, death in the stable.'

Why resting your elbows on the table should be considered rude is anyone's guess.

Always lay a table clockwise, or 'sunwise', as to do so the other way is to 'go against the sun'.

Whatever happens, never, ever sit thirteen down to a table for dinner, this is a sure sign that one of the party will die within the year. Folklorists almost universally maintain that the origin of this superstition is the Christian last supper, at which thirteen people were present.

The result of this is death, although there is some question as to which one of the thirteen at a dinner party is the most likely to die. Some believe that it is the last person to sit down, which has led some savvy hosts to insist that when the thirteenth guest is ready to sit down, the twelve already seated should all rise, so everyone can sit down simultaneously. Presumably this decreases the chances of death by twelve thirteenths. However, others maintain that the most likely to die will be the first one to rise.

Another common cure to the problem is to set a fourteenth place and sit a substitute in the stead of a real guest. The Savoy Hotel in London has a wooden cat called Kaspar who performs this invaluable function, just in case.

The accident of four people shaking hands across a table at the same time receives mixed reviews, some maintain that this is unlucky, while others believe that it portends that one of the four will be married within a year, which might also be unlucky, depending on how you feel about marriage.

Random objects

Here are a few more household objects with magic attached.

Books: if a book drops on a floor, step on it before you pick it up, or it's bad luck.

Candles: people generally use candle magic to grant wishes and desires, but you can burn candles of various colours for various effects: red for the courage to make changes; orange to inspire assertiveness and endurance or for happiness and health; yellow for travel or for help with communication; green for love and healing; blue for inner peace and tranquillity, but also for career, work and power; indigo for psychic development; lilac for relaxation and restful sleep; pink for love; brown for the house and home; silver for your secret desires; gold for success in business and for wealth; and to rid yourself of guilt, burn a black candle.

Chairs: never rock an empty chair and never spin a chair on one leg.

Keys: the Japanese use charms made of three keys joined together on the same key ring. Each key 'unlocks' a door leading to wisdom, life and love.

Soap: in Greece never pass soap, detergent or any other cleaning agent, including shampoo, by hand, as this has the effect of 'pushing bad luck' on to another person. Instead, put the cleaner down onto a table or tile and let the other person pick it up.

Stairs: it's bad luck to pass someone on the stairs, but if you do, it's even worse to stop, turn around and go back. To undo the bad luck, walk backwards down or up the stairs until you reach the landing, then start again. Stumbling while you're going up the stairs is good luck, but bad luck if you're on your way down.

thresholds

Stumbling anywhere is a sign that you've crossed someone's threshold. This is trespassing on magical territory and is unlucky. If you stumble, you must immediately turn around three times, clockwise, and incant: 'I turn myself three times about, and thus I put bad luck to rout.'

In Greece always cross any threshold into a building with your right foot first. The Roman aristocracy went so far as to place a slave at the door to ensure that everyone on festival days entered the house right foot first. This is the ancient origin of our modern footmen.

windows

If a bird bangs against any window, it's a bad sign, a portent of death to one of the members of the household. Introduce a cat to a new house by putting it through the window, rather than the front door. This will ensure that the cat will never run off.

In Greece, always cross a threshold with your right foot first.

eating and drinking with spirits

eating and drinking with spirits

Religions, customs and superstitions, both ancient and modern, have always had a lot to say about food. Eating is an intimate act. Foods are things we take in and they become a part of us. We are what we eat. No wonder there are superstitions about food. What can you eat? What can't you eat? When can you or can't you eat? What's poisonous? What's holy? What's profane?

Superstitions and rituals regarding the act of eating can be very elaborate. In some cultural systems the higher your status, the more restrictions there are, not only as to what you can eat, but also as to how you can eat and with whom you can eat. Many religious taboos relating to foods are well-known in the West, but some are better known than others. Whether these taboos among the big three religions—Judaism, Christianity and Islam—are 'superstition' or 'divine law' depends on your point of view, but they're included here to provide a cultural background and a better understanding of beliefs about food in general.

apples

In Western folklore the apple is the fruit of love and fertility, so many of the traditions to do with apples have to do with finding and keeping love. However, this doesn't stop the versatile apple from finding itself in other magic.

Cut an apple in half horizontally. Count the number of seeds that you see. This will tell you how many children you'll have.

If two or more people are gathered together, they can each peel an apple from top to bottom. The person with the longest unbroken peel will have the longest life.

Rubbing a peeled apple onto your wart, then giving the apple to a pig to eat is yet another wart remedy.

Beans

Pythagoras and his followers sought contact with the divine through dreams. Anything that could disrupt sleep was therefore suspect. He and his followers popularised the belief that beans were bad because they produce flatulence—their most famous side effect.

Another association that beans had going against them was their presumed resemblance to testicles. Eating beans, therefore, was a little too close to cannibalism to be comfortable. The Romans popularised another idea: that beans served to house the spirits of the dead. To eat beans was thus a form of spiritual cannibalism, denying them the opportunity to be reborn. Think magically. Souls leave the body, spend their time in testicles for a while, until they are put back in wombs to be reborn as babies. Some souls end up in beans before making the transition to testicles. It all makes sense.

There is also an association between beans and the dead between various Amerindian peoples, like the Pawnee of Nebraska, and there are friezes on the holy buildings of the pre-Inca Peruvian Mohica Indians that show figures that are half-bean, half-men. There is, however, no record of any bean-eating taboo in the Americas.

The Japanese have a slightly different take. In the Feast of Setsubun, which hails the coming of spring, people scatter soybeans throughout their houses chanting: *'Oni wa soto! Fuka wa uchi,'* which means: 'Evil demons out! Good luck home!' The family then eat plates of beans, one bean for every year of a person's life. This is a sort of internal immunisation against evil spirits.

Bread

The practice of eating bread as a form of devotion is an old one. The ancient Greeks and Egyptians ate bread especially dedicated to gods such as Dionysus and Osiris as an act of worship, partaking in the god's divine essence. This practice is the obvious historical precursor to the Christian consumption of the 'Body of Christ' during Holy communion. So powerful was communion bread that for centuries people used it in magical charms and as a folk medicine.

Bread is so important as the 'staff of life', that it was generally treated with great respect. As a result it was considered bad form to sing while making bread. When baking bread you should also mark it with a cross to 'protect' it. And if you're a woman, never prick bread. It's said that, 'She that pricks bread with fork or knife, will never be a happy maid or wife'.

Bread that splits open in the oven is a really bad sign. It portends a death in the family, as does bread with a hollow centre.

Don't turn the bread upside down after you've cut the first slice, or the 'head of the house' will fall ill. Bread that crumbles apart as you're cutting it portends a quarrel in the house. If you cut bread in an uneven manner, that's a sign that you've been telling lies.

To place a loaf of bread upside down on a table is unlucky, as is leaving any bread uneaten on your plate. It's unlucky to eat the last slice of bread on the table. It's up to the host to offer the last piece of bread to the 'lucky last', who will then be blessed with good luck.

Should the bread fall butter side down, it's a sign that a visitor will soon be arriving.

Bread should never be thrown out carelessly. In many countries it's customary to kiss leftover bread before putting it in the garbage, and in Greece eating the ends or 'heels' of a loaf of bread will make your mother-in-law love you. However, it's always preferable even to feed bread to the birds rather than throw it out, kiss or no kiss.

cereals

Grains are a big no-no among the Taoists of China and other nations in the Far East. The Taoists consider grains to be the principle food of P'o— evil spirits that live parasitically in the bones. The job of the P'o is to report back to heaven about all your misdeeds, so if you starve them of grains, they won't have the energy to give a bad report and make Destiny's Attendant knock years off your allotment in the Book of Life.

chicory and fern seed

In perfect silence and with a golden knife, cut chicory on the 25 July, the ancient Roman festival of Furinalia, then the power to become invisible, to open locks and to find hidden gold will be yours.

However, if you want power on a big scale, then put a silver bowl under a fern exactly at midnight on the Eve of St John (23 June), which is also Midsummer's Day in the Northern Hemisphere, and catch a seed that falls of its own accord (not shaken) into the bowl. Then hide the seed on your person and recite the following:

Fall free, fall free,
Where none shall see,
And give the same, great gift to me.

Should you accomplish this unlikely trick, then power over all living things shall be yours.

chopsticks

The Japanese never serve a bowl of rice with chopsticks sticking in them. The only occasion to do this is as an offering to the dead at funerals. If someone ever does this to you, then you know you are being either accidentally, or purposely, insulted.

christianity

Although Christians began as a sect of Judaism, they abandoned kashrut early on, under the direction of Saint Paul, although the *Bible* states quite specifically that Jesus Christ kept kosher. In the first century of the Common Era, Jews fasted on Mondays and Thursdays, but the early Christians fasted on Wednesdays and Fridays—because Jesus was arrested on a Wednesday and executed on a Friday. Many Orthodox Christians still keep these fasts, as did Protestants and Catholics until relatively recently. I should point out that 'fast' in this sense doesn't mean total abstinence from food, but avoidance of meat—hence the famous 'fish on Friday' meals. Even though Catholic Canon Law Number 1251 specifically states that Catholics should not eat meat on a Friday, Catholics as a whole now observe this fast haphazardly, many only observing it on Ash Wednesday and during the Fridays of Lent—the 40 days of abstinence leading up to Easter.

coffee

The Turkish believe that boys who drink coffee will not grow beards. In Greece it is bad luck to make toast with coffee.

eggs

Eggs generally have positive associations. They represent fertility, life and rebirth, and as such are a central motif in Easter celebrations and in the pagan festivals that preceded Easter. In spite of this, it's unlucky to use the word 'egg' aboard a ship.

In Siberia, certain natives believe that shamans are born from iron eggs laid in larch trees.

In China the layette, or clothing for a newborn child, often has designs featuring eggs to bring good luck. Eggs have 'eyes' to watch over the newborn.

If an egg accidentally falls and breaks, that's good luck, but if it falls and only fractures, or doesn't break at all, it's bad luck.

garlic and onion

Buddhists, Hindus, Jains and the Hare Krishnas refrain from eating the 'Five Pungent Spices'—onions, scallions, chives, leeks and garlic—on the grounds that: 'If these five are eaten cooked, they increase one's sexual desire; if they are eaten raw, they increase one's anger.' Since the discovery of chilli, some Buddhists have added this New World plant to the list.

Garlic, on a more magical note, is famous for keeping away vampires, who seem to have an allergy to the stuff. Garlic is also used in Greece as an all-purpose safety measure against the evil eye. Garlic is so effective in this role that it doesn't even have to be real. Bulbs of ceramic garlic are just as effective, and you can place them in your house, garden, car or anywhere else you want to protect from the evil eye.

hinduism

Hindu law says that you can't eat while standing up, or when you're lying naked. Eating while wearing wet clothes is out, as is eating out of a broken vessel. It's also defiling to eat when you have indigestion, and you should always leave the table a little hungry. You should only ever eat with the 'pure' right hand, and, if you're a Brahmin, your hands should never touch your lips or become contaminated with your saliva. If they do, you need to bathe and change clothing. Noisy eating is vulgar in the West, whereas a hearty belch is a sign of appreciation among the Arabs as is heartily slurping your noodles in Japan.

islam

The equivalent law to kashrut among Muslims is called halal. Similar in some respects to kashrut, halal also generally requires that hooved, cud-chewing animals be killed by slicing the neck and draining the body of blood. Halal shares the kashrut disgust with the flesh of the unclean pig, but permits the consumption of camel.

Even permitted animals though are *haram* (forbidden) if they have not been slaughtered in the name of God. Similarly, a permitted animal when shot, is halal if the hunter says, *'Bismillah. Allahu Akbar'*.

All dead meat is considered carrion and therefore haram, so, for example, fish caught alive is halal, but if was dead when it was caught it is haram.

Islam's notable innovation among the 'big three' religions is the prohibition on the consumption of alcohol.

In the case of the major religions, the penalty for violating food taboos is generally to put your soul in peril, whatever that might mean specifically.

Prohibitions on the preparation and consumption of various foods, the method of killing animals or the gathering of plants remain widespread in the cultures of the world. There are also many traditions of magical rites associated with foods. The penalties for violating these restrictions are often quite specific but can also be as vague as 'placing your soul in jeopardy'.

Prohibitions and restrictuions on the preparation and consumption of specific foods are almost universal among the cultures of the world.

Judaism

Kashrut is the body of Jewish dietary laws derived from the *Torah*, the first five books of the *Old Testament*. The word derives from the Semitic root *k-s-r* meaning 'correct' or 'proper'. From this we derive the adjective 'kosher'. Foods are kosher because they are 'allowed', kosher doesn't mean a particular style of cooking. All cloven-hooved animals that chew cud—cows, goats etc—are kosher as long as they're slaughtered by having their throats cut, and the resulting corpses are free of blemishes. All fruit and vegetables are kosher, but should be insect-free. The only exception is grape products. Jews can't eat grape products processed or made by non-Jews. Whole grapes, however, aren't a problem.

The Torah mentions that some insects are also kosher, but the specifics have been lost to history, so, except in some communities, all insects are now disallowed.

Forbidden foods, *treif*, include the following:

- 'Fish' without scales or fins. This includes all shellfish and crustaceans, as well as shark and leatherjacket.
- All reptiles and amphibians.
- All flesh-eating mammals or birds.
- Many vegetarian animals, such as camels, rabbits and pigs.

Even among the permitted animals, certain parts may not be eaten, such as the sciatic nerve and the fat surrounding vital organs. Blood in particular must completely drain from the corpse.

Wishbones

The traditions about wishbones, which in old England were called 'merrythoughts', can become quite complicated. The full ritual goes something like this: When with a friend, put the wishbone on your nose like a pair of spectacles and make a merry thought, or a wish that is equally applicable to both parties involved. Shake your head, thinking all the while about the wish. Let the wishbone fall off. Next each take one of the two ends of the wishbone in your little finger and pull. The person who pulls the longest part of the wishbone has the wish. However, the holder should now take both parts of the broken wishbone, put his hands behind his back and put one piece in each hand. He now brings both hands to the front and asks his friend to pick. The friend picks, and if she picks the long piece, the wish goes over to her. If she picks the short piece, the wish stays with the original winner.

The simpler version is just for each person to make separate wishes and try for the long piece. However, the older version is more generous in spirit, as there is a requirement that the wish be just as good if your friend gets it, as if you get it. Turkey wishbones are especially lucky.

There's a South American superstition that the younger of the pair of wishmakers will always pull the longer piece of the wishbone.

The tradition of the wishbone may come from fertility magic, in that the wishbone vaguely resembles the human female genitalia. It may also be related to an ancient method of divining the future, which involved burning the breastbone of a bird, and 'reading' the cracks or ridges, a practice called sternomancy.

magical food

The magical powers of foods are not restricted to shamans. The red squirrel of Africa makes its home hidden in the holes of trees. Among the Fang of Cameroon, Equatorial Guinea, Gabon and the Congo, pregnant women should not eat the flesh of the red squirrel, if they did their child might also want to live in a hole and refuse to be born. The Fang also refuse to eat the inside of an elephant's tusk. Not only does it not taste very good, but the Fang believe that its soft texture may deflate the penis.

meat

Buddhists are often vegetarians, although Buddha himself did not forbid the consumption of all flesh. Buddha was specific about people not eating other people, as well as bears, dogs, elephants, hyenas, lions, panthers, tigers and snakes. Tibetan Buddhists eat beef, and Buddha said it was also okay for monks to eat fish and non-forbidden meats, as long as the monk hadn't seen the animal being killed or as long as the monk did not believe that the animal had died on his behalf. In Japan, this get-out clause led to the development of a whole underclass of people, the Eta, who were permanently unclean because they did jobs like butchery and mortuary work.

Buddhists are often vegetarians although Buddha did not forbid the consumption of all meat.

According to Judaic dietary law, meat cannot be cooked in the milk of the same animal and you can't use the same utensils for preparing or serving meat and dairy foods. By extension, if you eat a dairy food, you have to allow half an hour to pass before you can eat meat and two hours must pass between eating meat and eating dairy foods. Other traditions also have restrictions on combining food. Chinese medicine frowns on eating quail with pork, or pheasant with walnuts. One also shouldn't eat the flesh of a black goat or ox with a white head, or any domestic animal that has died facing north. North is the direction in which the heads of human corpses are meant to be placed, so the direction is inauspicious. Avoid eating horse liver too, if you can, it's 'poisonous'.

Beef, a major food source in the developed West, is strictly forbidden to the hundreds of millions of Hindus, to whom the cow is sacred.

Among the villagers of Baan Phraan Muan in Thailand, you can eat duck whenever you want, except at weddings. The Phraan Muan observe that the duck is a rather laissez-faire mother, leaving her eggs alone and not bothering to hatch

The Masai Mara will consume a powerful purgative to rid their bodies of any traces of milk before they consume meat.

them, although anyone who has ever observed ducks will confirm that they are, in fact, attentive parents. Nevertheless, according to the Phraan Muan a bride-to-be may inherit the duck's purported lackadaisical parenting style if she were to eat duck during such an important transition in her life

milk

Even though Jews will not eat milk and meat in the same meal, the Masai of East Africa will go so far as to consume a powerful purgative to rid their bodies of any traces of milk before they consume meat. The Chinese traditionally avoid dairy products, and one source claims that drinking sheep or goats' milk with preserved fish will cause intestinal blockage. The avoidance of milk is widespread among non-Caucasians and for sound scientific reasons. Many non-Caucasian populations lack the proper digestive enzymes to assimilate milk properly, and this explains the absence of dairy foods in the cuisines of east Asia, among Amerindians and Australian Aborigines. The Kanuri of West Africa, who knew nothing of digestive enzymes, threw away powdered milk that relief agencies had given them during a time of famine, because they believed it was the food of evil spirits.

It is unlucky to spill milk, leading to the saying not to cry over it. In Ireland milk should not be sold or even given away on May Day (1 May, the ancient Celtic celebration of Beltane), and in Worcestershire, in central west England, it was bad luck to sell milk on Whitsunday.

If boiling milk spills over onto the fire it's considered unlucky, and the cow that gave the milk could suffer an udder infection or injury. The cure was to scatter salt over the fire upon which the milk had fallen.

salt

Prized in the ancient world for its power to preserve food and to add flavour, salt was once so valuable that the Roman Empire paid their troops with it, hence our word 'salary'.

Salt's preservative qualities meant that it was associated with purification and used in all manner of purification rituals. The ancient Greeks burned salt and flesh in their sacrifices to the gods. In Scotland salt was put on a corpse's chest, and Catholic priests add salt to water before blessing it to create Holy Water.

Spilling salt is, naturally, unlucky. The usual 'cure' is to pick up a pinch in the right hand and throw it over your left shoulder, right in the face of the evil spirit that caused you to spill the salt in the first place.

Another cure for spilt salt is to put it in the fire. This will burn away any tears that the spilt salt might portend.

Salt should always be the first thing you place on a table when setting it, and the last thing you should remove. There should always be salt within arm's reach of all guests at a table so that they can serve themselves. You should never pass salt to anyone, even if they ask for it: 'Pass me salt, pass me sorrow,' and 'Help to salt, help to sorrow.'

Swimming and eating

A very common superstition is that you should wait an hour after having a meal before going swimming. The consequences of not obeying this injunction are that you'll end up having a cramp so severe that you'll seize up, start sinking and drown. This is completely untrue. Swimming in no way inhibits or affects the natural process of digestion—or vice versa. About the only thing that can be said for this myth is that if you are one of the few people who experience a lot of gastric reflux, then it's probably not a good idea to go swimming on a full stomach, because choking on your vomit is bad enough, without having to concentrate on staying afloat at the same time. However, swimming does not cause stomach cramps.

TOTEMS

The most culturally important restrictions regarding foods depend on the concept of the totem animal. In many cultures certain members of a tribal group have a sacred animal. This animal is often an ancestor or ancestral spirit. It is forbidden for the member of a particular totem to eat or use any part of the totemic animal. Among the central Algonquin—of whom there are now only 11,000 left and mostly around the area of Quebec, Canada—it was forbidden for members of the Beaver Clan to swim across rivers, the Eagle Clan to wear feathers on their heads, the Fish Clan to eat fish or to build dams and the Thunder Clan (not all totems are animals) to undress before washing.

Because not all members of a tribe or tribal group have the same totem, it is not uncommon for a food to be forbidden to one member of a tribe, while completely permissible to another. To make matters even more complicated, and interesting, it's quite possible for some tribal members to kill their own totem animal, but not to eat it. They can, however, give the animal to fellow tribe members as food. The Bororo people of the Mato Grosso region of central Brazil, show yet another variation. To the Bororo, the only animal that they can't eat is the red deer, an animal that isn't a totem to any of them.

Sorcerers and shamans may have restrictions put on them because eating a particular animal may affect their capacity to do magic. A sorcerer among the Ndembu people of the Congo must not eat the flesh of the bushbuck, which has a spotted hide, or that of the zebra, which has a striped hide. If he did, his magic would wander or stray from its point of focus. Animals with dark coats would cast a shadow over his magical vision, and fish with sharp bones might prick his 'organ of divination'.

wine, beer and other alcohol

The Greeks believe that if you spill water at the dinner table you will soon come into money, but if you spill ouzo (the Greek aniseed-flavoured liqueur), then bad luck will come to your family. Spilling wine, however means that visitors are on their way.

Spilling wine accidentally is good luck, generally speaking. It's a fine thing if done while proposing a toast. It's especially good luck if you drop and break a glass full of wine. This is a sign of a happy, affectionate relationship between those sharing the wine, so it's especially good for married couples. And if you're unmarried in Greece, you should also try to drink the last serving of wine from a bottle. This means that you will marry well.

The Koreans believe that it's bad luck to order bottles of beer in even numbers, so don't order six-packs when you're with Korean friends, without buying a seventh bottle too.

It is forbidden for the member of a particular totem to eat or use any part of the totemic animal. Among the central Algonquin, for example, members of the Eagle Clan could not wear feathers on their heads.

making ends meet
without meeting
your end

making ends meet
without meeting your end

Practically everyone, at some stage of their lives, has to either take up a career as a writer or, alternatively, work for a living. However, some professions are more inherently risky than others. Here the universal principle applies: when all else fails, try magic. It's natural that magic should apply to jobs where the risk of injury, death or even just plain unemployment, is riskier than others—as in fishing, mining and acting. Even if all else succeeds, it's a good idea to try magic anyway, just to be on the safe side.

Actors

Generally speaking, actors share sailors' reluctance to whistle, for fear of attracting malicious spirits, although some superstitions are about not upsetting egos, which is why in a comedy duo you always bill the straight man above the comedian—hence Abbott and Costello, Laurel and Hardy, Rowan and Martin and Martin and Lewis.

Shakespeare's play *Macbeth* is considered unlucky, possibly because of the witches' scene. The play is never played in full until opening night—during rehearsals the last line is left unsaid—and some thespians are reluctant to call it by its name, referring to it instead as 'the Scottish play'. Actors never sing or hum during the rehearsals for *Macbeth*, especially during the witches' song itself.

There are many other perils of the stage. Never leave three candles lit, either on a stage or in a dressing room, as those in the same room as the candles will quarrel—not that actors generally need much excuse.

No actor should ever look over the shoulder of another in the dressing room mirror, or bad luck will befall the actor who is being overlooked. Also never write anything on your dressing room mirror.

Never mention the number of lines you have in a show or you'll forget some.

If an actor kicks off his shoes in the dressing room and they fall on their sides this is a sign of bad luck; if the shoes fall right side up this is lucky. It's good luck to spit on your dancing shoes before putting them on. If his shoes squeak when an actor walks on stage this is very good luck. Also tripping on your first entrance to a stage is one of the few times when tripping is supposed to be lucky.

Never take a wedding ring off to appear on stage, as this is bad luck for the actor's marriage. In fact film directors frequently use 'hand stand ins' for star parts where wedding rings are inappropriate.

Never use real flowers on stage, or accept a gift of real flowers over the footlights. Lilies, peacock feathers, knitting on stage, yellow in the set or green in a costume, wigs and crutches are all unlucky. However, walking canes are lucky.

Never read congratulatory telegrams, and if the play's a hit, use the same costume you used on opening night. Make repairs if necessary as you go, but don't change the clothing or you'll lose the luck. Never send out your laundry until after the final curtain on opening night.

And never, ever wish an actor good luck before a performance as this is extremely unlucky. This is why you always encourage them to 'break a leg', on the basis that if it's bad luck to wish someone good

Thespians have to deal with a lot of superstitious baggage to ensure that they stay employed and that their shows are a success.

luck, it's good luck to wish them bad luck. There is, however an alternative explanation for 'breaking a leg'. Before the tradition of throwing flowers on stage, actors who gave a good performance would be pelted with money. When they bent or kneeled to pick the money they'd 'break' their leg line, so the wish was that they'd give a great performance, and get plenty of tips.

Doctors

The first person to be treated in a new doctor's surgery, or in a new hospital will be sure to be cured.

However, it's not a good sign for the health of the patient, if you have to call a doctor on a Friday.

The best doctors, like the best sorcerers and mages, or magi, are the seventh sons of seventh sons (or the seventh daughters of seventh daughters).

fishing and seamanship

Fishermen are famously superstitious, and not surprisingly so. Going out into the ocean, often for weeks and months at a time, is asking for trouble. Storms, freak waves, sea-monsters and the ever-present danger of drowning have always made for a love–hate relationship with the sea. Of all the food-gathering professions, fishing was, and still is, the most dangerous. By extension, other types of mariners, traders, explorers and navymen inherited the traditions of fishermen. And yet, for all its risks, to dream of fishing is a sign of a peaceful life, and to dream of gathering a great pile of fish in your net is a great sign of fortune. Here are some other superstitions of the men who earn their living from the sea.

Women, ministers and pigs are really bad luck. Even the mention of these things is unlucky. Having a woman on a ship is inviting disaster.

Whistling is unlucky, because it invokes the spirits, but sailors can call a wind with a whistle. The reason that it's unlucky is because if the whistle is too loud, it can call up a gale, and there's no easy definition of what is 'too loud'.

Cats, who have a mixed reputation elsewhere, are lucky at sea. Besides being great rat catchers, sailors believe that if the cat walks towards you, you're in for some luck. If it turns away, then it's bad luck. At the start of a journey, if a cat cries, the passage will be rough. If it's playful, there'll be clear sailing. If it's restless, a storm's brewing. Cats can not only predict the weather, they can cause it. Never make a cat angry, or it will lash its tail and whip up a storm.

A knot hidden in a ship could cause it to founder. This superstition is particularly odd considering the number of knots on board a traditional sailing vessel.

Sneezing on the starboard side of a vessel is lucky, but sneezing on the portside means that there will be foul weather.

Japanese mariners refused to carry the following items on boats:

- beef
- rice boiled with red beans
- vinegar
- miso (bean paste)
- and *kayu* (rice gruel).

While the origin of some superstitions is difficult to fathom—no pun intended—the prohibition on miso and *kayu* might have to do with sympathetic magic. When miso is dissolved into hot water to make soup, or when rice is washed, the water becomes cloudy and resembles shallow seawater during rough weather, when waves stir up sand and silt. This unintended magic invites a storm.

At the time of the new moon, sailors and their families would greet the moon and chant: 'I see the moon and the moon sees me. God bless the sailors and the sea.'

Sailors in Devon, England, carried pincushions for good luck, but those who lost a mop or bucket over the side of the ship believed that their luck went with it. A more universal superstition was that wearing a gold earring in the left ear would prevent a sailor from drowning, which explains why pirates often wore one. With all their pillaging, they were some of the few sailors who could actually afford a gold earring.

Sharks following a ship is a sign of very bad luck, the implication being that somehow the sharks sense that there will soon be a death aboard and that a snack is coming, or that the whole ship is going to go down and that they are in for a feast.

Albatrosses following a ship are very good luck, but disaster will follow if the

albatross is hurt. Samuel Taylor Coleridge's famous poem related the tale of a hapless sailor who accidentally kills an albatross. The other sailors force the killer to wear the body of the dead bird around his neck as a punishment and penance, but the ship and the sailor are doomed, at least for a while.

In the north-east of Scotland, it was considered bad luck to name a boat before launching her. There is also a more general superstition about the naming of ships. Rather than risk annoying or angering the various gods—who seemed to have nothing better to do with eternity but to make life difficult for mortals— shipbuilders would avoid names like *Storm Master*, or anything else that smacked of hubris.

Tradition dies hard. When a ship was named, it used to be customary to offer a sacrifice to the gods for their good graces, so that even today we break a bottle of expensive champagne on the bow of a ship during its launch and say: 'May God bless her, and all who sail in her.'

It used to be considered very unlucky to rename a ship. If it had to be, the mast would have to be replaced. As this could be expensive, someone came up with the idea of putting an iron nail or knife into the mast, or putting a lucky coin under the mast. Still all references to the ship's old name had to be removed from documents, fittings, life jackets and lifeboats, and in some cases even plates and cutlery. The sailors would then ask Neptune, the god of the sea, and Aeolus, the god of the winds, to forget the ship's old name and accept its new one.

When you leave home to go to your ship at the beginning of a journey it's unlucky for anyone to look back, especially sailors. If a sailor forgot something, he'd have to leave it behind. The only way he could get it was if a family member ran after him to give it too him, but the sailor would have to receive the item from his front, he couldn't turn around for it. In the Shetland Islands, Scotland, it's good luck to come across a retarded or deformed person before setting out to sea.

The children of sailors customarily crushed the shells after eating boiled eggs and said the following rhyme:

*Oh, never leave your eggshells unbroken in
a cup,
Think of the poor sailor men and always
smash them up.
For witches come and find them and sail
away to sea,
And make a lot of misery for sailormen
like me.*

Once you're at sea, you should always throw back the first catch of the season for luck. It's a good idea to pour wine down the throat of the first fish. This will make it drunk. The other fish will make a rush for your nets in an effort to be caught and get drunk too. Little do they know …

Even recreational fishermen have inherited the superstitions of those whose living depends on it, for example:

- Always hook the bait with your right hand.
- Never let a woman step over your fishing lines, or you won't catch anything.
- Spit on your bait for luck.
- Never use an upturned bucket as a seat, you'll upset the spirits of the sea.

Fridays, saturdays and sundays

Perhaps because Fridays, Saturdays and Sundays are holy days for three major religions—Islam, Judaism and Christianity respectively—there are a number of religious prohibitions and superstitions about working on these days of the week. Jews can't even have anyone working for them on the Sabbath.

If you start a new project on a Friday, it will be unlucky. This is particularly true of making a garment, so don't start sewing or knitting a garment on a Friday, unless you can finish it on the same day.

If you start a new project on a Saturday, it will be seven Saturdays before completion.

Never hire anyone new on a weekend, as Saturday's servants never stay and Sunday's servants run away.

Feng shui for good fortune

The Chinese art of placement can become very complicated, but it has some general tips for both the home and office to ensure good luck:

- Always keep the toilet seat down when you're not using it.
- Keep mirrors, glass and any reflective surfaces clean.
- Never have an office or seating arrangement where your back is to the door.
- Your back can face a window, as long as it's not the west window.
- Even just sitting near a west-facing window in a room is problematic. If you have to, have a mirror placed in the room so that it faces out and reflects bad energy back out the window.
- Any place that holds cash should be coloured red to attract the energy of the red phoenix.
- Position your office desk facing south or southeast to attract both fame and fortune.
- Sit in the centre of the side of your desk, rather than nearer to one corner, to maintain a balance.
- If you work with a computer screen, it should be in front of you, rather than to your side.
- Have your in-tray on the right (in the wealth area) and your out tray on the left (in the health area).
- If you work on a computer, have a photo of your family or loved ones to the right of your screen and to the right of those is a good place to put your reference books. To the left of your screen have your computer hard drive itself, or your hard copy files, and to the left of those, that's where you keep your coffee, tea, biscuits and cakes.
- The general principle for workflow should be from right to left.

Hunters

There seem to be universal superstitions about hunting. Many of these concern the language that hunters can use while in pursuit of game. This practice arises out of the belief that if you use ordinary language, the animals will know what you're after. In Japan if you're hunting snakes you're looking for *naga mono* (long things), wolves become *yase* (leans), horses become *takase* (high backs) and a hare becomes a *yama no negi* (priest of the mountain). It's difficult to tell if this fools anything except the hunters. Animals are usually smarter than humans give them credit for.

Miners

Miners feel the same way about cats as sailors feel about pigs. It's unlucky to say the word 'cat' when you're down the mine. Miners also believe that it's bad luck to meet a woman or a cross-eyed person on the way to the mine, or to have a rabbit cross your path. Seeing a snail was also bad luck, but you could take a small pinch of tallow from your candle and drop it to the ground to defuse the bad magic. If they'd forgotten their lunch, miners would also prefer to go hungry all day rather than return home once they'd set out, because it was bad luck to go back.

Never wash a miner's back on a work day, as this might cause a cave in, and don't go into a mine at all on a day when you see a robin or a dove flying around a pithead.

Dreaming of broken shoes is a portent of disaster too.

Never wash a miner's back on a work day as this may cause a cave in.

Cornish tin miners believed in underground creatures called knockers. If you followed the sound of the knockers, they could lead you to rich veins of ore. Miners in Cornwall never wore crosses or made the sign of the cross underground, so as not to upset the knockers.

In Germany, if you were lucky enough to find a dwarf and do him a favour, he would reward you by giving you a heap of coals, which would magically turn into jewels when you took them home.

Pilots

During World War II a pilot would pick up a pebble from the ground and put it in his pocket just before going on a mission. On his return he'd put it back on the ground. Forgetting to pick up a pebble, or deliberately not doing so, was a sign that you didn't expect to come back. If a fellow member of one squadron didn't make it back, his best friend would take two pebbles on the next trip to make up for him.

To ensure that he would return, a pilot would leave some 'unfinished business' behind, like a half-written letter or giving a friend his wallet for safekeeping. Obviously you can't die because you still have to finish the letter or get your wallet back.

Royalty

Part of the social contract of royalty is to convince the peasants of the aristocracy's superiority. Because it's hard to sustain any mystique under close scrutiny, it's generally a good idea to create as much distance as possible between the royals and the rabble. One way to do this is to make royals taboo. In many cultures it used to be considered dangerous to look at monarchs, as you could be blinded or struck dead by their divine light. Touching royals was highly risky. Yet in Europe the belief arose that the touch of the king could cure diseases, in particular tuberculosis of the lymph glands (especially of the neck), historically known as scrofula, struma or 'the king's evil'. According to legend the English King Edward the Confessor (1003–1066) was supposed to have received the gift of the cure from St Remegius (437–533) during a spiritual visitation from the long-dead saint. Six hundred years later England's Charles II (1630–85) was still busy dispensing cures and supposedly touched 90,000 of his subjects. However, the practice stopped three kings and two queens later with George I (1660–1727). The French King Henry IV (1553–1610) was said to have cured as many as 1500 people at a time, and the practice continued in France until Louis XV (1710–1774). Scrofula is very rare nowadays, and responds to antibiotics and surgery.

As fountains of health, the health of a king was identified with the health of the country. This wasn't always a good thing for the king. In many cultures ceremonial kings became human sacrifices in the full bloom of their youth and power, in order to ensure the health of the realm. In England it was believed that the death of kings was preceded by the deaths of bay trees.

Taxi drivers

For cabbies, it's good luck to have the number seven on the taxi's number or on their licence plates. The letter 'U' is also beneficial because it resembles a horseshoe hung upside down, so that the luck doesn't run out. Catholic cab drivers, and in fact any superstitious drivers, would hang a medal of St Christopher from their rear-view mirror or elsewhere in the car for protective luck. St Christopher was actually in charge of the safe passage of the dead to the afterlife, but he also moonlighted as the patron saint of travellers and, less famously, of sports. Today St Christopher isn't quite as popular as he used to be, because in 1969 Pope Paul IV and the Vatican downgraded him to a local legend as there wasn't enough historical evidence for his existence.

money magic

Certain days of the week are luckier for business and investments:

Monday for health,
Tuesday for wealth,
Wednesday's the best day of all,
Thursday for crosses,
Friday for losses
And Saturday's the worst day of all.

Somebody obviously forgot to tell the universe this on Tuesday, 29 October 1929.

If you're building a new business premises, place a gold coin in the foundations for prosperity.

On the first day of trading in a new business, enter the premises through the front door, right foot first for good luck.

The jade plant, a small succulent with round fleshy leaves, is great to have growing outside your front door: 'Jade by the door, Poor no more.'

Never empty a purse of coins—always keep at least one in it for good luck. Also never give a wallet or purse as a gift without also putting money in it, otherwise you are wishing the receiver an 'empty wallet'.

Bent coins or coins with holes in them are lucky. Giving alms to the poor, even if you just throw coins to a beggar, is lucky. Tossing a coin into a fountain or a well is almost universally a good luck charm, but if you want the luck to be sure, throw the coin over your left shoulder.

Paint or draw the image of the cornucopia, or horn of plenty, and hang it in a prominent place. The Cornucopia looks like a large, hollow horn filled with fruit and grain, and it was the sacred symbol of goddesses with agricultural leanings, like Demeter, Fortuna and Hathor.

The image of an Abraxas might also help. Holding a shield of wisdom and a whip of power, the Abraxas is a creature with the head of a cock, the body of a man and snakes for legs. Try to avoid the obvious humour.

Gold charms in the shape of honeybees are handy for success in business. Gold has obvious associations with wealth and the bees represent industry and productivity. They also know how to protect their wealth with stings. Even their products—beeswax and honey—are golden. The Barberini Pope Urban VIII and Napoleon chose bees in their heraldry.

Agate was popular in ancient Persia to encourage money to come to you through inheritance or a will. In Europe florins and sixpences with crosses on them were lucky. They drove away the demon of poverty.

The Romans carried gold or silver charms carved with an image of a spider for similar reasons. They believed having spiders around was wonderful money luck, and if you see a spider in your house in the afternoon a gift will arrive soon. Dreaming of a spider means that money and success are coming, but if the spider bites you in the dream, prepare to lose money. Killing a spider is very bad luck and portends money losses. If you have to kill a spider, apologise first and make it clear that it's nothing personal.

In ancient China people observed that the cricket laid hundreds of eggs, so these insects became symbols of abundance and prosperity. If you saw one in your house, their magic would rub off on you and you'd be blessed with many children who would look after you in your old age. Some people even kept crickets in cages so the luck would stay around all the time. The song of the cricket means more money is on its way for any work you do that day. Having wild crickets come into your house is especially lucky, particularly if they settle on the fireplace hearth. Never kill the grasshopper or the cricket, or it will kill your luck.

Greet the new moon with three bows and say this rhyme to bring a gift into your life:

New Moon, New Moon,
First time I've seed'ee,
Hope before the week's out,
I'll have sommat gived to me.

If you hear the first cuckoo of spring, make a wish and turn the money in your pocket so it will grow.

On the first day of summer, if you meet a man wearing a straw hat, or eat from the first crop of strawberries, touch both your hands together, then both elbows and say:

Strawberry Man, Strawberry Man,
Bring me good luck,
Today or tomorrow,
To pick something up.

Then pick up any small object like a stone and throw it over your left shoulder.

On the first day of winter, fortune is coming to you if you see a red robin, while treading accidentally in manure is lucky and a sign that your business will grow.

If you lose gold, like a wedding ring, take a sprig from a yew tree and hold it out in front of you. The branch will turn in your hand, rather like a water diviner, and lead you to where the gold is.

And for the really big gold strike, find the end of a rainbow.

part two: Nature

Beyond the self and the world of society, there is the world of nature—filled with plants, animals, rocks and weather. These non-human things were, and to some extent still are, mysteries. They could be made less mysterious by giving them personalities, ascribing meaning to their actions, assuming that they had wants and desires and that they would try to manipulate you, if you couldn't manipulate them first. In short, humans created superstitions to some extent in order to treat the inhabitants of the world of nature just like people and so make them knowable. In spite of the disadvantages, the world of the superstitious is filled with meaning.

the superstitious rainbow

The superstitious rainbow

Humans are quite unusual among mammals in having colour vision. Most mammals see only in black and white, and rely more on their sense of smell than on their sense of sight. This may be a legacy from some groups of mammals having lost their ancestral reptilian colour-vision because they had to spend tens of millions of years avoiding dinosaurs and living nocturnally in circumstances where colour vision wasn't particularly useful. Some groups though, like primates, either held on to or re-evolved colour vision. However, while most humans see in colour, there aren't any culturally or historically universal ideas of what those colours actually mean. Surprisingly, even our linguistic definitions of colour differ around the world. Many languages make no distinction between green and blue, especially in Asia. In Korean, for example, both are called *purueda*. In Japanese both colours are called *ao*. On the other hand, Hungarian has two basic words for red—*piros* (used for inanimate objects) and *vooroos* (used for living things and emotional expressions). Considered individually the colours take on a significance that is as idiosyncratic as the cultures themselves.

black

In Western folklore black has the worst reputation among the colours. Black is the Devil's colour. Bats, dogs, hens, cocks, pigs, rabbits—you name it, if it's black, it's bad. Black cats especially, being witches' familiars, create a barrier, blocking you off from God. In Ireland, seeing a black cat portends death in an epidemic.

However, there are some exceptions.

- In Scotland seeing a black cat is a sign of prosperity.
- In Texas it's good luck if a black cat visits you, but only if it stays a while.
- Seeing an ambulance is bad luck until you see a brown or black dog.
- Seeing a black goat on the way to a wedding means that there's treasure hidden nearby.

- A visit by a black moth is actually a friendly visitation by the soul of a departed loved one.
- And meeting a chimney sweep, covered as they are from head to foot in black soot, is always lucky, especially if you kiss one.

Blue and indigo

Until recently the various lighter shades of blue, sky blue or turquoise were difficult for artists to reproduce. Plant blues didn't last and mineral blues were very rare. The most common, but still rare, blue was ground lapis lazuli and it commanded great prices. Blue was therefore a magical colour, the hue of heaven, hard for mortals to capture and very lucky—'touch blue and your wish will come true'.

On a more down-to-earth level, in much of today's Anglo-Saxon world, a blue movie is pornographic, whereas in France the same films are 'green'.

Blue represents one of the spirit colours, and candles that burn blue without any red in them are thought to predict death or the presence of ghosts. Some believe that blue light can paralyse the heart, and Goethe wrote that blue brings with it coldness and melancholy. Yet in the *Bible*, specifically *Numbers* 15:38, God calls upon the Israelites to fringe their garments with tassels of blue to remind them to keep His commandments.

There are a few spells that use the protective and healing properties of blue. In the mid-1650s wearing a garter of blue ribbon studded with shells of grey snails offered protection against the effects of gout. Cattle with cramps are supposedly 'elf shot' and chafing their afflicted parts with a blue bonnet can alleviate their symptoms. In England nursing mothers used to wear necklaces of blue woollen threads to protect their babies from fevers, and children would wear necklaces strung with blue beads to ward off colds, flu and bronchitis.

Depending on your cultural background, indigo is either a colour in its own right or just a darker shade of blue. There's reason to feel that they are different. Blue is the sky, while indigo is the sea. However, in the Anglo-Saxon world, some people feel that indigo isn't a real colour, but one invented by Sir Isaac Newton for superstitious reasons, because he felt that the number of colours in a rainbow or spectrum somehow had to match the mystical number of seven. So depending on whom you talk to and what sort of spectrum you're looking at, indigo is either a deep blue or a light violet, which leaves the real violet looking more like deep, rich, royal purple.

Feel free to decide for yourself whether or not 'indigo' is a real colour or just Sir Isaac Newton's superstition.

In India, blue is the colour of the fifth or 'throat' chakra. Invoking blue increases the capacity for articulating and communicating ideas and turning thought into action.

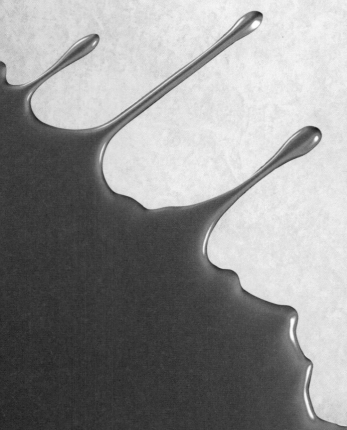

Brown

Brown, the colour of the earth, is generally lucky, and it's especially beneficial to see a brown hare. However, it's an ill omen if your chickens start laying dark brown eggs.

Brown is also the colour of the sixth or 'third eye' chakra. Invoking brown in meditations increases psychic ability and sensitivity.

Green

Green is the colour of plants, especially young crops and vegetables and springtime, so green signifies life and abundance. In Islamic tradition angels in green turbans visited Mohammed, and the prophet's banner is green. In honour of this, the flag of Saudi Arabia is green with white writing. The flag of Libya goes even further and is entirely green. In both cases it seems an optimistic colour choice for countries that are almost entirely desert. An old Turkish law also stipulated that only Muslims could wear green.

However, green is also a pagan colour. The Egyptian god Osiris was depicted as green. Some depictions of the Devil, based on the ancient god Pan, depict his colour as green. There is also the Green Man—a wood spirit who is often depicted with a face made of leaves—who represents the cycle of birth and rebirth. The Green Man is a common motif in the decoration of many churches, especially in Europe.

The Celts, especially the Irish, are the people most often associated with the colour green, but the relationship is a complex one. The green shamrock is lucky, but green is also the colour of the faerie folk, who, according to tradition, inhabited the British Isles before the coming of Man. Leprechauns nowadays are almost always depicted as wearing emerald green, but before the twentieth century they were always described as dressed in red. This is interesting as green and red are actually opposites on the colour wheel.

To catch a leprechaun may be a stroke of good fortune—they usually have a treasure buried nearby—but being faerie folk, leprechauns often outsmart dim-witted humans. In one famous story a young man captures a leprechaun and forces him to reveal the location of his treasure. The leprechaun says it is buried in an open field under a ragwort plant. The young man ties a red ribbon around the plant before going away to fetch a shovel. He makes the leprechaun promise not to remove the ribbon. The leprechaun keeps his promise, but when the young man returns, he finds that the wily leprechaun has tied a red ribbon around every ragwort plant in the field.

So because faeries are green, or wear green, and because faeries are unpredictable, the Celts have often considered green to be unlucky—especially *uaine* (bright green). Apparently the faeries think that any mortals to dare to wear their favourite colour are presumptuous. To wear green is to invite kidnapping by faeries, who will claim you as their own, so it is especially unlucky to dress a child in green. There is also a common belief that if you wear green it won't be long before you wear the black of mourning.

This reputed acquisitiveness may explain how green has become the colour of envy. Wearing green to a wedding is especially unlucky: 'Married in green, shame to be seen,' or 'Married in May and kirked in green, Baith bride and bridegroom winna lang be seen.' Also no green vegetables or foods should be served at a wedding.

To dream of the colour green is unlucky. And it isn't even easy to get rid of it: it's unlucky to burn green plants or twigs, if you do the plant you cut them will never thrive.

In the West we say 'green' to mean immature; in the East green is often associated with sickness. Green in Thai also means 'smelly' or 'putrid', which makes sense if you've ever been around rotting fruit or vegetables in the Tropics.

On a more positive note, green is associated with money and wealth, and many a magic spell to gain riches uses green objects. For a long time even accountants and ledger keepers were wont to use green ink to denote profit, and its opposite (red) to denote debt.

Green is the colour of the fourth or

'heart' chakra, and, in Indian belief, promotes the feelings of love and affinity.

Green has also now become a political colour, associated with environmental consciousness. And green is the symbol of immortality.

grey

Pull out a grey hair and ten more will grow in its place. If you happen to be passing a barn or an agricultural show, and there are nine cows all in a row with a grey bull at the end, you'll be granted a wish.

orange

In the Ayurvedic tradition, orange is the colour of the second or 'sacral' chakra, and orange stones such as tiger eye or carnelian or even doing orange visualisations, like seeing an orange flower opening up in your mind's eye, are supposed to induce emotional release and creativity.

red

Aside from black and white, red is the next most universally recognised colour, in so much as there is a word for red in almost every language.

Red has represented many different things but mostly strong feelings like anger, shame, danger and passion. Language reflects this in expressions like 'seeing red', 'red-faced', 'red alert'. Red is harlotry—red light districts—but also revolution—communism.

The origin of believing that redheads were hot-tempered or unlucky might have to do with the Norse invasions of the British Isles during the Dark Ages. If so, their descendants, legitimate or otherwise, have paid a high karmic price. In medieval times redheads were suspected of being—or at least prone to becoming—witches, werewolves or vampires. Redhaired children are supposed to come from unfaithful mothers. Sailors, already predisposed to find women unlucky, think a redhead especially so. Artists traditionally paint Judas Iscariot, the great betrayer of Jesus, as a redhead.

Red is blood. Sometimes this has meant that it is associated with death. Among the Maoris a canoe that had carried a corpse could never be used again. It was painted red then left on the shore. Red was sacred to the Maori and anything painted red became taboo. In Madagascar red is the colour of funerals, and shrouds are often dyed with red stripes.

However, red is also the colour of the heart, vitality and love. Strangely enough, the light from the 'heart' chakra in Hindu tradition is green, so instead red is the colour of the first chakra, and invoking red through the possession of red objects or meditations on red increases the sensitivity of your basic instincts for survival. However, you can go too far, and a red chakra that is too open leads to greed and emotional neediness.

Red is both lucky and unlucky, depending on the context.

In the true spirit of the contradictions that riddle the world of superstition, red is unlucky for lovers in some Western traditions, and love letters should never be written in red ink. Pick a red poppy and if one of the petals falls off, you'll be struck by lightning. If you wear a red rose and it loses its leaves this is a very bad omen. The cure for this possible bad luck is to set the fallen leaves on the ground and jump over them, backwards and forwards.

Red is lucky for card players, and a modern superstition has arisen that red cars are lucky. This latter is possibly due to reports that they are involved in fewer accidents, probably because they are more highly visible without being distractingly so.

Red, or burgundy, is the lucky colour for champion golfer Tiger Woods—he took US$100 million in earnings in 2007, so there might be something in this after all.

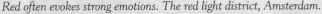
Red often evokes strong emotions. The red light district, Amsterdam.

violet

Purple has long been associated with royalty because the Romans adopted Tyrian Purple—which could range from a deep royal purple to a sort of dark red—as the colour of their aristocracy. Purple, or violet, is the colour of the seventh or 'crown' chakra. It is the light of pure understanding and wisdom, and purple stones, flowers or visualisations will help you achieve a contact with the Divine.

white

In the East white is the colour of ghosts and of the dead, and is generally considered unlucky. In the modern West, white represents purity but also sterility, and, even though black is the colour of mourning, there are still quite a few superstitions also associating white with bad luck.

If a fisherman on his way to his ship sees a woman wearing a white apron, he will go back home and wait until the next tide. The same was true for coal sellers on their way to the mines. Many believe that seeing a white bird, a white cat, a white weasel, mole or hare or having white flowers around is unlucky. Horses with four white fetlocks are so unlucky, you should only give them to your enemy. Three aren't much better, but two white fetlocks are good and one white fetlock is very good. Coming across a white horse is unlucky, but if you do, spit in its general direction, spit three time over your left shoulder or spit on the sole of your shoe and rub the spit into the ground. A white dog is good luck, though, especially if you see it before noon, and seeing three white dogs together is very lucky.

Purple is the colour of high-level spirituality and, by association, royalty.

yellow

The central colour of the spectrum, yellow is the colour of gold and of the sun. Pagans generally associated yellow with light, brightness and divinity—even love. This almost automatically created a negative reaction from early Christians, who wanted nothing to do with the pagan way of looking at things.

In the hands of Christian revisionists, yellow became the colour of carnality, prostitution, envy, treachery and cowardice. Artists traditionally painted Judas wearing yellow clothing. In Christian countries, the doors of criminals, especially traitors, were thus daubed with yellow paint, and yellow was the colour Jews were forced to wear, because the Jews were blamed for centuries, from medieval to modern times, for the crucifixion of Christ. And, as if Jewish persecution wasn't bad enough, the West later began to think about Asians as the 'yellow peril'.

Yellow, at least the drabber shades, became associated with sickness and disease, possibly because yellow is the colour of pus. Black and yellow would have been the colours most associated with the bubonic plague. A yellow banner flying on a ship, signalled that there was sickness on board and that the crew were under quarantine.

However, there are positive associations for the colour. Yellow is the colour of the third or 'solar plexus' chakra. Invoking yellow balances your judgement, and helps you to make sound decisions.

the animal kingdom

the animal kingdom

Animals have always been a part of the human experience, either as something to eat, something that might eat you or something mysterious, alien and yet familiar. Many traditions ascribe animals, or at least certain animals, the status of ancestors. As such, animals were often thought to be shape shifters, magically switching from animal to human form and back again, in some cases fathering or mothering half-divine mortals in the process. The Greek god Zeus took various forms, he once raped the princess Leda in the form of a swan, then Leda laid an egg, from which hatched Helen of Troy. The ancient Mexican god Quetzalcoatl shifted between the forms of a white-bearded man and a feathered serpent. Gods could also turn mortals into animals as punishment or reward, so if you encountered an animal in the wild, there was no way of telling who you were really meeting. Animals could also serve as divine informants, delivering messages to mortals wise enough to pay attention to the signs.

Animal hearts

There are many superstitions involving animal hearts, some of which are contradictory. In parts of Britain a scorned woman used to be able to take the heart of pigeon or a hare, stick it full of needles, pins and nails, then bury it near a tomb. As the heart rotted, so would the heart of her faithless lover sicken and die.

Farmers who suspected that their animals had died as a result of witchcraft would remove the hearts from the animals and stick it with nine new pins, nine new nails and nine new needles. The farmer could then either boil the heart or throw it on a rowan fire just before midnight. The burning heart would summon to the house the sorcerer or witch who had cast the spell, and he or she would knock on the door. On no account should the witch be allowed in, or the spell would break. A variation on this was to take the heart skewered with pins, needles and nails and hide it in the chimney, or somewhere else in the house or barn, in order to drive away the witch and protect the area.

ants

In Cornwall, England, people never used to kill ants because they were thought to be the shrivelled bodies of very ancient faeries in the last stages of their earthly existence. Killing them was unlucky, because as the faeries probably didn't appreciate being sent away from the earthly plane any sooner than they had to be.

bees

If a honeybee hovers near your head, don't panic. It's very good luck, as the bee is the most asset-rich of all insects—at least from a human perspective. Its presence heralds success. So don't shoo one away, especially as it might take offence. Hurting a bee or driving it away will drive away your good fortune.

However, in large numbers bees are unlucky. A swarm visiting your house is a bad portent for the future, unless the bees fly off after only a short while.

You should never buy honeybees, but swap them instead for something else of value. Bought bees will neither swarm nor ever make honey. You should buy them near Easter, but never bring them home until the morning of Good Friday, and if you ever have to move your bees, do so on Good Friday. The only other way of acquiring bees while keeping your good luck is to have someone give them to you. If you must buy bees, never pay for them with silver, they must be bought with gold.

Bees will die if they are made to cross water. They're also sensitive to bad language and fighting, so they will leave a household full of swearing and quarrels. Bees swarming on dead wood are a sign of death. If bees desert you, then at best your good luck will leave you, at worst it is a sign that death will visit your house soon.

Bees should never be inadvertently exposed to death. If a death does occur, it's polite to inform the bees and to drape black mourning cloth over them before turning the hives away from the house in which the person died.

In fact, you should always keep bees in the loop. If bees visit a wedding or a funeral, someone should tell them who is getting married or who has died. If they're not told, they'll get angry and sting all the attendees.

Butterflies

The Greeks believed that butterflies were the souls of the dead. Their word 'psyche' meant both butterfly and spirit, and the idea has come down to us as the root word for both the mind, as in 'psychology', and the paranormal, as in 'psychic'. You can ask for a sign that your recently departed loved ones are happy in the afterlife, and seeing a butterfly is a sure sign that all's right with the world beyond, because the butterfly is actually the soul of your departed loved one paying you a visit.

It's lucky to see the first white butterfly of spring.

Cats

The Egyptians regarded the cat as sacred. Their cat-headed goddess Bast (or Bastet) was the goddess of pleasure and healing, and she was invoked to protect people from sickness and evil. The Egyptians mummified hundreds of thousands of cats—cat mummies far outnumber those of people. Cats even had their own heaven, filled with fields of greenery and mice to torture and eat. The Egyptians depicted Bast as a black cat, or as woman with a black cat's head. Ironically, this is the origin of all the later negative associations with black cats.

The Hebrews, who spent some time in Egypt, were the first to associate the cat with the evils of Egyptian religion. Jews believed that if they ate the ashes of a black kitten, they would be able to see demons. In the Middle Ages black cats were often suspected of being familiars (companions) to

witches or to be the witches themselves in their favourite animal form.

In spite of this, black cats have their uses. If you have a sty in your eye, stroke the tail of a black cat over it and incant:

I poke thee,
I don't poke thee,
I poke the queff that's under the eye,
O qualyway, O qualyway.

You can use the tail of a tortoiseshell cat in a similar way to cure warts, while holding the skin of a cat of any colour next to your face was supposed to cure a toothache. A more general cure, in fact for all that ailed a person, was to wash the patient while keeping the water, then to throw the water over a cat.

Chinese emperors slept on cat-shaped pillows for luck.

There's a widely held superstition that if you have to change houses, you shouldn't take your cat with you. It's bad luck to move a cat. Ideally, the new people who move in should take the cat as a package deal. There are numerous stories of people losing their cats (or dogs) after they've moved house. The animals use their incredible sense of direction to find their way back to their original home—sometimes over hundreds, even thousands, of miles,. There are too many verified accounts of this happening, so if you ever hear of this phenomenon, don't count it as a superstition.

The Azande believe that some women give birth to cats, but if you see this happen you will die, so there aren't any witnesses around to refute this belief.

Superstitious chickens

Psychologists have known for quite a while now that you can make chickens superstitious. Really! In the 1970s a group of boffins designed an experiment. Every time that a chicken scratched the ground three times with its left leg, they gave it a food pellet. Pretty soon the chicken caught on, and from then onwards, every time the chicken ate anything, she'd do her leg trick—even after the experiment ended.

This sort of thing gives us an insight as to how people become superstitious too. It only takes a few instances of 'good luck' to be associated with some sort of behaviour, and the superstition comes into being.

cobras

A superstition has it that if you kill a cobra, you have to dispose of the body thoroughly, or at least far away from your home. If you don't and the spouse of the dead cobra finds the body, it will see you, the murderer, reflected in the eyes of its dead mate. It will then seek you out and pursue you ceaselessly until it exacts its revenge.

Unfortunately for the romantics among us, eyes are not cameras. They don't store images, and snakes have poor eyesight anyway, preferring to hunt through smell and taste—which is what all that tongue flicking is about. Furthermore, cobras just aren't like that. During mating season a male cobra competes with other males for females and if successful, he'll stay with her only for a short time until she lays a clutch of eggs. Then she leaves him, for good. He hangs around for three months to protect the nest, but once his children hatch, he abandons them. That's about the extent of cobra family ties.

cormorants

Cormorants are elegant birds. In many parts of the world fishermen train them to catch fish by diving for them. The fisherman put a tight ring around their necks to stop them eating bigger fish and they can't fly away because their wings are clipped. Superstitiously, an old cure for a stomach ache is to tie cormorant skin to your belly.

cranes

In Japan the oriental white crane is a sacred animal, symbolising wholeness and happiness. One of the simplest folds in the art of origami is the crane, and if someone is sick, it's customary to fold cranes and send them to the patient. There is an old belief that whoever folds or receives a thousand cranes will have their wish granted. In cases of extreme or life-threatening illness, people have been know to fold over a thousand cranes in the hopes that their loved one will recover, and in Japan you can buy *zenzabaru* sets—kits containing just over one thousand squares of paper along with the string to hold the completed cranes all together.

In Japan, the oriental white crane is a sacred animal symbolising wholeness and happiness.

All the crane folding didn't help Sadako Sasaki, who died in 1955 at the age of twelve from the effects of the Hiroshima atomic bomb, in spite of having folded over a thousand cranes, and having thousands more given to her. However, her courage and tenacity in fighting her illness, and in being a martyr to the horrors of war, have been an inspiration to many people since. People still fold cranes and send them to Sadako's monument in Hiroshima, praying for peace or perhaps that the spirit of Sadako can do for others what she was not able to do for herself.

crickets

A cricket in the house has various meanings depending on the cricket's colour: black means illness, grey means money and green, hope. In contrast to the beliefs of the lucky cricket in Europe, Africa and China, in north-east Brazil a cricket in the house portends death and the cricket is immediately killed.

Elsewhere in the country, a cricket's constant chirping predicts a pregnancy in the house or is a harbinger of rain. This is especially true of the mole cricket, which burrows in the ground prior to a storm.

Amazingly the snowy tree cricket can actually tell you the temperature outside:

- Count the number of chirps per minute.
- Subtract 40.
- Divide the result by four, then add 50.
- The result is the outside temperature in degrees Fahrenheit. To convert to Celsius, subtract 32, multiply by five and divide by nine.

crows, ravens and rooks

Being large and black, and not having the most attractive of calls, crows, ravens and rooks are bad luck birds. Meeting a single crow in your travels is a bad sign and especially bad if you hear one croaking to your left in the morning. If a crow flutters over you or flutters outside your window, this is an omen of death.

If rooks leave the rookery, it's a bit like rats leaving a sinking ship, a sign that all is lost—you'll leave too if you know what's good for you.

Crickets are symbols of abundance and prosperity.

The raven too, crows evil. However, there is an old superstition that there are at least six ravens resident in the Tower of London at any one time. Legend has it that if the ravens ever leave, the Tower itself (the White Tower), the monarchy and the kingdom will fall. This seemed close when there was only one surviving raven in the Tower after World War II—a bird called Grip. Ravens can live a long time—over 40 years. Today there are nine ravens in residence at the Tower, and their names are rather whimsical: the males are called Gwylum, Thor, Bran, Gundulf and Baldrick, while the females are Hugin, Munin, Fleur and Branwen.

DOGS

Dogs and humans have a history together that stretches back tens of thousands, perhaps hundreds of thousands of years. There's been ample time for humans to ascribe all sorts of superstitions to dogs.

Many Muslims regard dogs as 'unclean' and they cause *hadath* (impurity) if touched. Moroccans regard a man who kills a dog as unclean. Animals that have been killed by hunting dogs are unclean unless you chant '*bismillah*', meaning 'in the name of Allah'.

In Europe, dogs are generally good guys. They are considered masculine animals, whereas cats are perceived to be feminine, so where witches would have cats as their familiars, dogs—particularly black, menacing-looking ones—would be the familiars of sorcerers and warlocks. The popular media seems to like this idea, so bad guys nearly always have Doberman watchdogs, and Dobermans are the 'hound of choice' for Satan and his minions.

Eating dog is a bad idea in many cultures, sometimes because they are impure, sometimes for the opposite reason. To the Zoroastrians, dogs are sacred. To the Hare of Canada's north-west territories, dogs were literally their best friends and the idea of eating dog would be as unthinkable as cannibalism. However, to Polynesians, like the Tahitians, Hawaiians and the Maori, dogs were a food source, and to the Chinese and many South East Asian cultures they influenced they still are. To many tribes in Nigeria, dog meat is medicinal, as it is in Korea, and soups made from dog meat are supposed to be powerful tonics. Over 6000 restaurants in South Korea specialise in dog meat dishes.

In many parts of the world dogs are assumed to have more acute psychic vision than humans and they are supposed to be able to see ghosts, phantoms and spirits more easily than people. In China if a dog howls continuously and can't be settled, it's supposed to portend an imminent death, because the dog can see death approaching. It stands to reason, therefore, that if you take a dog's tear and put it in your own, you acquire, for a time, the ability to see the spirit world and the ghosts of your ancestors. There is a danger to this practice, and some believe that without proper preparation, you can die from the shock of seeing the usually hidden afterlife. Mediums, who are presumably professionals, use the technique to help them with their exorcisms.

To add to the presumed psychic abilities of dogs, it's commonly held that dogs can smell blood on the hands of a murderer, even years after the event. It would be amazing if this were true, but, even though the appropriately named bloodhound has 220 million scent receptors in its nasal armoury—as opposed to a human's five million—the coldest trail that it can usually track is about five days old—assuming that there's been no intervening rain or snow to wash away any traces of the crime.

In Tibet dogs are useful as psychic garbage disposals. If you're having a run of bad luck, make a dog biscuit from dough that looks like you and give all your bad luck to it. Then, let the dog eat it, and it will eat your bad luck with it.

There is an old wives' tale that a dog's saliva is cleaner than a human's, so if you scrape your knee it's a good idea if you can persuade your dog to lick it clean for you.

This is crazy. Dogs never brush their teeth, their tongues are not only 'shower cloths' but also their toilet paper, and if you've ever seen a dog eating faeces … need I go on?

For all their questionable hygiene, dogs remain man's best friend. Their loyalty is famous and there are many stories of dogs who refused to leave the graves of their former masters. The Skye Terrier Greyfriars Bobby stayed close to the grave of his owner, nightwatchman John Gray, for fourteen years, and became so famous in his home city of Edinburgh that the Lord Provost paid for the renewal of his licence so that Bobby would become the responsibility of the whole city. When Bobby died in 1872, he was buried just outside the church grounds near John Gray's grave. In Japan a white Akita named Hachiko waited to greet his master at the end of every day at Shibuya station, Tokyo, and he continued to do this after his master died. When Hachiko's story became widely known, he became a sensation, and probably saved his breed from extinction, as there were only 30 purebred Akitas still alive when Hachiko died in 1935. Given this sort of history, it's no wonder that many people believe that dogs and their masters have a profound spiritual link. Dogs are commonly believed to howl, whimper and otherwise exhibit signs of grief when their masters die, especially if the death is violent, and even if the death is hundreds or thousands of miles away.

doves

Ever since Noah set free a dove after the 40 days and 40 nights of flood, and the dove returned holding an olive branch in its beak, the dove has been a symbol of peace and hope. Killing a dove is atrociously bad luck. Muslims believe that doves nestling in the eaves of a house bring good fortune to the family.

fish

If you dream of a fish, it's a sign of good luck. If the fish is in water, you'll receive unexpected favours. However, dreaming of a dead fish is a sign that you'll lose something, and gutting and cleaning a mackerel is bad luck—a sign of deceit and bad news.

foxes

Foxes don't have much luck in the West or the East. Symbols of cunning, treachery and trickery in Europe, in Japan the fox is a demon that takes the form of a beautiful woman who seduces lecherous men and sucks the life force out of them. Foxes around your house portend death and disaster, and heaven help you if you come across several all at the same time.

frogs

There are a number of spells involving frogs, nearly all of them bad for the frog. Rubbing a frog across a wart, then impaling the poor thing on a thorn tree was supposed to cure the wart. Ironically, science has established that because frogs live in wet environments, which often encourage the growth of parasites and diseases, their skins secrete a host of antibacterial and anti-viral substances, so there may be some truth to such superstitions. However, even if it is true, killing the frog is completely unnecessary.

Frogs were sacred to Egyptian midwives, and frog-shaped charms helped ensure an easy delivery.

goats

The goat was sacred to the Greek god Chronos—Saturn in Roman mythology—also known as Father Time, so goats symbolised the patience, perseverance and time to acquire wealth. The cornucopia, the horn of plenty, is a goat's horn, and amulets depicting goats or cornucopia are given to encourage wealth.

Horses

You'd think that horses would be lucky animals because they wear horseshoes all the time, but even horses have to be careful. Horses blow on water before drinking it in the morning, because the water falls asleep at night. It will die if it drinks the sleeping water.

It's bad luck to meet a white horse or a piebald horse. Spit three times to ward off the bad luck.

A concoction made from hocks, the rear 'knees', of a horse, imbibed every two hours used to be given as a treatment for epilepsy.

kingfishers

These birds, of which the Australian kookaburra is a particularly large species, are supposed to have skin and feathers that never rot, so they have the power to preserve any material they touch. Housewives used to place kingfisher feathers in drawers to preserve linen. Tradition states that when the kingfisher breeds, the weather remains fine and there are no storms at sea.

Kookaburras, like all other kingfishers, are supposed to have skin and feathers that never rot so they have the power to preserve any material they touch.

Ladybirds

These little insects are lucky. If one lands on you, don't brush it off; let it fly off on its own. Count the number of spots, as you'll have one month of good luck for each spot, and the deeper the red of the ladybird, the luckier you'll be.

The ladybird's name comes from the medieval belief that the insect was a favourite of the Virgin Mary, mother of Jesus Christ. Ladybirds would bestow blessings on anyone who found them, including newborn babies, which is why in Italy they've been called *commaruccia* (little midwives).

Needless to say, killing a ladybird is very bad luck. If you do, you'll be in the Virgin Mary's bad books for nine days. Killing a ladybird is also stupid, they are great hunters of aphids, mites, white flies, cabbage moth larvae and broccoli worms.

oysters

The Anglo-Saxon world is responsible for the belief that oysters are poisonous during months with an 'r' in their name. Although untrue, this myth allows the oysters time to prepare to spawn. Oysters are edible from September to April, but they're not at their best in the Northern Hemisphere.

pigs

Today pigs are an important food source for many people; historically, they've had mixed reviews. In the West calling someone a pig is, of course, an insult, while Jews and Muslims, and cultures these religions have influenced, have always considered pigs unclean. Even the ancient Celts had an antipathy towards them. Well into the 1800s, it was difficult to persuade anyone in the northern British Isles to have anything to do with them. In these areas, a pig

crossing your path had the same negative connotation usually ascribed to black cats, especially if the pig crossed the path of a wedding, christening or funeral party. British fishermen would refuse to go to sea for the day if a pig crossed their path while they were on their way to their boats. Fishermen considered the animal so unlucky that they'd refuse to carry a ham onboard or even mention pigs—doing so while baiting the lines could ruin the catch. Some people believed that touching wood, nails or other 'cold iron' could dispel the bad luck of the word.

Southern landlubbers weren't so squeamish.

In Somerset, England, people were known to take the snout of a freshly killed pig in their right hand, and stand in front of their house with their back to it.

They would then try to throw the snout over their head and over their house. If the snout landed in the back garden, it brought good luck, if it hit the roof and stayed there, bad luck.

If a pig died suddenly in your house, there would be sickness soon. However, pigs could be useful. It was commonly believed that you could rub a sick child's head onto a pig's back, and disease would go from the child to the pig. This was supposed to be particularly effective for mumps.

Pigs are supposed to be able see the wind, if one runs towards you with straw in its mouth, rain is coming, if one squeals loudly then a storm is coming.

In contrast to the West, the Chinese consider pigs to be a symbol of luck, wealth, fertility and virility, and the

In the West, pigs are generally regarded negatively, whereas the Chinese
consider pigs to be a sympol of luck, wealth, fertility and virility.

words 'pig' and 'God' sound very similar in some dialects. The pig is the twelfth sign of the Chinese zodiac, and children born in a pig year will grow to be happy, honest, patient people. On the negative side they can also be materialistic, gullible and naïve. Nevertheless, some Chinese are squeamish about mentioning the pig directly, and use the euphemism 'long-nosed general' to refer to them.

Pigs are also associated with money in the West. Irish farmers sold pigs to pay the rent, and the Irish generally feel good about pigs. However a piggy bank is bad luck unless you chip it or knock one ear off.

In Sumatra pigs are given a lot of respect, and natives hang the jawbones of slaughtered pigs from the ceilings of their houses for a while to save the souls of the pigs.

Animal faeces

In the developed, urban world, dung is seen as dirty and disgusting, and its proper place is in a septic tank or a sewer. People who live in the country or in societies that are a little more connected to the earth see it as a resource, mostly as a fertiliser, but dried it is in fact one of the world's major cooking fuels.

There are a few superstitions connected to dung. For pubescent boys who can't wait to grow up, pigeon droppings smeared on the face is supposed to promote the growth of moustaches and beards. Goose droppings are recommended to cure baldness of the head.

In Europe a poultice of cow manure and milk used to be considered efficacious in the treatment of frostbite. The English used to apply goose dung mixed with elder bark to burns. One source states that:

the consumption of fresh, warm camel faeces has been recommended by Bedouins as a remedy for bacterial dysentery; its efficacy (probably attributable to the antibiotic subtilism from Bacillus subtilis) was confirmed by German soldiers in Africa during World War II.

Accidentally treading in doggie-do, or any other 'do' for that matter, is generally considered lucky. Wedding guests who tread in faeces shouldn't wipe it off. If an animal defecates in front of your front door this is very good luck, and in parts of rural Britain, some people put horse manure near their front door—or even inside their houses—for luck and protection against the evil eye. Many people today still say: 'Where there's muck, there's luck.'

possums

The Hua people of China have an interesting attitude towards possums, at least the men do. Male Hua claim publicly that the possum is the symbol of female reproductive power, and that if a man eats possum meat he will become pregnant. Without the right magic his body will rupture, and he will die when the foetus within him cuts its first two bottom teeth. Privately, male Hua eat possum meat during special ceremonies, and they even have a special place in which to do so, the *zga zu* (possum house). The men claim that eating possum is actually a way of gaining great health—the catch is that women aren't supposed to know this, and no female Hua will ever admit that she knows anything about this secret men's business.

Rabbits and hares

The name Easter comes from the name of the west Germanic goddess Eostre, the deity of the dawn and of the first month of the year (which corresponds roughly to present-day April), and by extension rebirth and new beginnings, even resurrection. The hare was sacred to Eostre and this explains why rabbit's feet are supposed to be lucky. It also explains the curious appearance of the Easter bunny, an animal not usually associated with eggs at any other time.

In other traditions the hare is unlucky, believed to be a favourite animal for witches to turn into. So if a rabbit crosses your path, it's bad luck, unless it's behind you, which means that your bad luck is also behind you. To counter any rabbit bad luck, spit in its direction, cross yourself, draw an 'X' in the road or cross your fingers … you get the idea.

Rats

The rat is not the most beloved of creatures, which is a real pity because rats are highly intelligent and resourceful. When humans become extinct, it will be the rats that take over the world. Perhaps if their tales weren't so scaly and their teeth so yellow, rats would have a better public image, although it doesn't help matters that they break into food stores.

A magical formula for getting rid of rats is to write them a letter in which you politely, but assertively, and to the fullest extent of the lore, suggest that they may be happier elsewhere. Perhaps the building next door? You then cover the letter with grease—bacon fat is especially good— and push it down the rat hole. Since rats usually can't read, they eat the letter and digest the message along with it.

Nonetheless, rats can be useful. Eating dried rats' tails is supposed to be good for colds.

Robins

Robins are lucky. Never kill a robin, don't steal or break its eggs, don't even disturb its nest. Break something of the robin, and something of yours will be broken too. Witches take nasty revenge on anyone who hurts a robin. A robin flying into your house is very good luck.

scarab beetles

A beetle that makes its living by gathering balls of shit became sacred to the Egyptians because they believed that there was a celestial scarab that moved the sun across the sky. It's unclear whether the Egyptians believed that the sun was actually a huge ball of burning dung, but they might have, considering that there are few trees in Egypt and dried dung was used—and is still used by millions of people throughout the world—as a fuel for cooking fires. Because the sun is 'reborn' each day, the scarab, by association, became the symbol of rebirth and immortality, and scarab amulets are among the most ancient good luck charms known.

slugs and snails

Slugs live in similar environments to frogs and their skins are also full of parasite- and disease-killing goodies. In northern Europe, folk used to make a cough syrup, which was apparently quite effective, by dissolving slugs in sugar.

Prick a snail and let the liquid that comes out fall into an ear to treat earache.

snakes

Although the story of the Garden of Eden has guaranteed bad press for the snake in the Western world, in the East the snake is revered for its wisdom. Many cultures thought that the shedding of a snakeskin indicated that the animal was immortal. Snake venom is not universally lethal and in many traditions snakes are symbols of healing. Cast-off snakeskin wrapped around the head is a treatment for headaches. The ancient Greek *caduceus* wand—still the symbol of medicine and doctors in the West—shows two snakes wrapped around a staff topped with a pair of wings. The symbolism is rich, originally representing the Mesopotamian serpent god Ningishzida, messenger of the goddess Ishtar and the patron of medicine. The Greeks borrowed the symbol 1000 years later and added a legend too.

Before he lost his sight, the blind prophet of Thebes, Tiresias, came upon two copulating snakes. He tried to separate them with his staff, he failed and was turned into a woman for seven years until he could find another pair of copulating snakes and repeat the act. The god Hermes, messenger to the gods and also of commerce, later acquired the staff. The symbol was originally one of messengers and messages, but Hermes was also the god of alchemists, producers of medicines, hence the link. The real symbol for medicine is actually the rod of Asclepius that depicts a single snake of healing wrapped around a wand. Asclepius was the son of Apollo, the Greek god of medicine, and Asclepius himself was a gifted healer. In Indian tradition the sexual energy that travels up the backbone, the kundalini, is depicted as a coiled snake or pair of coiled snakes at the base of the spine. When the energy is invoked, the kundalini rises and the snake, or snakes, travel up and entwine along the spine.

One popular belief is that baby snakes are more venomous than adults. In fact this is true—fortunately babies are much less practiced at biting than adults, so if they lunge, they're more likely to miss. Further on the upside, only about ten to fifteen per cent of all snakes throughout the world are venomous.

Snakes can only be successfully killed during daylight. Never attempt to kill a snake after dark, because it will not die.

sparrows

Christian tradition maintains that a sparrow betrayed Jesus to the Romans in the garden of Gethsemane, so the sparrow is an unlucky bird. If a sparrow enters your house, that's unlucky. It's very unlucky to keep a sparrow in a cage and it's even unlucky to kill one.

spiders and their webs

Cobwebs are supposed to stop bleeding in small cuts. Rolled into pills, spider webs can be swallowed to relieve ague and asthma, and to help restless people sleep.

storks

The original superstition was that a stork flies over a house where a child is about to be born. This eventually mutated into a story that storks actually brought babies, a convenient tale for parents who aren't prepared to explain sex to five-year-olds.

Storks, like albatrosses, emperor penguins and several other animals, mate for life. As such, they are symbols of fidelity.

swans

Swans are lucky and very bad luck to kill. The Roman nobility often served swans at their feasts, which might explain why so many of them had such violent and short lives. There is a superstition that swan eggs will only hatch during thunder and lightning, and that the usually silent swan sings beautifully before its death.

toads

Among the Amerindians toads are lucky, but killing one brings a storm.

In England, toads used to be considered to be emissaries of Satan. Charms involving toads make strong black magic, but use such charms at your peril, as any bad you bring to another comes back three times over to you. One farmer's spell is to burn a toad alive at midnight if he believes that someone has hexed his cows.

In spite of the toad's bad reputation the English also believed that old toads possessed a small gem in their heads. These 'toadstones' were highly valued because people believed that the stones changed colour in the presence of poison. Toadstones were also powerful protective charms for newborns and their mothers against malicious faeries.

Toads are thought to be able to cure certain medical problems. An old treatment to stop bleeding involved putting a dead toad in a bag and wearing it around your neck. In West Africa if an epidemic has struck your village, you can drag a toad through the streets to absorb the plague. You then throw the toad into the forest, and he takes the plague with him.

There is a common belief that toads give you warts. This is a myth. In humans there's a group of about 70 viruses called papilloma viruses, and they are the real cause of warts. Toads don't have papilloma viruses—they can't even carry them, but if you do want warts, you can encourage them through eating raw meat or raw fish. People who work processing meat or raw fish often have 'butcher's warts'.

tortoises

What do tortoises, dogs and incest have in common? Read on.

Among the Baan Phraan Muan villagers of north-eastern Thailand, marriages between even second cousins are considered incestuous and invite the attention of punitive spirits. Should such a marriage take place, the bride and groom have to eat rice served in the shell of the *lang diaw* (tortoise). The reasoning is that eating like this resembles the way a dog eats. The spirits accept that dogs are incestuous, so eating out of the tortoise shell fools the spirits into thinking that the bride and groom are actually dogs and don't need to be punished.

In the East tortoise charms ensure long life, because the tortoise itself lives for such a long time. Tortoises obviously have magical protection to live so long, so amulets made from tortoise shell also protect against the evil eye.

In ancient Greece the tortoise was sacred to Hermes, the messenger of the gods, who also had a role in diplomacy as a peacemaker. Tortoise charms thus promote peace between enemies.

whippoorwills

This small, dark, nocturnal bird, native to North America, has a bad reputation because you can hear its slightly eerie cry at about dawn, the time when the spirits of the night have their last chance to do whatever it is that they do.

Whippoorwills nest on the ground, and usually lay two eggs at a time, so watch your step. Never destroy the eggs of the whippoorwill, for every egg you destroy, a member of your family suffer a misfortune.

Hear the whippoorwill near your house and the bird might be warning you of an impending death.

The Amerindians believed that two whippoorwills were always a bad sign.

If you heard two whippoorwills carrying on a conversation, shout 'No!' If the birds stop, the listener can expect to die soon, if the birds continue, then the listener will have a long life. Whippoorwills are, however, solitary birds, and you'll seldom hear two calling at the same time.

New Englanders believe that the whippoorwill can sense the departing soul and will catch it as it leaves the body. To counter this magic, point your finger in the direction of the call of the whippoorwill and say 'shoot it'.

A young woman who hears the first call of the whippoorwill in spring is receiving a more benign message. If she hears one call, the man of her dreams will appear, two calls means that she will have to wait another year.

More in the menagerie of magic

And the list of animal superstitions doesn't end there:

Bears: sleeping on bearskin is supposed to accelerate the healing process of wounds.

Beetles: if a black beetle crawls over your shoe, this is an omen of death.

Birds' nests: never rob a bird's nest. It will bring the wrath of heaven upon you.

Cows: the Hindus believe that cows are sacred and will never harm anyone. A Hindu could be starving but would never eat beef.

Donkeys: to treat scarlet fever, take a lock of the patient's hair and stuff it down the throat of a donkey.

Lambs: the first lamb of spring is lucky, especially if it's black. Make a wish when you see a black lamb, as it's sure to be fulfilled. The birth of a black lamb is lucky for the flock. Leap years, however, are never good for sheep, at least according to the Scots.

Lice: eating nine lice on a piece of bread and butter was a treatment for jaundice.

Owls: like so many animals of the night, owls are unlucky. An owl visiting you in the daytime is an omen of death. If the owl's hoot resembles your name, then you're really in trouble.

Peacocks: it is very unlucky to bring peacock feathers indoors. Some maintain that in a house where peacock feathers are, no child will be born.

Roosters: expect a visit from a stranger if your rooster crows while facing your front door.

the superstitious gardener

The superstitious gardener

Where possible, human settlements nearly always start near a body of freshwater, like a lake, stream or river, near the edge of the forest. It is here, at the boundary between field and forest, that there is the greatest opportunity for foraging. For most people, plants make up the bulk of their diet although, like animals, plants have always been with us, it's only after own deaths that we generally become food for them.

Our relationship with plants is thus mostly benign, but no less mysterious. Lesser gods and spirits usually inhabit the bodies of herbs and trees, and people usually think of plants, especially medicinal plants, as gifts from the gods. Sometimes the gods even turned people into plants, especially trees.

Ancient pantheons tended to divide supernatural beings into good gods and bad gods, benign and evil spirits, with a smattering of others who could be either good or bad depending on how they felt on the day.

As the tears, or sometimes the blood, of gods fell on the earth, plants would grow and it followed that food plants and healing plants came from good gods and noxious plants came from bad. To make matters even more confusing, whether a plant heals or hurts often depends on the concentration of its extract, or what part of the plant you use.

Christian myth, for example, tells us that after the fall of Adam and Eve, Satan walked out of the Garden of Eden and that from his left footprint sprang garlic, and from his right, onions.

Only rarely are plants absolutely poisonous or evil, and whether good or bad, plants too have a rich lore of superstition associated with them. Whole compendia of plant-medicine lore, known as 'herbals' are full of plant cures for diseases, while the treatments of the alternative medicine industry fill whole libraries. Below though, you'll find uses and attributes assigned to plants that can best be described as 'magical'.

Apple trees

By weight, more apples are harvested than any other fruit, making them the most popular fruit in the world. There's a considerable amount of lore about apples.

Apple orchards have to be coaxed into producing lots of fruit by singing to the trees and leaving pieces of toast soaked in cider for the god of the orchard. You have to bury the corpse of an animal under a newly planted tree, or the tree will not bear fruit. In west England there is a superstition that the orchard will bear more fruit in the following year, if you let children steal any apples left over on the tree after the main harvest is finished, so you never pick all the apples from a tree the first time around, in order to allow for the 'piskies harvest'. To get the most out of your apple trees, and any other fruit trees for that matter, you should prune and graft during the increase of the moon's cycle.

It's considered extremely bad luck to burn apple branches for firewood and you should never bring the cuttings of apple trees into your house.

Ash trees

Ash trees were sacred to the Norse, and their great 'world tree' Yggdrasil was an ash. Ashes are used in a variety of spells as a general protection against evil and to cure diverse illnesses. Magic wands made of ash were second only to hazel in effectiveness.

To cure whooping cough, cut a lock of hair from the sufferer and attach it to an ash tree. To cure warts, stick pins into an ash, then pull them out and stick them into the warts.

Never bring the cuttings of apple trees into your house.

Rickets, a childhood condition that causes deformation of bones, especially leg bones, because of a deficiency of vitamin D, can be cured in the following manner. Find an ash sapling and split it in two down the middle. Pass the child nine times through the tree. Then bind the tree up again. If the tree healed, so would the child. This same method could be used to leave behind other diseases or ills, or to make a symbolic 'new beginning' if you were leaving your old life behind.

Carrying an ash twig was supposed to help rheumatism. Ash sap (like rowan sap) protected newborn children from faeries. Christian legend has it that the Virgin Mary burned ash to warm the baby Jesus, so English mothers used to rock cradles under ash trees. If you want your child to grow up to be a good singer, bury the child's first fingernail parings under an ash tree.

Asparagus

In ancient Greece wild asparagus was a lucky plant and was used in wedding garlands. It was also considered a good idea to leave one stem of the asparagus uncut and to allow it to flower, which is more sensible than superstitious, since asparagus is tricky to grow and the plant takes seven years to mature.

Bananas

In the 1960s it was fashionable for a time to smoke dried banana skins on the assumption that it was a hallucinogen. In spite of some positive responses, bananas have no hallucinogenic qualities at all and any hippies who tripped out on the stuff were getting high on their imagination rather than on chemistry.

In the Bismarck Archipelago, off the north-eastern coast of New Guinea, you should always dispose of a banana skin carefully, as a witch may retrieve it and burn it causing you to die a painful death.

Bay and laurel leaves

Although bay leaves in the modern world end up flavouring stews and casseroles, in ancient times it was a herb of prophecy. At the Oracle of Delphi, some traditions say that the seeress, the Pythia, would inhale smoke from burning bay leaves to contact the god Apollo and make her predictions. Other traditions say, however, that the

Pythia only *held* the bay leaves as she sat on a three-legged stool in front of a hole in the ground to inhale sulphurus fumes, which were sacred to Apollo.

Later in history people would throw bay leaves on a fire. If they crackled, that was a good omen, but a bad sign if they burned silently.

If you wrap a wolf's tooth in a bay leaf, then put it under your pillow, your dreams will tell you where someone has hidden money they've stolen from you. If you can't get your hands on any wolves' teeth, you can still put bay leaves under your pillows for sweet dreams.

Beans

When the broad bean is in flower, accidents, madness and other lunacies are more prevalent.

Some traditions have it that broad bean flowers are sweet because they contain the souls of the dead, so never eat these flowers, as they will give you bad dreams.

cabbages

A cabbage that grows with widely spaced leaves is lucky, and a double cabbage, where two heads grow from the one root, is very lucky. Some folk cures for sore throats involve cabbage, and there may be something in them, because cabbages are high in vitamin C. The more intelligent sea captains took along pickled cabbage and rationed it among the sailors to prevent scurvy. One treatment for hoarseness or laryngitis that was not likely to work was to tie cabbage leaves around the throat. More efficacious probably was another treatment, to mix cabbage juice with honey and swallow the mixture.

In parts of northern France and southern Belgium, children don't think that storks deliver babies, but that babies grow in cabbage patches—white cabbages for boys and red for girls.

chrysanthemums

It's never a good idea to give chrysanthemums to Europeans, since the flower, especially the white variety, is associated with death and funerals.

To the Chinese, however, they are symbols of autumn, and in Japan they resemble the sun, so much so that they are the sacred flowers of the Japanese emperors, who are descended from the sun goddess and who sit on the chrysanthemum throne.

cloves

According to James Frazer, in *The Golden Bough* (1890):

In the Moluccas, when the clove trees are in blossom, they are treated like pregnant women.

No noise may be made near them. No one may approach them with his hat on. All must uncover in their presence.

These precautions are observed lest the tree should be alarmed and bear no fruit, or should drop its fruit too soon, like the untimely delivery of a woman who has been frightened in her pregnancy.

Four-leaf clovers

The shamrock is one of the luckiest of plants. Consider the following rhyme:

One leaf for fame,
And one for wealth,
And one for a faithful lover,
And one to bring you glorious health,
Are all in a four-leaf clover.

cucumbers

Cucumber was originally considered an aphrodisiac, perhaps because of its shape. It was also prescribed as a cure for rabies.

Hawthorn and hazel trees

Although unrelated botanically, many traditions associated with the hawthorn also apply to the hazel. Hawthorn was used to make Christ's crown of thorns, but nevertheless crowns made from the flowering hawthorn or hazel are supposed to be very lucky and will make your wishes come true.

juniper

Gin, the spirit flavoured with juniper berries, served with or without tonic water is supposed to be good for fevers, and it may surprise some gin and tonic drinkers to learn that quinine, the additive that gives tonic water its distinctive bitter taste, was originally used as—and still is—an effective treatment for malaria. An old English cure for fever is to drink gin with powdered mole for nine consecutive days.

Lavender

Lavender is a paradoxical plant that is said to provoke passion but also encourage chastity, which sounds like the medieval ideal of courtly love. Today lavender is burned as an essential oil in hospitals to encourage calm and healing, and it is especially popular in cardiac wards.

Mandrake

Traditionally used to cure skin complaints and chronic liver diseases, as an anaesthetic or as a powerful medicine to 'expel demons from the sick', mandrake was a dangerous plant to gather. When pulled out of the ground, it was supposed to emit a scream that was lethal or at the very least that would make you mad. To avoid these fates, gatherers would dig around the mandrake root, then tie a rope to it and a dog to the other end of the rope. After moving a safe distance away, they'd call the dog, which would pull the root out.

Some believed that the dog would then die instead of you.

It stands to reason that it would be less expensive to use deaf dogs, but then, of course, the dog wouldn't hear you when you called, so you'd have to find another way of signalling to it. However, when people observed that dogs used in this way didn't die, people assumed it was not because the mandrake didn't really scream, but because dogs were immune to it. This is classic magical thinking, where you'll do anything to keep a good story, rather than confuse the issue with facts and less romantic explanations.

Mint

Growing mint in the garden attracts prosperity. It's only a coincidence that the buildings in which money is made are also called mints. 'Mint' for plant comes from the Greek, 'minthos', which became the West Germanic 'minta'. 'Mint' for coin production facilities comes from the Latin word for money, 'moneta', which became the West

Germanic 'munita'. However, using the magical principle of similarities and that green is the colour of mint, green is the colour most associated with money, not only in the modern world, but also in spells to increase the flow of money.

mistletoe

For a parasite that can only live by sucking the sap from a tree unfortunate enough to be its host, the mistletoe has a good reputation as a plant of magic and power. It was sacred to the Druids, and, as an emblem of peace, warring Celtic tribes would sit beneath it when engaged in negotiations to cease hostilities. Mistletoe also had a reputation as a cure for all sorts of illness and as a plant that could boost fertility in women. This again is ironic, because mistletoe is highly poisonous.

moss

Scrape off some moss that's been growing on a human skull. Dry it and use it like snuff to treat a headache.

mugwort

Use mugwort tea to wash any tools that you are going to use to divine the future, as mugwort is the medieval witch's herb of choice for prophecy. You can also rub the tools with mugwort. Burn mugwort and inhale the smoke for prophetic visions or put dried mugwort into your pillows for prophetic dreams. Use mugwort with care, however, as in large quantities it is toxic.

oak trees and acorns

The oak was sacred to Thor, the Norse god of Storms, so the Vikings put acorns in their windowsills reasoning that Thor would not strike his own tree.

However in other traditions, people believed that the oak tree, among others, actually attracted lightning, as well as bad poetry:

Beware the oak,
It draws the stroke
Beware the ash,
It courts the flash,
Creep under the thorn,
'Twill protect you from harm.

onions

Eating onion is supposed to be good for the ears in the same way that eating carrots is supposed to be good for the eyes.

If you dream of onions, you'll be facing some arguments in the home or some other domestic strife.

parsley

To the ancient Greeks, parsley was an unlucky plant, a symbol of mourning. If you encountered parsley while you were marching to war, it was a very bad omen. The English inherited similar prejudices against parsley and some refused to cut it, give it away, transplant it or even to grown it in the first place.

poplar trees

Some people say that the cross upon which Christ died was made of poplar wood, which explains why the leaves of the poplar are always trembling; other traditions say the cross was made of ash, oak or even pine.

potatoes

Cut a potato in half and put it in your pocket. As the potato shrivels so does your arthritis.

Americans apply mashed potatoes—presumably cold—to heal burns.

It's commonly thought that if a potato has any green in its skin or under its skin, it is poisonous. Although it is true that a completely green potato is likely to contain enough of the green-tinged poison solanine to kill you, it would taste so bad that you wouldn't eat it in the first place. For more normal-looking potatoes, if there's a little green tinge on the skin, just cut it off.

Some gardeners recommend that you plant potatoes with the eyes up, so that they can see in which direction they are supposed to grow.

All the members of the family should eat some of the first potatoes of the season or else the remaining potatoes will feel unappreciated and rot in the fields, or fail to keep in the pantry.

roses

The rose was especially sacred to the Christians because it was the flower of the Virgin Mary. However, many also consider it unlucky.

Roses were often associated with death. White roses would be planted on the grave of a virgin, red on the grave of a person noted for their charity.

In Scotland, if a rose blooms out of season, there will be a shipwreck.

You should never scatter red rose petals on the ground. It's bad luck, because it looks like spilled blood. However, the Romans showered their emperors, triumphant generals and anyone who did anything noteworthy with rose petals as a sign of respect.

Roses could also protect. If you place wild roses over the gate of a cow pasture, witches won't be able to enter the field and ride on the cows.

However, these days roses are mostly associated with love and beauty. Different types of roses have different meanings in the language of flowers:

- bridal roses: happiness in love
- burgundy roses: beauty without self-consciousness
- cabbage roses: love
- damask roses: to enhance the complexion
- deep red roses: to communicate shame
- dog roses: to speak of pleasure and pain
- the rosa mundi: to signal variety
- thornless roses: early attachment, love in a hurry.

Rosemary

Since the time of the ancient Greeks, rosemary was associated with memory, so students used to make garlands of it and wear it on their heads during examinations.

This is especially important in a culture where, even if you knew how to read and write, things were very seldom written down, and people often memorised whole books by heart.

In the modern world, if you want the advantages of rosemary without being conspicuous, apply rosemary oil to your temples.

Rue

In Dark Age Europe, the rue plant was thought to protect against all evil, strengthen vision, cure snakebites and keep the plague away. Because superstition survives even in the face of evidence, facts and logic, the failure of any amount of rue to save the lives of millions of people during the Black Death, hasn't stopped herbalists prescribing it as a liver and blood 'cleanser' even today.

The Ancient Greeks associated rosemary with memory.

People who ate sage regularly were supposed to live long and happy lives.

sage

This herb was supposed to be good for just about everything. People that ate sage regularly were supposed to live long and healthy lives and, as the name implies, increase their wisdom. Even after death the plant was helpful and it was often planted on graves to prevent evil spirits from rising and haunting the living.

Sage is used in many rituals of cleansing, but it should never be used near pregnant women, as it may 'cleanse' them of the baby. A common use of sage is to dry it in a bundle, then to burn it to 'smudge' an area. This drives away bad energy and evil influences. Even non-burning sage is effective. If you grow sage in your garden, the health and vigour of the plant is indicative of your prosperity, so it's a good idea to keep your sage happy. It will grow better if you have rue as its companion plant.

st john's wort

This is a lucky plant that you can also use in a charm against witches:
Trefoil (clover), Vervain, St John's Wort and Dill, Hinder witches of their will.
St John's Wort was also grown as a protection against faeries, although it was also supposed to be sacred to female horses, mares, or female horse spirits, *maers*. Maers lived in the woods, but would come out of the forest at night and settle on sleepers, choking their breath and causing 'nightmares'.

If you put St John's Wort in a pillow St John himself might appear in a dream and give you his protection and blessing for the coming year.

Today herbalists use St John's Wort to treat insomnia, as an anti-depressant and as a treatment for anxiety attacks, a use for St John's Wort long known to the women of Europe.

strawberries

Faeries and elves are supposed to be fond of strawberries, so in Bavaria farmers tie them to the horns of cattle to stop the spirit folk casting spells on the cattle.

In Michigan, superstitious farmers would never eat the first strawberry to ripen in the field because it would give the strawberry plants the impression making lots of fruit would be of no use, and they would stop producing in despair. They'd throw the first strawberry to the birds instead.

timber

To get the most durability out of certain cut woods, you should only chop down a tree at a specific time in August. For hickory, maple, pine or any other white wood, cut these trees in the morning, any time when the moon is waxing. For chestnut and oak, choose the first morning after the first full moon of August.

Since there's a spirit inhabiting every tree, it is considered polite to ask the forgiveness of the spirit before you cut the tree down.

Further faith in flora

Basil: a herb of peace. Grow it in the garden to encourage domestic harmony.

Cinnamon: hung in the house this will increase the happiness of the household.

Cress: eating cress is supposed to make you witty.

Cypress trees: in the Mediterranean, cypress trees are supposed to offer shelter to the spirits of the dead during storms.

Elder trees: unlucky, because it was from an elder tree that Judas Iscariot chose to hang himself.

Endive: when growing in the garden, endives are supposed to open their leaves at eight o'clock in the morning and close them promptly at four in the afternoon.

Fig trees: in Greece, never sleep beneath a fig tree.

Lettuce: no woman will conceive a child in a house that has a garden with too many lettuces growing in it, although it's pretty vague as to how many is 'too many'.

Lilies: steep the petals of a Madonna Lily in brandy and apply them to the skin, rough side down, to treat boils.

Nutmeg: hand three nutmegs or a bag of camphor around the neck to relieve boils.

Oranges: stuffing a small thin piece of orange rind up each nostril is good for colds.

Pine trees: pine-bark tea is good for stomach aches.

Radishes: dry some radish pulp and use it like snuff to alleviate a headache.

Tobacco: blowing tobacco smoke into the ears is supposed to be good for earaches.

Turnips: eating turnip is good for fevers, but if a German farmer digs up a turnip in the shape of a shrivelled hand it is a powerful sign that his own hand will shrivel.

Vervain: nowadays found in herbal tea, vervain is supposed to help people deal with grief.

Watermelons: eating watermelon is good for fevers.

Yew trees: never injure a yew tree, it's very bad luck, but it's okay to steal the branches in order to make magic wands.

the magic of
rocks
and stones

The magic of rocks and stones

Since the early days of agriculture, farmers observed that they could plough a field and remove all the surface rocks but eventually other rocks would rise to the surface. Unaware of the complex processes of settlement, erosion and other facts of geology, farmers naturally assumed that the rocks must be breeding in some way. In many traditions rocks, and in particular gemstones, are thought to be alive, or at the very least imbued with a life force, like a spiritual battery. How else can you explain their beauty, especially if they seem to glow with an interior light? Stones could even be the 'frozen' tears of a god, storing or focusing power, for good or bad. And, of course, once again, the gods could turn you into a stone too.

Most significantly, gemstones were thought to protect people from the evil eye or other malevolent influences, and one of the most important functions of jewellery was that it protected the openings of the body from becoming entry points for evil spirits. Earrings in particular kept evil from entering through the ears, and even lipstick served the same purpose for the mouth. Following the same logic, doors and windows were the openings to the house and so stones could protect those too.

The technical term for seeing signs and divining the future through the use of rocks and stones is 'lithomancy'.

Metals too have their magical properties, specific metals being associated with particular gods or spirits. Metals hardly ever occur in their raw form in nature, the ore had to be mined, then smelted—separating the metal from whatever else it was bound to. The implication here is that the gods of the earth don't give up their treasures easily, so anything that's this difficult to reach must be worth having.

agate

The magical uses of agate have included powers as wide ranging as the ability to calm thunder and lightning, to secure the help of the powerful and to bring victory over enemies. Wearing agate was also supposed to increase the gift of the gab, and orators used it when they needed to be more eloquent. Moss agate is also useful when gardening or in any situation that requires a grasp on the lore of plants.

coral

Coral not only increased wisdom in its possessor, but it also helped prevent storms and floods.

Coral beads supposedly change colour depending on the health of the wearer—they pale as the wearer sickens, but recover their colour when the patient recovers. Mothers also put coral necklaces on children in order to help the teething process.

diamonds

The hardest known natural substance, diamonds are much more common than people think, but they remain highly prized and are generally considered good luck. Many old traditions credit diamonds with the power to drive off evil spirits, because the spirits can't stand to see their own reflection shone back at them through a diamond's many facets. When held on the left side, diamonds are supposed to ward off violence in the form of arguments, brawls and physical attacks from enemies or wild or venomous animals. Diamonds also protect the wearer from insanity.

However, there are some exceptions to this idea. There are cursed diamonds that bring all manner of trouble. The famous Koh-I-Noor (Mountain of Light) was

Coral beads are considered to have healing properties.

once the largest known diamond in the world and was stolen from the Indians by the British. Prince Albert had the stone cut, by a huge 42 per cent, to its present size of 21.61 grams (105.602 carats). After Prime Minister Benjamin Disraeli proclaimed Queen Victoria Empress of India, it became part of the crown jewels and currently resides in the Tower of London, set into the crown of Elizabeth II. The Koh-I-Noor is supposed to be very unlucky to its male owners, but lucky to its female owners. This superstition probably stems from the stone's long—possibly 5000-year-long—history of ownership by kings and emperors and the fact that the diamond has often changed hands as a spoil of war.

The curse of the blue, currently 9.32-gram (45.52 carat) Hope Diamond is somewhat stronger. Legend has it that it was stolen in India, from the eye of a statue of the goddess Sita. It went to France and into the hands of Louis

The crown jewels currently reside in the Tower of London.

XIV in 1668. He had the stone cut from 22.4 grams to 13.4 grams. Almost all of Louis's legitimate children died during childhood and, in a remarkable two years—1711 and 1712—Louis lost his eldest son suddenly as well as his grandson and his eldest great-grandson to smallpox. The only surviving heir was Louis's younger great-grandson, who became Louis XV in 1715.

Historians generally look upon Louis XV as having been amazingly ineffective in his 59-year reign. He too lost his son and was succeeded by his grandson, who became Louis XVI. Louis XVI gave the diamond, long ignored, to his wife Marie Antoinette. Louis and Marie both died in 1793, beheaded in the turmoil of the French Revolution. Their eight-year-old son, Louis XVII, was imprisoned and lived in squalor, dying of the cumulative effects of abuse and neglect at the age of ten in 1795.

A thief named Guillot had stolen the diamond in 1792, eventually taking it to London. In 1796 he tried to sell it. The prospective buyer had Guillot put into prison. The diamond then mysteriously 'disappeared' until the 20-year French statute of limitations expired in 1812. Somehow it ended up in the collection of millionaire Henry Philip Hope. When he died childless in 1839, his three nephews fought over his inheritance for ten years, until Henry Hope finally won through. Two generations later it was in the hands of Henry's grandson, also called Henry. This Henry went bankrupt and his wife left him, but he was finally able to sell the stone to a London dealer, who sold it to an American dealer, who eventually

sold it to one Salomon Habib. Habib went bankrupt and the diamond was sold to a French dealer, who sold it to Pierre Cartier in 1910.

Cartier had the stone reset and sold it the next year to Edward Beale McLean, who would go on to be the owner of the *Washington Post*. McLean bought the diamond on a whim for his wife, socialite Evalyn Walsh McLean. They had four children. Their eldest son Vinson was an epileptic who died in a traffic accident at the age of nine. Their daughter committed suicide at the age of 25. Edward turned out to be an unfaithful alcoholic and Evalyn acquired an addiction to morphine. Edward and Evalyn divorced in 1929, shortly after Edward became bankrupt in the Wall Street Crash. His binge drinking took a toll on his sanity and he ended his life in a private 'psychiatric facility' in 1941. In 1932 Evalyn was cheated out of $100,000 by Gaston Means, who claimed to be a private investigator who had managed to broker a deal to rescue the Lindbergh baby. This loss, however, was just a drop in the bucket compared to the millions that Evalyn and Edward had managed to waste during their lives. Together the couple ruined two family fortunes and when Evalyn died in 1947, her assets had to be sold to cover her debts.

New York Jeweller Harry Winston bought Evalyn's collection in 1949 and escaped the curse by sending the Hope Diamond on a fund-raising tour for charity. He had the stone recut to its present size to increase its brilliance and ultimately donated the stone to the Smithsonian Institution, in 1958, sending the diamond through the post in a brown paper bag. Winston died at age 82 in 1978 after a long, happy and prosperous life. Maybe the curse just ran out.

Emeralds

This precious green gem was thought to come from the nests of griffins. Those who possessed emeralds would gain increased memory, intelligence and understanding as well as riches. An emerald placed under the tongue would enable a man to see and speak the future.

Gold

The sacred metal that never rusted represented heaven, the pure, the incorruptible. To ancient Mesoamericans gold was the 'sweat of the sun'. Gold has formed a part of many medical prescriptions and many people still eat gold leaf in the belief that it will confer vitality. There are numerous gold baths in various hotels throughout Asia, and some are leased on by the quarter-hour. Bathing in these baths for even this short amount of time is supposed to add years to your life.

At a smaller scale, wedding rings, made of 18-carat gold, are often applied to infected eyelids to 'charm away' a sty. In some cases you need to rub the ring on cloth until it becomes hot before you apply

it to the sty. If there is any efficacy to this at all, it is because the heat encourages the activity of the body's natural defences to accelerate the progress of the disease, so that the sty goes through its 'life cycle' more quickly.

Heliotropes (bloodstones)

If the heliotrope stone is used in conjunction with the heliotrope flower, the combined properties would render the wearer invisible.

To many cultures, gold represents eternal life.

Birthstones

Like so many other things in the realm of magic or superstition, which birthstone belongs to what depends on whom you talk to. Folklorists, or anyone else with a vested interest, promote the birthstone idea and assign particular stones to each star sign. In either case, if you wear or have your birthstone in your possession, it's supposed to increase your luck or heighten whatever positive qualities your sign has. It can also make it easier for you to reach your goals. Birthstones can be either precious or semiprecious, so it's a less expensive proposition for some people to acquire their birthstones than others. Many lists offer less-expensive alternatives for the big-ticket rocks. Birthstone aficionados suggest that where there is more than one alternative, you should take some time to feel which one works best for you.

In this table, the 'modern' list by month is endorsed by the American Gem Society. The 'modern' list has been derived from considerations of the practical availability of stones from the latter half of the 20th century. The 'traditional' list comes from the Western European traditions of the mid-19th to mid-20th centuries, with the 15th to 20th' century list being almost identical, but include stones that were more popular and fashionable in earlier centuries dating from the Renaissance. The 'mystical' list comes from alchemical traditions and assumes that the wearer is interested creating magic, whereas the 'Ayurvedic' comes from the health-promotion traditions of India.

Birthstones by month

Month	Modern	Traditional	Mystical	Ayurvedic	15th–20th centuries
January	Garnet	Garnet	Emerald	Garnet	Garnet
February	Amethyst	Amethyst	Bloodstone	Amethyst	Amethyst, Pearl
March	Aquamarine	Bloodstone	Jade	Bloodstone	Bloodstone, Jasper
April	Diamond	Diamond	Opal	Diamond	Diamond, Sapphire
May	Emerald	Emerald	Sapphire	Agate	Agate, Emerald
June	Pearl, Moonstone	Alexandrite, Turquoise	Moonstone	Pearl	Agate, Cat's eye,
July	Ruby	Ruby	Ruby	Ruby	Onyx, Turquoise
August	Peridot Sardonyx, Topaz	Sardonyx	Diamond	Sapphire	Carnelian, Moonstone
September	Sapphire	Sapphire	Agate	Moonstone	Chrysolite
October	Opal, Tourmaline	Tourmaline	Jasper	Opal	Beryl, Opal
November	Yellow topaz, Citrine	Citrine	Pearl	Topaz	Pearl, Topaz
December	Blue topaz, Turquoise	Zircon, Turquoise, Lapis lazuli	Onyx	Ruby	Bloodstone, Ruby

Birthstones by zodiac

With zodiac birthstones people make distinctions between the stone assigned to that sign, the stone assigned to the planet of that sign, or a stone that is particularly lucky for that sign, even though it's not strictly speaking the birthstone for that sign.

Sign	Gem and birthstone	Planetary stone	Lucky charm
Capricorn (22 Dec–19 Jan)	Agate, Garnet, Ruby	Lapis lazuli	Ruby
Aquarius (20 Jan–18 Feb)	Amethyst, Garnet, Moss agate, Opal	Turquoise	Garnet, Hyacinth
Pisces (19 Feb–20 Mar)	Amethyst, Bloodstone, Rock crystal, Sapphire	Aquamarine	Amethyst
Aries (21 Mar–19 Apr)	Bloodstone, Diamond Jasper	Jasper	Bloodstone, Diamond
Taurus (20 Apr–20 May)	Amber, Blood coral, Emerald, Sapphire, Turquoise	Aventurine, Emerald	Diamond, Sapphire
Gemini (21 May–20 Jun)	Agate, Chrysoprase, Pearl	Tiger eye	Agate, Emerald
Cancer (21 Jun–22 Jul)	Emerald, Moonstone, Pearl, Ruby	Moonstone Emerald	Agate, Chalcedony
Leo (23 Jul–22 Aug)	Onyx, Sardonyx, Tourmaline	Rock crystal	Amber, Onyx, Peridot
Virgo (23 Aug–22 Sep)	Carnelian, Jade, Jasper, Sapphire	Citrine	Carnelian, Sardonyx
Libra (23 Sep–22 Oct)	Lapis lazuli, Opal, Peridot Sardonyx	Sapphire	Opal, Chrysolite
Scorpio (23 Oct–21 Nov)	Aquamarine, Topaz	Garnet, Ruby	Aquamarine, Beryl
Sagittarius (22 Nov–21 Dec)	Amethyst, Sapphire, Topaz, Turquoise	Topaz	Pearl, Topaz

Iron

The most magically protective of all metals is iron, particularly cold iron. The most obvious reason is that blood, which is the liquid of life, smells strongly of the iron bound up in its haemoglobin. Iron, the blood metal, is therefore the metal most closely associated with the life force. Even its oxide—rust—is the colour of blood, and iron ore deposits were considered the blood of the earth.

The Iron Age was a recent development in the history of human technology, because the temperatures required to smelt iron are much higher than that necessary to smelt copper or the tin you mix with copper to make bronze. Iron swords are far tougher than copper or bronze, and an army with iron weapons has a huge advantage over soldiers still fighting with bronze.

When people finally learned how to smelt iron from ore, they must have felt that they were really onto something magical. And when people discovered that meteorites that fell from the sky magnetically attracted iron, they made a connection between the life force of the earth and gifts from heaven. The Hittites, early discoverers of iron, guarded the secret of their techniques jealously. The Greek historian Plutarch considered iron to be the 'bones' of the gods.

Somehow the magic of iron developed into a protective element against faeries, ghosts, witches or anyone else supernatural. In the West only dwarfs who lived in mountains could work iron with impunity. As far as Europeans were concerned, any magic you wanted to work against the presumed wickedness of faeries needed to involve 'cold iron'— hence the number of spells involving

Iron is considered the most magically protective of all metals.

pins, tacks, nails, chains and pokers. People even wore iron rings to ward off disease.

However, it was considered bad luck to bring old iron into the house. Iron had to be new, and in good shape, which must have kept the blacksmiths busy. And, however practical it might have been, in parts of Europe it was considered bad luck to use iron-tipped ploughshares, as this would alienate all the good faeries who could help with the growing, reaping and gathering of the harvest, and no plant cut for magical purposes could ever be cut with iron.

By extension, it was a bad idea to construct any sacred dwelling with iron. This makes most of our modern cities, with their copious use of iron and steel, decidedly profane, and may explain why modern city dwellers never see faeries.

Eastern faeries don't seem to have the same allergy to iron as those in Europe, and you need to resort to other means to get rid of them, such as spells and incantations, folkloric knowledge about the habits of spirits and also the use of sacred writings on signs to ward off evil.

Iron magic was used to treat nosebleeds. Place a knife under the bleeding nose or push a cold door key down the back of the bleeder.

The Maori of New Zealand are among the many peoples of the world who value jade.

Jade

Highly prized, especially in the Orient, among the Maori of New Zealand and among the Mesoamericans, jade has a long history in sculpture and jewellery. The Chinese believed jade could confer immortality—and luck in gambling—and some nobles of China's Han Dynasty were buried in jade suits, in the belief that the suits would prevent the decay of the body. In other traditions if jade were placed on the eyelids or in the mouth of a dead body, the spirit of that body would return to another life on earth.

Jasper

This stone will cure madness or increase the powers of the intellect if you don't have any madness to cure.

Magnets

You see them in cheesy advertisements in cheap magazines or on infomercials for vulnerable insomniacs at 3.00 a.m., amulets, bracelets, back braces and even mattress covers and pillows that have small magnets in them. These are claimed to perform all sorts of miracles, everything from improving circulation—because magnets 'draw' blood cells to an affected area—reducing inflammation. A group of bandage-shaped products have been designed to help sports injuries to heal faster. And there are even magnetic pillows that can help you to sleep—pay attention, insomniacs! However, put a magnet against your skin and you'll find that it doesn't get redder, because the iron in your blood is molecularly bonded to haemoglobin. The iron in your blood is no more magnetic than the iron in rust. Furthermore, even if the magnetic field in these small magnets worked, the field is so weak it could barely penetrate the skin, much less reach tendons, ligaments and bones.

The myth that magnetic fields help in the healing process comes from studies done on bone healing using special pulsed magnetic fields, far stronger and more focused than anything in a small fridge magnet. According to these studies, pulsed magnetic fields may have some therapeutic benefits, but the jury is still out on many of these experimental treatments and the research continues. In any case, the belief that small fridge magnets have any benefit seems to be about as hokey as believing that you can get computer processing power out of a grain of sand as easily as you can out of a microchip, just because both are made of silica.

Mercury

Alchemists prized mercury highly because it has such unusual properties. It's the only metal that is liquid at room temperature. What really impressed the protochemists was its transformation from ore to metal. Cinnabar, the principle ore of mercury, is a deep red crystal, easily ground to a powder in a mortar and pestle. However, when smelted the mercury emerges as a bright, heavy, silver liquid.

The Romans were well aware that cinnabar was poisonous, so to mine it they used condemned criminals. It's odd, however, that they never recognised the deadliness of the lead that they used to make their pipes. Chinese alchemists decided that cinnabar was a path to immortality and that ingesting it would confer eternal life. Quite a few Chinese nobles and emperors died of mercury poisoning as a result. However, Chinese healers also recognised mercury as a poison, and used it on the principle of 'fighting fire with fire' or 'poison with poison'. It was said to reduce excess 'heat' in the body. In more recent times mercury was used to treat syphilis. The treatments were successful, but at the high cost of toxic side effects. In any case there was little alternative until the development of antibiotics.

opals

The opal has had a mixed history. The Romans thought that it was a piece of solidified rainbow and very lucky. Scientifically, the Romans weren't far from wrong as both the opal and the rainbow gain their colours from the same mechanism of prismatic bending of white light into its separate hues. The Arabs believed that opals fell directly from heaven.

Christianity had a different take. In the thirteenth century the German philosopher and alchemist Albertus Magnus wrote that the opal was the 'patron of thieves', and that if you took an opal and wrapped it in bay leaves it would make the bearer invisible. The English writer Sir Walter Scott is probably responsible for starting the modern world belief that opals are unlucky. In his 1829 novel *Anne of Geierstein*, the character Hermione, who may be a witch or a faerie, always wore a brilliant opal in her hair. However, she falls sick, then dies and crumbles to ashes when her husband touches the opal with a drop of holy water. The rumour began to spread that opals were unlucky except if they were your birthstone, which it is if you happen to be either a Libran or born in October, depending on who you talk to.

Opals have been very lucky for Australia—it produces 96 per cent of the world's opal trade, worth tens of millions of dollars. It's the country's national gemstone, and with one of the highest standards of living in the world Australia could hardly be thought of as an unlucky country.

pearls

In the Middle Ages pearls were thought to be solidified tears and to be very unlucky, especially to prospective brides and grooms. They were disastrous if mounted in engagement rings, as they would bring tears to the marriage. Brides should not wear pearls at their weddings for the same reason.

Today pearls are considered very lucky. Some believe that you can tell real pearls from fake by running a string of them across your teeth. One socialite once rudely grabbed pearls from around the neck of American writer Dorothy Parker. After performing the test, she said, 'They're fake!' To which Dorothy replied, 'How can you tell—with false teeth?'

rubies

Rubies will protect the wearer from thinking impure thoughts, and they'll bring peace of mind. Priests and monks in the Middle Ages would wear them to make chastity easier to bear. On the downside, their blood-red colour was also thought to attract werewolves.

sapphires

Sapphires will dispose a man to be cool, calm, collected and peaceful, and they can even make him devout.

silver

The 'tears of the moon' to the Mesoamericans, silver seems to have always been associated with the moon and many magic spells and rituals that use the moon also use silver. Since the time that Queen Elizabeth I first minted the silver sixpence, the coin was considered lucky. It used to be considered especially good luck for a bride to receive the lucky sixpence prior to her wedding. The modern custom is for the father of the bride to place a silver sixpence in the left shoe of the bride to wish the couple health and wealth.

On a more occult note, silver is famously effective against werewolves.

Gemstones for healing

Many traditions ascribe curative and healing powers to gemstones, although some sources are careful to point out that the way you cut a stone will affect its healing properties. Since most of the stones that you find in shops are rounded, the properties listed below are for round, or 'pebble', cuts and are specifically to do with the stones' healing powers.

The stones can be placed for a few minutes on the affected body part, gazed at or held during meditation, or slept with, in a pillow or under a mattress cover.

Agate: thought to help the eyes or any eye ailments. Also thought to be an antivenin, which would heal snakebites and scorpion stings, and that it would prevent the contagion of other diseases (see also Moss and Tree agate).

Amazonite: a confidence booster that improves one's sense of self-worth.

Amber: creates lightness—excellent if you feel 'weighed down' by circumstances.

Amethyst: reputed to increase connectedness with one's spiritual nature, probably because of the links between the colour purple and the divine. In ancient times amethyst was also thought to prevent drunkenness. Now gem healers use it to help their patients with stomach and liver problems.

Apatite: promotes effective and clear communication. Also helps with viral infections.

Aquamarine: increases awareness of the love in a situation, so it's useful in resolving difficult, dark situations, like conflict or grief.

Aventurine (blue): emotionally uplifting, improves circulation and clears congestion.

Aventurine (green): boosts the healing process, but the stone should be washed every day in cold running water for a few minutes, in order to clear accumulated negative energy.

Black obsidian: a powerful stone to gain insights into situations.

Cape amethyst: also called chevron amethyst, with its white banding, the stone is used to balance the spiritual, emotional, mental and physical energies, thus liberating energy. Pressed on acupressure points it will clear energy blockages, and wrapped around joints helps with arthritis.

Carnelian: promotes creative thinking.

Citrine: an emotional booster that helps the flow of energy in the spine.

Coral: grounding and emotionally stabilising, in ancient times coral was supposed to help staunch blood flow and given to babies to help with their teething.

Diamond: the stone of clarity. Wearing diamond clears away uncertainty and puts you back in touch with your higher purpose. In ancient times diamonds warded off madness.

Emerald: a powerful stone to aid all healing processes, whether physical or emotional.

Fluorite: helps periods of transition or stimulates change where you need it.

Fluorite (green): useful for treating premenstrual syndrome or any other hormonal imbalance or transition, such as occurs during puberty and menopause.

Freshwater pearls: increase the sense of deservingness, so that you can more easily accept the generosity of others.

Jade: relaxant and tension reducer.

Kunzite: helps to promote synergy between thoughts and feelings.

Lapis lazuli: useful for mental expansion and broadening you inner vision.

Leopardskin jasper: will help bring what you need into your life and support you if required.

Mahogany obsidian: promotes effective decision-making.

Malachite: Used in meditation this stone increases the awareness of a situation and brings the right knowledge at the right time.

Moldavite: brings you back to earth and in touch with physical reality.

Moonstone (white): all moonstones boost the effects of other stones by making you more accepting of their energies and qualities. If you find the effect of white too strong, use orange instead. Grey moonstone clears mental and emotional blocks but can create a lot of self-confrontation and awareness of 'home truths'.

Moss agate: a great support stone in herbal healing as it increases the intuitive use of plants.

Mother of pearl: offers protection in emotionally difficult undertakings.

Onyx (black): a support stone for when one wishes to change bad habits. Mexican onyx promotes healthy sleep in cases of insomnia.

Opal: a vision expander that helps you see your true potential, either when resolving a conflict or in general personal development. Black opal is the most powerful variety, but other types are gentler and may be more suitable for certain people.

Peridot: used with conscious intent to channel new energy into a situation.

Poppy jasper: increases positivity.

Quartz (frosted or cloudy): soothing and balancing, especially settling if healing makes you feel a little raw or frayed at the edges.

Rhodochrosite: supportive in making big changes.

Rhodonite: helpful in making emotionally difficult transitions.

Rose quartz: opens the 'heart' chakra and increases receptivity to and the expression of love. Overdoing rose quartz may create attractions that are too intense and need to be balanced.

Ruby: increases courage and fearlessness.

Sapphire: increases mental clarity.

Sodalite: creates a field of protection against negative energies, whether psychic or electromagnetic.

Sugilite: uplifting and clearing of the subtle auric energies.

Sunstone: increases the capacity to remember dreams and gain the wisdom of their insights.

Tanzanite: change facilitator.

Tourmaline: enhances balance, healing and protection. Use the green variety for men and the pink for women.

Tree agate: helps with any introspective process and helps you to see your role and power in a situation.

Unakite: helps to align and clarify the way that emotions are expressed in the body.

heavens above

heavens above

Of all the forces of nature, the things that lived in the sky—the sun, the moon, the planets and comets, thunder and lightning, the wind and the rain—were the most unreachable, the most intangible and the most mysterious.

Across the world's cultures, the supreme gods were nearly always gods of the sky, and life or death depended on them. They could warm the earth with the sun, or hold it back and bring the biting cold. They could bring enough rain to nourish the soil, or too much to drown it in floods, or too little to parch it with drought.

You needed to know how to read the signs of such gods, since they always spoke indirectly, and you had to work out what they were saying. It's as if all of life were an intelligence test, a constant game of intellectual and emotional cat and mouse, since you dared not do anything that might anger them. Instead you'd try anything, anything at all, to keep them happy.

fair weather signs

There's an old proverb:
Red in the morning
Sailors take warning
Red at night
Sailor's delight.
This portent is even in the *Bible*, in *Matthew* (16:2–3): 'When it is evening, you say, "It will be fair weather, for the sky is red." And in the morning, "Today there will be a storm, for the sky is red and lowering"'.

It turns out that this superstition is actually true to some extent. In the world's middle latitudes, storm fronts move from east to west, so when the morning sun rises on a storm front, its light shines on the clouds, and refraction turns them red. In the evening, the setting sun illuminates clouds that are travelling west and away from the observer, so the high-pressure zone and its good weather is heading towards you from the east. Unfortunately, this only works if the weather is travelling from east to west. If you live in an area where weather patterns are different, the red sky rules don't apply. Sayings about the weather can often be accurate, but only if the superstition arose in your neck of the woods.

Other signs that it'll be fine include:

- Ants piling up hills in the early morning.
- Cobwebs on grass in the morning.
- High-flying swallows.
- Rooks nesting high in trees.
- Dandelions opening their petals early.

Lightning

To be struck by lighting—besides frequently being fatal—is not only considered unlucky, but was seen to be a sign that the gods were picking you out specifically for punishment.

It is absolutely untrue that lighting never strikes twice in the same place. Anything that obviously sticks out high into the sky relative to its surroundings is a candidate for multiple strikes. The Empire State Building in New York is struck about 23 times per year.

American Park Ranger Roy Cleveland Sullivan continues to hold the record for being a human lightning rod. He was struck seven times between 1942 and 1977, mostly in and around Shenandoah National Park in Virginia. There is no evidence that any god had it in for him, although one source claims that he suspected it at one point.

Lightning isn't always unlucky. New Zealand's and Australia's most famous racehorse of 1926–1932, Phar Lap, was named after the Zhuang/Thai word for lightning. Phar Lap won the modern equivalent of about $US50 million in prize money during his career, although, considering the manner of his death and possible assassination, perhaps he wasn't so lucky after all.

Superstitions to protect yourself from being struck by lightning include: wrapping yourself up in a feather quilt, sleeping with a thimble under your pillow or cutting a piece of hawthorn on Holy Thursday (the day before Easter Friday) and putting the wood in your house. Finding a piece of coal under a mugwort plant on Midsummer Day is also supposed to protect you from strikes. It is also said that lightning will never strike elm or walnut trees.

In western North America, lightning strikes may be lucky, as there's a belief that where lightning strikes, you'll find oil.

the moon

Long a symbol of love, and curiously linked to the menstrual periods of women, the moon has always exerted a powerful force on our imagination.

To cure a sick person, carry them outside on the night of the new moon, blow on them nine times and say:

What I see,
May it increase,
What I see,
May it decrease,
In the name of the Father,
Son and Holy Ghost.

For a further dose of new moon magic, gather the rays of the new moon in a dry silver dish and 'wash' your hands in it. Incant:

I wash my hands in this thy dish,
O Man in the Moon,
Do grant my wish,
And come take this away.

Never look at the new moon—the time when the moon is at its darkest and just beginning to wax again—through glass.

This is 'disrespectful'.

The full moon is especially lucky. Bow three times to the full moon for luck, and wishes made beneath a full moon are more likely to come true.

If you practise magic, cast spells of increase—for example, more health, more wealth, more love—when the moon is waxing (getting bigger). Likewise when the moon is waning (getting smaller), then it's time to cast spells of decrease—for example, a spell to remove a wart, or a lover who's become a pest. Hence there is the superstition that you should cut your hair during a waxing moon if you want your hair to grow and during a waning moon if you want your hair to stop growing. The most enduring superstition about the full moon is that it makes people and animals crazy and that it brings out all the nutcases—consider the semantic origin of the word 'lunatic'. Full moons do provide an air of excitement and mystery, and people are much more likely to go out at night when the moon is full, especially when the weather is warm. Even though crime statistics show no connection between the phases of the moon and crime rates, lovers and young women should beware, as there are hints that some serial killers prefer to do their murdering during the full moon. David Berkowitz, known as 'The Son of Sam', killed five of his eight victims during a full moon, and doctors and nurses in emergency departments in hospitals routinely believe that they are much busier during full moons than at other times of the month, with a marked increase in the incidence of animal bites. So maybe the statisticians should be looking at hospital records, rather than reported crimes, to see if there's any truth to this superstition after all.

RAIN

To bring rain, stick a spade in the ground, burn ferns or heather or carry a statue of your favourite saint into a stream and give it a dunk. You can also kill a big, black beetle or spider, although I wouldn't recommend the latter. Should you accidentally kill a beetle and not want it to rain you should bury it in a matchbox. Giving the beetle a 'proper burial' will reverse the magic.

Alternatively, you can wash your car or hose your lawn. Many people swear by this.

Signs of rain include:

- Cats sneezing or licking their fur in a direction opposite to the way the fur runs.
- Chickweed closing up.
- Dogs eating grass.
- Frogs croaking during the day.
- Gulls flying inland.
- Horses gathering in the corners of fields.
- Low flying swallows.
- Moles casting up their hills.
- Smoke hanging low to the ground.
- The sky appearing greenish at the horizon.
- Spiders deserting their webs.

In fact any signs of restlessness in animals is assumed to mean that a storm is coming. If a pig's tail straightens, you're in for a big storm.

Whatever you do, never open an umbrella indoors—it's very bad luck, not because you could hurt someone or knock something over, but because the sun god Apollo will take offence that you're trying to shield yourself of his rays even indoors.

seasons

There are quite a few signs that indicate when we're in for a bad winter:

- Bees storing large amounts of honey.
- Cornhusks that are hard to pull apart.
- Heavy coats on foxes.
- A large nut harvest.
- Large numbers of wild geese migrating.
- Skunks coming in from the forest earlier than usual to make their winter homes in barns.
- Oysters bedding deep.

Or, if you're a New Englander, take a look at your onions:

Onion's skin very thin
Mild winter coming in.
Onion's skin, thick and tough
Coming winter cold and rough.

the sun

The sun is one of the most awesome objects in our experience. As the source of all life, it represents health and vitality, but because you can get too much of a good thing, the sun can also represent uncontained power, and many ancient peoples considered the sun a god. Perhaps this is the origin of the belief that pointing at the sun is unlucky, in the sense that it is rude to point at God. Why anyone should ever need to point to the sun is a little hard to imagine, since its location is usually self-evident.

Being the obvious symbol of power the more megalomaniacal of rulers have used the sun to confer on themselves a certain cachet. Alexander the Great was a 'Sun God', and in 274 CE, the Roman Emperor Aurelian created the state religion/cult of *Deus Sol Invictus* (the Invincible Sun God). The birthday of the unconquered sun was 25th December—sound familiar?—and the Emperor Constantine created the first Sunday as a day of rest on 7 March 321 CE. Royal families as far flung as the Egyptians, the Aztecs, the Inca and the Maya, all claimed descent from a sun god or, exceptionally in the case of the Japanese Emperors, from a sun goddess.

In the Northern Hemisphere, especially in the higher latitudes, in order to look at the sun you need to face south. From this point of view the sun moves in a clockwise direction. In fact the very reason that clocks move 'clockwise' is that their designers took their cue from the movement of the sun, and the movement of shadows in sundials, so strictly speaking clocks

actually move in a sunwise, or to use a wonderful old English word, a 'deasil' direction.

Clockwise, sunwise or deasil thus became the 'natural' flow for the movement of life and to go anti-clockwise, or to use another wonderful old English word 'widdershins', was to go against the flow. Pots that brewed herbs for good magic were always stirred deasil, black magic was stirred widdershins. By extension any cooking in general was stirred deasil, unless your intention was to do the magical dirty on your guests.

In Devonshire, England, the hour before sunrise on a Thursday is considered unlucky.

Tornadoes

The myth that tornadoes do not strike cities and cannot cross water is completely untrue. Major American cities, such as St Louis, Missouri and Denver, have had tornadoes go through their streets, while the deadliest ever recorded, the Tri-State tornado of 18 March 1925, crossed the Mississippi River from Missouri to Illinois during its journey of destruction, which claimed the lives of 695 people. One sobering fact is that 40 per cent of all Americans who have died in a tornado lived in a caravan—but this is because of caravans' lack of foundations, not because tornadoes are somehow 'attracted' to caravan parks, as another superstition has it.

part three:
Beyond nature

Imagine a world without electricity, when most of the world's people still lived outside cities. Then imagine a night of the full moon, or worse, a night of the new moon. Imagine the darkness. Imagine the silence.

Fertile ground for the human imagination to grow whatever it wanted, spreading its roots in the soil of primal fear and fed with stories of ghosts, ghouls and all manner of things. At this point we leave further behind the connection to the real world, whatever that might mean, and we enter the realm of things that exist only in our imaginations. Or maybe they do exist, but most of us are simply not sensitive enough or attuned enough to see or hear them.

Superstitions and the supernatural are intimately entwined and often difficult to tell apart. Follwoing are beliefs that some people might have a scientific explanation for, but that are perhaps easier to deal with as supernatural, even when they don't directly involve ghosts or spirits.

the spirit world

the spirit world

There's a traditional Scottish prayer that goes:
From ghoulies and ghosties,
And long-leggedy beasties,
And things that go bump in the night,
Good Lord, deliver us!

evil spirits

The Chinese believe that spirits can only travel in straight lines, so they build bridges with curving spans to thwart and confine them. Many cultures also maintain that witches and demons can't cross running water, so crossing a river is another good way of avoiding them.

If you think that a spirit is vexing you, try this ancient Babylonian remedy: make an image of the spirit out of anything at hand, maybe clay. Put the figure into a small boat then push the boat out onto open water, like a pond, lake or even the sea, then incant any spell of your choice to make the boat sink.

ghosts

The general theory of ghosts is that they are souls trapped on earth because they are cursed or have certain obsessions that prevent them from letting go and getting on with their afterlives. One way of getting rid of a ghost is simply to ask it what it wants. This is supposed to bring the ghost to its senses and it leaves, never to return.

People often use the terms 'ghosts' and 'spirits' interchangeably. It's perhaps more precise to think of spirits as non-corporeal beings of any description, whereas ghosts are

non-corporeal beings who were at one time corporeal. In other words a ghost is the non-physical remains of a dead person or animal. However, there are exceptions even to this rule. There are numerous stories of ghostly vehicles, such as carriages, cars, trains or ships. And there are tales of ghost buildings and even whole ghost cities—the spiritual remnants of artefacts now gone to ruin.

An even more striking idea is the possibility that ghosts are the spirits of people yet to be born. Even spookier is the possibility that ghosts are the astral bodies of people asleep, either in this world or in another. We might all be ghosts, haunting ourselves or others in realms beyond our own.

One characteristic of ghosts is that they tend to be local. The most common ghosts are spirits of dead people who have died under traumatic circumstances—the victims of accidents or foul play. Typically a murder victim haunts the site of their death, until someone pays attention and solves the mystery of their death. Sometimes, though, the death may not in itself have been traumatic, but there remain unresolved things. Either way, the ghost's behaviour resembles that of a severe case of shock or post-traumatic stress syndrome. The ghost may not even be aware that they are dead, or that they are trapped between the world of the living and the proper abode of the dead—wherever that might be. Those with a talent for seeing ghosts and conducting them into the white light for the next stage of the afterlife, or 'ghost whisperers' maintain that ghosts are, in fact, well aware that they are dead, but in many cases are just being ornery.

In some cases the ghost is earthbound because of bad timing. There is one superstition that says that the spirit of the first person to die in the year has the responsibility of calling the dead for the next 12 months, performing the function of the 'grim reaper', riding around the parish in a ghostly horse-drawn cart. Only at the end of this period are they allowed to leave the earth and move on to their heavenly reward.

In Asia there is a long-standing belief that ghosts continue to require nourishment from the material world in some form or another. What these 'hungry ghosts' feed on depends to some extent on the way that they behaved while they were alive. Buddhist philosophies of karma have obviously influenced this sort of thinking. If you were a particularly bad person your afterlife 'diet' would be appropriately unpleasant. In India these hungry ghosts are called *preta*, in Japan *gaki*. They are said to have very thin throats, which force them to

feed continuously as they can never get much down in one swallow. Among the various foods of the hungry ghosts are the following, in order of increasing unpleasantness—depending on your point of view:

- nothing (which in some Buddhist philosophies is a sort of something)
- water
- dharma (a word with many meanings, but in this case a sort of by-product of existence. Think of it as a temporary manifestation of consciousness, as if the ghosts could eat your dreams or desires)
- incense smoke
- saliva
- blood
- semen
- ashes from tombs
- excrement
- poison
- fire
- infants.

There are a few things that you can do to prevent your house from being invaded by ghosts:

- Draw an unbroken chalk line across the threshold—an extension of the belief that no evil spirit can harm you if you are within a circle
- Remove a door and rehang it with the hinges on the other side.
- Place an iron poker perpendicular to the top bar of the grate in your fireplace, so the it forms a cross that is visible to any ghosts who might want to enter through the chimney.

The smell of burning incense drives away evil spirits as well as being 'food' to appease hungry ghosts.

The house of murder

Even if you'd never heard the superstition that buying a house in which a murder has taken place is bad luck, there is such an obvious case of 'guilt by association' that you'd be likely to make up the superstition on the spot. You can imagine any amount of hauntings, or at the very least that the aura of 'evil' will cling to a house and make life hell for anyone foolish enough to ignore it. It's a powerful, dramatic and completely understandable sentiment, from a psychological point of view.

There was a house at 10050 Cielo Drive, Bel Air, California, that belonged to Doris Day's son Terry Melcher. It was there, on 9 August 1969 that the Manson 'Family' murdered actress Sharon Tate and her guests. In 1994 the house had to be demolished, as no one wanted to buy it. A new Italian-style mansion was built in its place, and it was originally listed with a sales price of $12.5 million. The price was later reduced to $7.7 million. Most agents refuse to list it and the house has remained vacant for years.

At 8213 West Summerdale Avenue, Norwood Park Township, Norwood Park, Chicago, Illinois where American serial killer John Wayne Gacy murdered over 20 young men in the 1970s had to be demolished in April 1979. For years nothing, not even weeds, would grow on the empty lot. Later, new owners built another house on the site, with a new address. The grass grew again.

The building on the corner of 63rd and South Wallace in Chicago, where serial murderer par excellence HH Holmes may have killed hundreds of people between 1891 and 1894 was dubbed 'Murder Castle' and attracted thousands of sightseers. One entrepreneur bought Murder Castle and was going to turn it into a tour-guided museum, but before it could be opened, shortly after midnight on 19 August 1895, the building burned to the ground under suspicious circumstances. In 1938 a post office was built on the site. The place remained a focal point of strange tales and bizarre happenings. Residents claimed they couldn't even walk their dogs on the same side of the street. The animals would start whining and howling.

Occupancy rates in the street in Milwaukee where the notorious serial killer and cannibal Jeffrey Dahmer lived fell from 80 to 20 per cent. A developer had to demolish the whole apartment block. The house at 722 Elm Drive in Beverly Hills where the Menendez brothers murdered their parents on 20 August 1989 sat unoccupied for years before selling at a fraction of its former value. Ditto the house at 875 South Bundy Drive, Brentwood, Los Angeles, where Nicole Brown Simpson and Ron Goldman died on 12 June 1994.

Some real-estate agents think that it takes up to a generation, 25 years, before the taint of a murder house fades. This is one superstition that is unlikely to go away, ever.

shadows

Shadows and ghosts are close cousins, it's even common to refer to ghosts as 'shades', and many, but not all superstitions relating to shadows are similar to those relating to ghosts and to omens of death.

For example, it's bad luck to see your shadow when it's cast from moonlight.

A Jewish tradition states that at nightfall on Hosannah Rabbah—the seventh day of the Feast of Sukkoth—if a man cannot see his shadow, then he will die within the year.

Similar in logic to the belief that driving a nail into someone's footprint will make them lame, there are superstitions that any injury you do to someone's shadow will happen to them too. Never step on someone else's shadow, or you'll damage their soul. There's an Arabian superstition that shows a complicated 'scissors, rocks, paper'-like relationship between hyenas, dogs and people: if a hyena steps on a man's shadow, the man will become mute; a dog can make a hyena mute by stepping on its shadow; and if a dog is higher up than a hyena when the hyena steps into the dog's shadow, then the hyena will be jerked to the ground as if by a rope.

There's an old superstition that, 'if Candlemas Day (2 February) is bright and clear, there'll be two winters in the year.' This is the origin of the Groundhog Day celebration of Punxsutawney, Pennsylvania. Here the town gathers to see a groundhog called Punxsutawney Phil emerge from hibernation. If the groundhog sees its shadow, because the day is clear and bright, the groundhog will return to hibernation and the region is due for six more weeks of winter.

Unfortunately for groundhog lovers everywhere, the facts show that Phil is only right about 39 per cent of the time. Considering that Phil's predictions are actually worse than the 50 per cent of chance, Phil is actually a good indicator of what won't happen, rather than what will. Maybe Phil just likes his sleep.

vampires

Blood-drinking immortals are among the most famous and ancient of supernatural beings, and even the Mesopotamians who flourished a couple of millennia BCE had stories of vampire-like beings. However, the modern image of the vampire comes down to us mostly from southern-eastern Europe, from an oral folk tradition that was finally turned into literature in the early 1700s.

Descriptions of vampires vary widely, but there are common elements. Vampires are always associated with graves and some form of 'coming back from the dead'. They are usually nocturnal, and sleep in their own graves during the day. Traditionally they were not thought to be vulnerable to sunlight and in Bram Stoker's novel *Dracula* the blood-sucking count has no trouble walking in the day. The idea that sunlight is a vampire killer arose in popular culture only in the 20th century, probably as early as F W Murnau's film *Nosferatu* (1922). Not all folkloric vampires suck blood; often, as

A superstition about Candlemas Day is the origin of the Groundhog Day celebration.

in China, they might be involved in a more mysterious process of draining the *chi*, or 'life essence' of their victims. Some, like the *manananggal* of the Philippines, feed off the unborn foetuses in sleeping pregnant women or even the phlegm of sick people—so snot-eating vampires are not unknown.

Among the blood drinkers, most would be pale and thin until they had blood, after which they would be bloated and ruddy, which makes them sound a little like leeches. Red hair was a common vampire trait, and they were supposed to have the ability to change into various 'creatures of the night', most commonly bats, dogs, wolves and rats.

Creating a vampire could be as easy as having an animal jump over a grave or as complicated as being bitten three times by another vampire.

If you wanted to make absolutely sure that your loved ones wouldn't come back as the 'undead' then you had to:

- dig up the corpse
- drive a wooden stake through its heart
- cut off the head
- place the head between the corpse's legs
- stuff the mouth with garlic
- re-bury the corpse
- lightly sprinkle it with holy water for good measure.

Just to be on the safe side, you could also bury the body with a sickle, a scythe or a wax cross and a piece of pottery with 'Jesus Christ Conquers' written in Greek. Scattering millet, poppy seed or sand over the gravesite might also help. It doesn't actually prevent the vampire coming into being, but it's good to know that they suffer from an obsessive–compulsive trait. If a vampire ever chases you, simply scatter any seeds in their path. They'll have to stop and count them. Poppy seed has the obvious advantage in that it is small and black. In China you throw rice, just as you do to ward off other evil spirits.

Getting a naked virgin boy or girl to ride a horse over a grave was a good way of identifying a vampire, as the horse would rear over the vampire's sleeping place. Holes appearing over graves were suspicious, and if you dug down and found corpses that still looked vaguely healthy and that refused to decompose— well, that was obviously suspect.

Garlic, mustard seeds crucifixes and other religious symbols and substances such as Holy Water were supposed to be effective in warding off vampires. Crucifixes, crosses with the likeness of Jesus on them, were what worked, not crosses by themselves. Even crucifixes and Holy Water have no power if you have no Christian faith to back them up. Vampires can't walk on consecrated ground—which makes you wonder how they get out of their graves—they can't cross running water and, as mentioned previously, because they have no soul, they have no reflection in a mirror and cast no shadow.

A wooden stake through the heart was always the best way to kill a vampire, especially if the stake were made of ash or hawthorn. Gypsies preferred to drive iron needles into the heart. Heavy-duty cases required decapitation, garlic in the mouth (or a lemon in Saxony) and burning

the corpse to cinders with a sprinkling of holy water for good measure.

werewolves

The name comes from the Old English word *were* (man), and werewolves were men who would turn into a wolf, or a wolf-like man, a lycanthrope, in the light of the full moon. The modern myth is that the werewolf usually only comes into being if another werewolf bit him, which begs the question of where the first werewolf came from. Greek legend has it that Lycaon, the first werewolf, came down with his condition after having consumed human flesh. Older legends give a more satisfying origin story. A man could become a werewolf or any other 'were' creature, such as a werefox or a werecat, if he drank water that he had poured into the footprint of the animal in question, or if he made a pact with the Devil.

Historically the legend of the werewolf may have come from people who had been bitten by dogs or wolves suffering from rabies. Although rare, rabies is a terrible way to die. It causes inflammation of the brain, uncontrollable salivation and tearing, an inability to swallow and accompanying hallucinations and insanity.

Having eyebrows that met in the middle or hairy palms or suffering from epilepsy are supposed to be indicators of werewolfhood.

Werewolves are pretty indestructible, having even fewer weaknesses than vampires. They are said to be allergic to the plant wolfsbane, and their true form is revealed if you throw an iron object over them. Later legend has it that they could only be killed with a silver knife, arrow or bullet. One possible cure includes striking the wolf three times on the forehead with a knife, or drawing at least three drops of blood from a werewolf.

whistling

Muslims associate whistling with the casting of spells and invocations for the Devil. Whistling is a way to communicate with the Jinn, spirits formed of 'smokeless fire' who may or may not be benevolent. The belief that whistling is a way to talk with supernatural beings is widespread. Whistling isn't talking and it's a lot like birdsong, so it's natural to assume that nature spirits would use it and because nature spirits are notoriously fickle, unreliable, capricious and unpredictable, careless whistle might attract the attention of beings that are best left undisturbed. For many, whistling is just plain bad luck.

witches

Witches were feared for centuries, and in many parts of the world they still are. Witches were usually considered to be women who had made a pact with Satan. The Devil could have their souls in exchange for supernatural powers, especially over their fellow countrymen. Society in general had a very ambivalent relationship with witches and their rarer male equivalents, warlocks. On the one hand, witches could be useful to cast spells on unreachable enemies; on the other hand, if you thought they could harm you, you wanted them out of the way. They made very good scapegoats too, and you could blame them for all sorts of evils.

Because witches could look like everyone else if they chose to, it became important to be able to identify them. It was believed that witches had a physical mark, placed by the Devil in order to seal his pact with her.

This witch's teat could be a third nipple, from which the Devil would suckle at night. It could be on any part of the witch's body, but was usually in a 'hidden place'—in an armpit, under an eyelid and even on an internal organ. Any birthmark or scar could be a witch's teat, and suspected witches were shaved in order to find any mark hidden under the head hair. The mark was supposed to be impervious to pain, and if stabbed, the witch would not react. Enthusiastic and unscrupulous witch-finders were not above having special daggers made with retractable blades for this purpose. If you couldn't get close enough to a witch to stab or shave her, you could drive a pin into her footprint. If she really was a witch, she would be compelled to return and to remove it.

Wearing a blue bead could protect you from witches, not all of them, but at least the less powerful ones.

superstitions
all year round

superstitions all year round

One peculiarity of the planet on which we live is that the distribution of land over the earth is uneven. Another is that the earth's axis tilts (currently) at 23.5 degrees from perpendicular. This is why we have seasons. At one part of the year, the north receives more light and heat, six months later the south receives more light and heat. When you combine these two factors you become aware that most of the world's population, and most of its dominant cultures, live in areas with pronounced seasonal variation. If you live in cities and buy your food from supermarkets, this only means that you have to deal with weather and air-conditioning and heating bills, but if your livelihood depends on it, then seasons shape your whole world view, and days you dedicate to gods and their festivals become imbued with their own magic and their fair share of superstitions—365¼ days a year.

Bearing all this in mind, we shouldn't be surprised that the vast majority of the world's superstitions relating to dates come from a perspective based in the Northern Hemisphere, although the cultures and civilisations of the Tropics have their own superstitions, often blended under the powerful influence of the 'dominant' cultures of the higher latitudes.

You should note one important point: the date of midsummer and midwinter and the first day of autumn and of spring and midwinter change over time. The modern calendar is supposed to compensate for this, nevertheless their traditional dates are now often a few days after the actual astronomical time they occur. It's up to you to decide whether to go with tradition or reality. If you want to go with reality, you should talk to your local observatory, where the resident astronomers will be able to tell you the exact date and time that a particular event like the vernal equinox, the first day of spring, takes place. Traditionally, the vernal equinox is not only the first day of spring, but the first day of the New Year.

January

The first water drawn from a well or a spring on New Year's Day is very lucky and brings health, wealth and happiness to those who drink it.

In Greece on New Year's Day throw a pomegranate against your front door. The number of seeds that fly out will equal the amount of money you make that year. One would assume that, given how tough pomegranates are, you either need to pick an overripe one, throw it very hard, or assume that each seed is worth about $10,000.

Take note about how you feel about your first guest of the New Year. Your feelings will tell you whether good luck or bad luck will follow. It's probably best to hedge your bets and to invite someone you like to cross your threshold at 12:01 am. According to the British custom of 'footing', however, it was bad luck for a woman or a blond man to be the first to cross your threshold, and married men weren't as good as bachelors. Dark-haired bachelors would thus usually have a great time on New Year's Day, bringing luck to all the households whose thresholds they crossed. The first footer would also bring coal, to help keep the fires going in the depths of winter.

In Scotland it was the custom to invite a dog to the door on New Year's Day, give him a piece of bread, then shoo him away. The dog would take away all the ills, troubles and evils that were going to

The Aztec calendar combines a 365-day solar calendar and a 260-day sacred cycle that together form a 52-year 'century' the end of which marked a time of disaster.

visit you during the year. This is a case of a scapedog, rather than a scapegoat. The Bhotiya people of the western Himalayas have a similar ceremony, but they play the game harder. When they shoo the dog away out of the village they chase it, catch it, then beat or stone it to death.

If the fire went out on New Year's Day, so would the luck for the whole year. There was no cure for this, because if a neighbour lit a fire for you from their own hearth, they'd be giving away their luck too, and if you tried to steal someone else's fire, it would be even worse for you.

Nothing should be thrown out on New Year's Day, not even the rubbish, and the larder should be well stocked; if it's empty on New Year's Day, it will be empty all year.

On the morning of New Year's Day, if a girl gets up, looks out the window and sees a man passing by, she can count on being married before the end of the year.

In the Philippines people wear polka dots at New Year's to symbolise money and to attract it. The same logic dictates that you should open all your windows, doors and even cupboards and wardrobes to let the good luck in, and lay your table with round food, like pizzas, cakes, fruit and pies.

february

The 1 February used to be known as Candlemas Eve, and in Scotland people would dress a sheaf of oats in women's clothing and invoke St Brigid: 'Brigid, Brigid, come in, your bed is ready.' Brigid would then help ensure a good year's growing, in keeping with the ancient pagan traditions of the Bride of Spring, by wedding the soil.

It was also important around this time that all Christmas decorations should be gone from the Church (if they hadn't been taken down already). Any decoration left behind would signify a death within the year in the family whose pew was closest to the remaining decoration.

It was important that the weather be bad on 2 February, as fine weather on Candlemas Day was a sign of a long winter—'When the wind's in the east on Candlemas Day, There it will stick till the second of May.'

Shrove Tuesday, called Mardi Gras (Fat Tuesday) in French, is the last big indulgence before the austerity of the 40 days of Lent. It usually falls in early February. The tradition is to make pancakes. If you do, throw one into the henhouse. If the rooster eats it all, that's a bad sign, but if the hens get most of it, that's good luck. On the following day, Ash Wednesday, eat pea soup for luck and don't sell any cattle.

chinese new year

The Chinese, like the Jews and Arabs, observe a sacred calendar based on the cycles of the moon. Lunar calendars don't align precisely with the Western solar calendar, so festival days don't fall on the same solar date from year to year. Even in the West, the Christian churches calculate the date of Easter based on the movements of the moon, and even here there's disagreement. In fact, one of the major reasons that the Eastern and Western Christian churches finally split in 1054 was because they couldn't agree on how to calculate the date of Easter.

On the other side of the world, the Chinese, by sheer force of numbers, have influenced the cultures all around them, and much of Asia celebrates Chinese New Year, which, in the Western Gregorian calendrical scheme of things, usually falls in early February and, more rarely, in late January.

According to ancient legend, it was around mid-winter that a man-eating monster, the Nian, would come out of seclusion to hunt and devour humans. The celebrations of New Year, with their eating, drinking, lion dances and loud bangs of fireworks in streets decorated with red lanterns and banners, have managed to frighten away the Nian for thousands of years.

The Chinese believe that New Year's Holidays, especially the first three days, are a very unlucky time to make any business decisions. Houses are cleaned prior to this time, to sweep out the old year's bad luck and make room for the new year's good luck. On New Year's Eve houses serve fish for fortune—as the word for 'fish' sounds the same as the word for 'surplus'—and dumplings for wealth, as dumplings resemble ingots of precious metal. There are additional decorations of plum blossoms and sunflowers for luck, kumquat, narcissus and koi fish for prosperity, and chrysanthemum for longevity.

There should always be more food than people can eat, because it's good luck in all years to have a surplus. The leftovers are eaten on New Year's Day, although some Buddhists will not eat meat on New Year's Day out of the belief that abstention will lengthen their life. Another charming custom, especially

Fireworks in Victoria Harbour, Hong Kong, during Chinese new year.

popular among the children who receive them, is to give money wrapped in red paper parcels.

Because it's one of those liminal moments of the year, symbolically, whatever happens on New Year's could profoundly affect the coming 12 months. Gamblers will often gamble on New Year's for luck, but this is a risky business. If you win, you'll win all year, if you lose, well …

New Year's is also a time when evil spirits have the opportunity to work mischief, so there are plenty of superstitions to encourage good luck and to avoid or mitigate the bad.

Bathe in bathwater with pomelo leaves on New Year's Eve, and you'll be healthy for the next 12 months. If you can't find pomelo, use grapefruit.

On New Year's Day eat sweet cakes to have a sweet year. Open all the windows and doors of the house to allow the maximum amount of good luck to enter. Switch on all the lights to scare away ghosts. If you wear slippers that you've bought at the end of last year for the first time on New Year's, you'll 'step' on the people that are gossiping about you. Don't, however, buy shoes during New Year's, as this will invite evil, because the word for 'shoe' and 'evil' sound the same in Mandarin. Don't buy books, because 'book' sounds like 'lose'. Buying a pair of pants is either good or bad, because one word for trousers or pants sounds like 'bitter' and another sounds like 'wealth' in Cantonese. If you have

A Chinese Lunar New Year performance in Beijing.

to buy clothes, don't buy black, as that means bad luck, and don't buy white, as it's the colour of death.

Don't wash your hair in the first days of the New Year, as this will wash away luck. And if you break something, wish everyone peace throughout the ages, because 'shatter' sounds like 'ages'.

On the second day of the New Year's celebrations, the Chinese are kind to dogs as this is the birthday of all dogs.

It is bad luck to visit relatives or friends on the third day of the year, because of the belief that all the fried food that people have been eating in the first two days will make them argumentative. The third day is usually reserved for visiting graves and honouring the dead. The fifth day is the birthday of the God of Wealth and businesses reopen on that day.

The seventh day is the birthday of men, on which everyone is counted as a year older.

The fifteenth day is the day of the Lantern Festival—the day when candles and lanterns are lit outside houses to guide the wandering spirits of the dead home, presumably because they became lost in all the fun.

march

The word 'Easter' on its own is generally shorthand for Easter Sunday, which falls in late March or April. Roughly every two out of three years, it also falls on different days depending on whether you follow the Western or the Eastern Orthodox version of Christianity. It's related to the Jewish festival of Passover.

The body of legend and lore of Easter and Passover are considerable, being of primary importance to the Jews and central to the whole Christian experience. Following are some Easter superstitions:

- Rings blessed on Easter will protect the wearer from illness for the whole year.
- Keep some of the hot cross buns you make at Easter for the whole year, as they are an effective treatment against whooping cough. Bread baked on Good Friday will also cure many an ill and anything baked on Easter will never go mouldy.
- Parsley sown on Good Friday will come up double.
- Do nothing that recalls the crucifixion during Easter—don't hammer any nails, and don't plough or spade the earth, or nothing will grow in that ground that year.
- Don't hang up clothes, they will spot with blood, but wearing new clothes that have never been worn before is extremely good luck.
- At dawn on Easter Sunday, it is said that you can see the Lamb of God in the rising sun. If the sun is shining, it will shine 50 days later on Pentecost. If it rains, it will rain for the next seven Sundays.
- There was a Teutonic belief, related to the goddess Eostre, that rabbits laid eggs on Easter and that to refuse an Easter egg from someone, was to refuse that person's friendship. Eggs blessed at Easter are also great for keeping sickness away.

Some people decorated boiled Easter eggs, but to do an Easter egg 'roll' you need uncooked ones. The Easter egg roll at the White House in Washington DC is the most famous one, but to do it yourself, gather your friends together at the top of a hill and roll the eggs down repeatedly. Gradually all will break except one. The owner of the longest-lasting egg will be rewarded with a year of good luck, but if any broken Easter eggs contain two yolks that is very lucky too.

April

The origin of April Fool's Day is lost to history, but it may have grown out of earlier New Year's Day celebrations, especially among the French. There is a superstition that if you do want to play practical joke, you should do so in the morning; pranking in the afternoon will give the prankster bad luck. If a pretty girl fools you on 1 April, you'll marry her, or at least be good friends.

Men married on April Fool's Day will always be ruled by their wives. Children born on 1 April will be lucky all their lives, except when it comes to gambling.

May

The Greeks believe that you should collect wild flowers on May Day (1 May) and make a wreath. Then, on the feast of St John the Divine (8 May), burn the wreath for good luck.

In the pagan world, the festival of Beltane, celebrated on or about 1 May, was one of the most important dates in the sacred year, marking the midpoint between the vernal equinox (the first day of spring) and the summer solstice. It was a time of purification, and people would light fires on Beltane and jump over them to cleanse themselves of evil and bad luck.

The Greeks believe that you should collect wild flowers on May Day—1 May.

Water, the most purifying of all things, is especially beneficial on May Day. If rain falls on your head on May Day, you won't suffer a headache for the rest of the year. If women wash their faces in dew gathered at daybreak, it will preserve their complexions. In Spain and France, people used to roll naked in May Day dew to protect themselves from skin diseases. Peasants in Slavic countries also used to gather May Day dew, but they put it on their cows to protect them against witchcraft.

Cattle were once thought to be especially vulnerable to magic on May Day, and people used to kill any hares found near the cows, in the belief that they were witches who planned to harm the cows. People placed branches against the sides of their houses, planted a maypole near the cow barn or decorated the barn with branches of rowan to ensure that the cows would continue to produce plenty of milk. Some recommended singeing the cows with burning straw, bleeding them and burning the blood on May Day, for extra protection.

Wear a garland on May Day, and you will find love that year. Eat sage on May Day and you will live forever.

Ascension day happens at the end of Lent, and Christians celebrate it 40 days after Easter, which generally places the date any time in May. If it rains on Ascension Day the harvest will be poor and the cattle sick, but the consolation prize is that the rainwater collected on the day is good for eye troubles.

Make a wish as the sun rises on Ascension Day, and if the day is sunny the weather will be fair for the whole of summer. Always take the Thursday before Ascension off, or you will have an accident at work. In Switzerland girls ring the bells in church towers on Ascension Day to bode a good flax harvest.

June

Midsummer has traditionally been celebrated on 24 June, although the real Midsummer's Day is now on 21 June. A girl has a good chance of meeting the man she will marry on Midsummer Eve if she fasts all day. She is supposed to set a table with a clean cloth, bread, cheese and ale, then, at midnight, sit down as though to eat. Mr Right is then supposed to come through the door and bow to her. If this doesn't work, she can pluck a rose on Midsummer's Day and put it away. If it is still fresh on Christmas Day—freezing it would be an idea—she should wear it to church. The man who takes it from her will be her future husband. A woman who wants to conceive a child should go out naked into the garden at midnight on Midsummer Eve and pick some St John's Wort.

July

St Swithin's Day is 15 July, and if it rains on this day, during the height of the northern summer, it will rain for the next 40 days.

August

The ancient Irish festival of Lughnasadh used to be celebrated on 1 August to commemorate the death of Tailtiu, the mother of the god Lugh. Tailtiu is said to have died of exhaustion after clearing the forests of Ireland to make room for agriculture. The festival commemorates the harvest. On Lughnasadh, couples commence trial marriages lasting a year, at the end of which they could formalise their union, or part without shame.

Lughnasadh is another one of those days when you have an increased chance of meeting your true love—especially if you're a man, as in this traditional Irish song *Star of the County Down*:

At the harvest fair, she'll be surely there
So I'll dress in my Sunday clothes,
With my shoes shone bright and my hat cocked right,
For a smile from my nut-brown rose.
No pipe I'll smoke, no horse I'll yoke,
'Til my plough is a rust-coloured brown,
'Til a smiling bride by my own fireside
Sits the Star of the County Down.

So on 1 August, dress up and be on your best behaviour, and the luck of the Irish might rub off on you too.

september

Michaelmas is on 29 September, the Feast of St Michael the Archangel. Traditionally, Satan was banished from heaven on this day and landed in a blackberry bush, cursing the brambles. In yearly commemoration the devil now puts his foot on the blackberry on this day, so people will not pick blackberries at Michaelmas, perchance to come across Satan himself.

Observe the moon on Michaelmas, count the number of days since the last new moon and this will give you the number of days of flooding that will follow Michaelmas.

People celebrating the Summer Solstice—21 June in the Northern Hemishpere—at Stonehenge.

october

The day called All Hallows Eve or Halloween, 31 October, had its origin in Samhain, or the Celtic New Year. It's traditionally the day when the spirits of the dead are out and about, enjoying a good haunting before All Saint's Day puts a wet blanket on their fun. It's also the day when witches feel at their most powerful.

On Halloween, the wind will blow and sigh against the windows of those who will die within the next 12 months. If you go to a crossroads on Halloween and listen to the wind, it will tell you what will happen to you in the next year. If you're in a really ghoulish mood, sit on a three-legged stool at a crossroads when the church bells strike midnight on 31 October, and the wind will tell you the names of all those who will die in the parish in the next year.

If you are a gambler and you missed the Michaelmas opportunity to make your acquaintance with the Lord of Darkness, you can always hide under a blackberry bush on Halloween, ask the Devil for help and you will win at cards. A non-gambling man will see the shadow of his future wife under a blackberry bush, whether or not he invokes the Devil. There are in fact a whole host of 'find your future spouse' superstitions associated with Halloween. One is that a woman should stand before a mirror and eat an apple. Her future husband's image will appear beside her reflection. Alternatively, she can catch a snail, leave it on a covered dish overnight, and the next day the snail's trail will be in the shape of the initial of her future man.

Apples and Halloween mix well. You can bob for them, and if you want to play for higher stakes, people can carve their names in apples and throw them into the tub. You then bob for them blindfolded. The apple that you pick out of the tub will be the one belonging to your future mate. If that doesn't work, you can peel new apples—as long as you can keep the peel in a single, unbroken piece—then throw the peel over your left shoulder and see what initial forms. Then to determine how you're going to plan all these weddings, you can take some apples and attach strings to them. Give each person a stringed apple and tell them to whirl it about. The first person whose apple flies off the string will be the first one to marry.

Bobbing for apples at Halloween will help you identify your future mate.

november

In Mexico, 1 November and 2 November, or All Saints' Day and All Souls' Day respectively, comprise a two-day festival for the dead. People make food and drink offerings for the dead, and even though they eat and drink the offerings themselves, they believe that on these days the dead will have partaken of the 'spiritual essence' of the food, so it has no nutritional value, including, supposedly, calories.

The simplest way to commemorate the dead on the night of 2 November is to light a candle in the window of the room of a person who died in that household—one candle for each person. As people so seldom die at home any more, it also works to light a candle in their former room.

december

In the West, and increasingly in the East, the traditions and attached superstitions of December are almost totally dominated by Christmas and New Year's Eve.

Never throw out your Christmas tree or put away your Christmas decorations before Twelfth Night, 6 January, or you'll be throwing away your prosperity for the coming year. Never let a fire leave the house on Christmas and never cut the Christmas cake before Christmas Eve.

Things you can do to have good luck on Christmas Eve and Christmas itself include the following.

Bringing holly into the house, at any other time it's bad luck. At midnight on the 24th, open all the windows and doors to let the evil spirits out and the good ones in. Always have holly and ivy as part of your Christmas decorations, as holly is lucky for males and ivy is lucky for females.

If you want your fruit trees to be abundant, tie a rock to a branch or tie bunches of wet straw to the trunk on Christmas Eve.

Christmas is another one of those nights, like Halloween, when magic to find your future spouse is especially potent. A woman can profit if there's a pear tree about. Walk towards it backward, circle it nine times, then tap it—you'll see an image of your future husband. Or go into the garden at midnight and pick 12 sage leaves for the same result.

Go to a henhouse on Christmas Eve and tap it sharply. If the rooster crows first, you'll be married within the year, if you hear the hens cackle, you won't. If you can arrange it, become engaged at Christmas—it's very good luck.

On Christmas Day itself, just as at New Year's, don't go out until you receive a visit from a dark-haired man, if a woman visits, that's very bad luck.

If Christmas Day is overcast, the harvest will be rich.

It's also said that ghosts never appear at Christmas, and that a child born at Christmas will be lucky all its life, or at least will never be hanged. However, in Greece a Christmas child is believed to be a wandering spirit, and in Poland, Christmas children run the risk of growing up to be werewolves.

A candle burning in the window on Christmas night will mean good luck to the household for the whole year if the candle stays lit. If it putters or blows out before dawn on the 26th, then it's bad luck. This may not be as bad as you think, as a windy Christmas is supposed to be very good luck.

Leave a loaf of uneaten bread on the table on Christmas night and you'll have no lack of bread for the rest of the year.

Kissing under the mistletoe for luck evolved out of ancient Celtic beliefs that mistletoe was a plant of peace and reconciliation. Nowadays it's the only time that men and women can kiss each other when no one will think twice about it, regardless of the marital status of the participants.

There is an urban myth that more people commit suicide between Christmas and New Year than at any other time of the year. This doesn't seem to be true, at least in America. The US National Centre for Health Statistics has found that, sadly, the highest incidents of suicide are in the northern spring, which is why April is Suicide Prevention Month. And although women are more likely to attempt suicide than men, men are twice as likely to actually succeed. The peak time for female attempted suicide? Valentine's Day.

In Greece on New Year's Eve people leave an onion outside their front door to repel evil spirits for the next 12 months.

And don't kill flies on the last days of the year, you'll lose US$100 dollars for every fly you kill.

A candle burning in the window on Christmas night will mean good luck to the household for the year.

unlucky days

Oxford mathematician Arthur Hopton was interested in telling the future. In 1612 he published a book called *A Concordance of Years*, or an *Exact Computation of Time*. His chapter on 'fatall dayes of the years' lists the following really unlucky days, derived probably from astrological calculations that you can extrapolate to any year, if you're so inclined:

- 3 January
- 30 April
- 1 July
- 1 August
- 31 August
- 7 October.

If perchance you fall ill on one of these days then you will 'hardly ever escape'. Hopton's prognostications were part of a more general attitude that existed at the time about unlucky days and he died in

November 1614 at the age of just 26. You can read whatever you like into that fact.

In *The Complete Book of Superstition, Prophecy and Luck*, author Leonard Ashley quoted the following translation of the Latin text of the *Old Sarum Missal*, a rite still used to celebrate mass in the Western Orthodox Church. The Sarum rite became the basis of the 1549 *English book of common prayer*. Here it lists evil days too:

January

Of this first month, the opening day
And seventh like a sword will slay.

February

The fourth day bringeth down to death;
The third will stop a strong man's breath.

March

The first the greedy glutton slays;
The fourth cuts short the drunkard's days.

April

The tenth, and the eleventh too,
Are ready death's fell work to do.

May

The third to slay poor man hath power;
The seventh destroyeth in an hour.

June

The tenth a pallid visage shows;
No faith nor truth the fifteenth knows.

July

The thirteenth is a fatal day;
The tenth alike will mortals slay.

August

The first kills strong ones at a blow;
The second lays a cohort low.

September

The third day of the month of September,
And tenth, bring evil to each member.

October

The third and tenth, with poisoned breath,
To man are foes as foul as death.

November

The fifth bears scorpion sting of deadly
pain; The third is tinctured with
destruction's train.

December

The seventh's a fatal day to human life;
The tenth is with a serpent's venom rife.

playing the
numbers

playing the numbers

It's often true that human beings lapse into a worldview in which they are too clever for their own good. People invented numbers and counting to make some sense of what was around them and to quantify things. Human culture may be based on language, but human civilisation is based on numbers. True to form, it wasn't enough that people could just stop with the very useful invention of numerals and arithmetic. They had to go on and put a whole lot of extra baggage onto numbers.

In the West you can blame Pythagoras for much of our numerical superstitions. Well known for his theorem of squares built on the sides of right-angled triangles, Pythagoras is less well known for his mystical attitude towards numbers, an attitude that was quite common in ancient Greece. Like Pi, the square root of two is irrational—a fraction without end. There is a legend among historians of mathematics that in Ancient Greece someone had to commit suicide if they uncovered the fact that the square root of two was irrational. Although most people don't take numerology as seriously as this, many still believe that numbers have meanings beyond their strict functional values, especially when people start mixing numbers up with astrology, as in the following list:

- **Zero:** The number of the planet Pluto—although it's no longer officially a planet—and lucky for Scorpio.
- **One:** The number of the Sun and lucky for Aries and Leo.
- **Two:** The number of the Moon and lucky for Gemini and Pisces.
- **Three:** The number of Jupiter and lucky for Sagittarius. Three has the distinction of being a magical or sacred number across a wide range of cultures. It is the number of corners and sides in the equilateral triangle (naturally), and this way one of the Pythagoreans' 'perfect shapes' and is of course the number of the Christian Trinity of Father, Son and Holy Spirit.

- **Four:** The number of Mars, also lucky for Leos or Scorpios, depending on whom you talk to. Also a sacred numeral by being the number of corner and sides in the square—another 'perfect' shape.
- **Five:** The number of Mercury and lucky for Gemini and Virgo.
- **Six:** The number of Venus, lucky for Libra and Taurus.
- **Seven:** The number of Neptune and lucky for Cancer or Pisces. Being the sum of three and four, seven has a special place in human imagination, hence seven colours in the rainbow and seven days of the week, of which the seventh is reserved for the Deity. The Bible is a great fan of the number seven, it mentions seven or groups of seven about 300 times throughout its text. Jericho fell when seven priests blew seven rams horns before the Ark of the Covenant for seven days. On the seventh day they walked around the walls of the city seven times and at the end of the seventh circuit, they blew their horns and the walls came tumbling down. There were originally only supposed to be seven planets, which meant a lot of doubling up among the twelve signs of the zodiac.
- **Eight:** The number of Saturn and lucky for Capricorn.
- **Nine:** the number of Uranus and lucky for Aquarius, it's especially lucky being three times three.

In the Far East many cultures have a slightly different take on numbers due to linguistic coincidences. One is unlucky because it sounds like the Chinese Mandarin verb 'to lack' or 'to want'. Four is especially unlucky because it sounds like the word for death or the verb 'to die'. If your office extension number is '1414', saying it out loud can sound like you're saying 'I want death'. Chinese people consider the number four to be so unlucky that they don't have it on hotel room numbers, and high-rise buildings don't have a fourth floor because nobody wants to live or work on the 'floor of death'.

Eight, however, is very auspicious—it sounds like the word for 'prosperity' and is the number of wealth and good fortune. People are willing to pay a premium for numbers with a lot of eights in them. In August 2003 Sichuan Airlines in China paid 2.33 million Yuan (190,000 pounds or $350,000 in 2008) to acquire 8888 8888 as their 24-hour customer service hotline. Everyone at the company thought that paying for eight eights was money well spent. People will pay higher prices for houses with an eight in the street number or

for car licence plates with eights. Bank accounts with lots of eights are great too. This contrasts with Western numerology. In the West, both four and eight are money numbers, but four means money going in and staying there, while eight means money going in and money going out. You can assume then that fours are lucky numbers to have for investment accounts, whereas eights are good for current accounts—as long as the cash flow is positive.

The number **Ten** is so basic to our system of arithmetic that it doesn't seem to have acquired much superstitious baggage, but go one up to **Eleven**, and suddenly you are in another space altogether. Eleven is considered a highly spiritual number, elevated above earthly concerns. Also great are 22 and 33. The Japanese believe that it's lucky to climb Mount Fuji, especially so on your 33rd and—would you believe it—88th ascents. Yet there is a saying in Japan, that the man who climbs Mount Fuji once is wise, but the man who climbs Mount Fuji twice is a fool.

Twelve is another utilitarian number, more versatile than ten and easily divided by two, three, four and six. The ancient Jews considered it an ideal number for organisation, thus twelve tribes of Israel and twelve apostles. In Babylon, twelve was sacred to their male gods, and we've inherited twelve months from them. The Babylonians originally had a thirteenth month, called 'the month of the unlucky raven', so they may have devised the twelve-month year to avoid the unlucky month altogether.

The number of numerological systems that people have devised over the millennia would fill a large book all on their own. They all have their

individual interpretations of what the basic numbers mean and how to predict personality, compatibility and the future by playing around with them. However, a few examples should show how this sort of thinking works and how differently people perceive numbers depending on their historical background and culture.

The first meaning given for each number below comes from the *Bible*:

- **One:** Unity
- **Two:** Division, but in other cultures simply 'duality' and in China double of anything is good luck, which explains brand names like Double Happiness for items as varied as table tennis equipment, medicines and even cigarettes.
- **Three:** The divine perfection of the Trinity and the Resurrection. This idea permeated the realm of music, where composers preferred the 3/4 time signature for sacred music—the beat of the waltz—because it was 'perfect' time.
- **Four:** Earth as in the 'four corners of' and the four seasons, four winds, four directions—north, south, east and west—and four 'elements', fire, earth, air and water.
- **Five:** Has no special meaning in the Bible, but Islam has five 'pillars' of wisdom. In Asia there are five directions, the Western four, plus 'centre', and five elements, earth, fire and water, plus metal and wood. In Cantonese, 'five' sounds like 'not' and in front of a number, cancels its effect, so '58' is not lucky.

- **Six:** Man was created on the sixth day, and six is one short of seven, which is perfection, so 'man falls short of God's perfection' (Romans 3:23). The number 666 is the 'number of the beast', the signature of Satan himself. However, in Cantonese the word for six sounds like easy, so the number '666' is considered very lucky. Anything with this number attached to it will always go smoothly.
- **Seven:** Perfection. Seven has been revered throughout the ages, possibly because it's deeply rooted in the way that human brains are wired. Psychologist George A. Miller explored this in some depth in his landmark 1956 paper, "The Lucky Number Seven, Plus or Minus Two". However, in China seven is associated with the spirit world and the seventh month of the Chinese year is the 'month of ghosts'.
- **Eight:** The New Beginning after the end of a 'perfect seven' cycle. China has eight immortals and Buddhism has the Eightfold Noble Path. The official time for the opening of the Summer Olympic Games in Beijing was 8/8/08 at 8:08:08 p.m.
- **Nine:** The Holy Spirit has nine fruits—nine qualities that come from God: Love, Joy, Peace, Longsuffering, Kindness, Goodness, Faithfulness, Gentleness and Self-Control. Human gestation takes nine months, so nine is therefore the number of generation. Nine is lucky in China, symbolising power, but it's unlucky in Japan.

number thirteen

Thirteen was sacred in many Pagan traditions, being the number of real months (moons) in the year. Thirteen is thus identified with the moon and therefore usually with the principle female deity in the pantheon of your choice. So thirteen was very lucky to certain pagans.

Naturally, when Christianity came along thirteen became unlucky, but they may have inherited their prejudice from the Romans, one group of pagans who did think that the number thirteen was unlucky. The soothsayer famously told Caesar to 'beware the Ides of March' shortly before his assassination. The Ides, or midpoint of the month, usually fell on the 13th, but they were on the 15 May, July, October and March. In spite of this, the number fifteen never became unlucky.

Even without the Romans, it didn't help that there were thirteen diners at the Last Supper, and that Christ died on a Friday, which is why Friday the Thirteenth, which happens on average twice a year, is especially unlucky. The number thirteen used to have the same significance to Europeans and European-influenced cultures as the number four has in the East, which is why you can still see houses with the street number '12A' and many older aeroplanes don't have a Row 13. Nevertheless, not all of Europe thought that thirteen was bad. In the past, Orthodox Greeks who had a 'glass is half full attitude' felt that thirteen was a good number, standing for Christ plus the twelve apostles. More recently Greeks have become influenced by the more general aversion to thirteen, although Tuesday the Thirteenth is more unlucky there than Friday the Thirteenth. This superstition harks back to a particular date. On Tuesday 29 May 1453, the city of Constantinople, capital of the Eastern Roman Empire, fell to the Turks, ending one thousand years of Byzantine

Constantinople, today known as Istanbul, fell to the Turks on a Tuesday, a day of the week still considered unlucky there.

civilisation. To this day Greeks will not start a new business venture or project on a Tuesday. Tuesday the Thirteenth is also unlucky in South America.

Today, traditional Christian thinking has evolved and there has been recent upsurge of 'New Age' thinking. The 'goddess' and the 'feminine principle' are back in fashion and the number thirteen is once again seen as a good thing. Regardless, there have always been a small number of contrary souls who have always sworn by 'lucky thirteen' anyway.

your Birth Number

You can use numerology to find exceptions to the general rules about what is or isn't lucky and to discover what is lucky for you in particular. Take the colour green, which is generally considered unlucky. Apparently it isn't unlucky for you if your Birth Number is a two. So you can fight magic with more magic.

To determine your 'Birth Number', using a traditional Western method, add the digits of your birthday date until you are left with a single digit. For example, if you were born on the 29th of the month, add the numbers as follows:

$2 + 9 = 11$ then $1 + 1 = 2$

This is your Birth Number.

The lucky colours for each number are:

- **One**: All shades of gold, yellow, bronze to golden brown.
- **Two**: All shades of green, cream or white.
- **Three**: Mauve, violet and purple.
- **Four**: Electric blues and all shades of grey.
- **Five**: Light grey, white and any shiny or glistening colours or materials.
- **Six**: All shades of blue as well as rose and pink.
- **Seven**: All shades of green, white and yellow.
- **Eight**: The 'bruise' colours, black, dark blue and purple.
- **Nine**: Crimson, rose and pink.

You can also match your Birth Number to your lucky stone:
- **One**: Topaz, amber, citrine or yellow diamond.
- **Two**: Moonstones and jade.
- **Three**: Amethyst.
- **Four**: Sapphire.
- **Five**: Diamond.
- **Six**: Turquoise.
- **Seven**: Pearls and moonstones.
- **Eight**: Amethyst or any dark-toned sapphire.
- **Nine**: Ruby, garnet, blackstone.

You can also use the ever-versatile Birth Number to determine which days of the week are luckier for you than others.
- **One**: Sundays and Mondays.
- **Two**: Sundays, Mondays and Fridays.
- **Three**: Thursdays, Fridays and Tuesdays.
- **Four**: Saturdays, Sundays and Mondays.
- **Five**: Wednesdays and Fridays.
- **Six**: Tuesdays, Thursdays and Fridays.
- **Seven**: Sundays and Mondays.
- **Eight**: Saturdays, Sundays and Mondays.
- **Nine**: Tuesdays, Thursdays and Fridays.

your name number

Numerology, or arithomancy if you're using it to predict the future, is a bit like astrology—a realm for experts and the initiated. As much of numerology involves converting names to numbers, logomancy (working with words) and onomancy (letters in a name) are related ideas.

Here's just a taste of how complicated it can become.

Use the table to find the numerical values of the letters in your name and add them together. For example:

XAVIER WATERKEYN

6+1+4+9+5+9 +

5+1+2+5+9+2+5+7+5 = 75

Then, in the same way that you found your Birth Number, see above, keep adding the letter values of your name until you are left with single digit, which is your Name Number. For example:

75 = 7+5 = 12 = 1+2 = 3

Your name number is supposed to give you an insight on the best area in which to focus your achievements:

1 – Action, 2 – Relationships, 3 – Self-Expression, 4 – Stability, 5 – Travel, 6 – Truth, 7 – Spirituality, 8 – Business and 9 – Intellect.

To confuse matters, some authorities say that you shouldn't reduce any number lower than 66 because these numbers all mean something, with special significance to the numbers 1 to 16 as well as 22 and 33.

Consult a numerologist for further guidance, but be warned, numerologist are like lawyers: consult two and you get three opinions.

Some people, however, prefer to use the so-called Chaldean numerology grid. They feel it gives better results.

Letters and their associated numbers

1	2	3	4	5	6	7	8	9
A	B	C	D	E	F	G	H	I
J	K	L	M	N	O	P	Q	R
S	T	U	V	W	X	Y	Z	

Chaldean numerology grid

1	2	3	4	5	6	7	8
A	B	C	D	E	U	O	F
I	K	G	M	H	V	Z	P
Q	R	L	T	N	W		
J		S		X			
Y							

Note that if you use the Chaldean numbers the only way to reach a nine is by addition of the letter values. Chaldean numerologists also find further special significance in the numbers 40, 44, 55, 66, 77, 88, 99. Again, for specifics you'll need to go to an expert. Those in the know don't give up their esoteric knowledge without charging for it, rather like investment advisors—with rather the same rate of success.

Adding up the values for your full date of birth can give you another Birth Number, say:

$29/7/1965 = 2+9+7+1+9+6+5 = 39 = 3+9 = 12 = 1+2 = 3$

your current year number

Another useful number is the Current Year Number. This will tell you what sort of year you're going to have. You generate the Current Year Number by adding the numbers of your birthday in the current year. Say:

$29/7/2012 = 2+9+7+2+0+1+2 = 23 = 2+3 = 5$

Do it for yourself and see what type of year you're going to have:

- One: A year of new beginnings, a lucky time to start new projects, endeavours or businesses.
- Two: A year for forming relationships or achieving harmony in your current ones. The things you began in a '1' year will now start to bear fruit if you're patient and you don't get in the way.
- Three: A year of gradual change and expansion but also of revelation, when things long hidden may become uncovered.
- Four: A year of consolidation, a steady time of trimming and tidying up. Work hard this year and you'll reap greater financial rewards.
- Five: A year of sudden changes and the destruction of routine. A year of opportunity through disruption.
- Six: A year focused on the home and family and dealing with any issues with relatives.
- Seven: A year of turning inward, spending time alone and becoming reacquainted with yourself. A 'me'-focused year.
- Eight: A year of recognition. This is the year when people will acknowledge and celebrate your achievements. A great year for self-promotion and building up your reputation.
- Nine: A year of review, discarding the old and making way for the new. Good luck will come to those who get rid of any objects, patterns or even

relationships that no longer serve them during this year.

As you can see, you can play around with numbers and link them to all sorts of other traditions and practices. Feel free to create your own, once you've done a few psychic development exercises. Your intuitions are probably as good as anyone else's.

lucky numbers, from eastern traditions

If Chinese thinking has intuitive appeal for you, here is a simple way to determine all sorts of luck using feng shui.

If you're **female**, calculate your Lucky Number as follows:

- Take the last two digits of your birth year, eg 1965 = 65.
- Subtract four, eg 65 − 4 = 61.
- Divide this number by 9, eg 61 / 9 = 6 remainder 7.
- The remainder is your Lucky Number.
- If there is no remainder your Lucky Number is 9.
- If you were born in 2000 then start with 100, which makes 1 your Lucky Number.

However, in this system the number 5 is never a Lucky Number, and a 5 is converted to an 8 if you are a female.

If you're **male**, calculate your Lucky Number as follows:

- Take the last two digits of your birth year, eg 1965 = 65.
- Subtract this number from 100, eg 100 − 65 = 35.
- Divide this number by 9, eg 35 / 9 = 4 remainder 8.

- The remainder is your Lucky Number.
- If there is no remainder your Lucky Number is 9.

As for females, 5 is never a Lucky Number, and a 5 is automatically converted to a 2 if you are a male.

Now you're ready to refer to your number in the Lo Shu Magic Square, in which all the numbers in a single row or single column add up to 15.

Within each square is your lucky number along with other corresponding lucky factors that you can use to increase your luck, in this order:

- Colour: By wearing it.
- Season: By doing things that require more energy or risk at this time of the year.
- Lucky Element: By incorporating this element physically or symbolically as a booster in various parts of your home or workplace.
- Lucky Direction: By placing your desk facing this direction, or by using your Lucky Element in this direction. (Elements come in 'greater' and 'lesser' forms. If yours is a greater element, use it in a big way; if yours is a lesser element, take a more subtle approach.)
- Unlucky Direction: By using your Lucky Element to cancel bad luck coming from this direction.

For example if your lucky number is 3, you could choose to put a large metal sculpture against the east wall of your office and another against the west wall, to increase your luck. You might also choose spring to be the time to begin or undertake the hardest part of a major project, when you'll need the smoothest sailing.

Lo Shu Magic Square

4 Orange Early summer Lesser water South-east North	9 Red Summer Greater water South North-east	2 Pink Late summer Lesser wood South-west North-west
3 Green or gold Spring Greater metal East West	5 Earth Centre	7 White Autumn Greater wood West East
8 Purple Late winter Lesser metal North-east South	1 Indigo Winter Greater fire North South-east	6 Blue Early winter Lesser fire North-west South-west

your chinese birth year

If you want to go even deeper in determining your luck, then it's a good idea to determine your Chinese Birth Year. Since the Chinese years are based on a lunar calendar the start and finishing dates change from year to year.

For each year there is a corresponding animal sign. The legend is that the Buddha once asked for a meeting of all the animals but only 12 or so showed up: rat, ox, tiger, hare (or rabbit), dragon, snake, horse, sheep (or ram or goat), monkey, rooster, dog and pig.

Consult the following table for any year from 1924 to 2008. For years beyond 2008 go to page 252. For years before 1924 go to any number of websites like this one: www.paranormality.com/birth_signs.html.

You'll note that for each sign there is a corresponding best or luckiest time of the year and of the day and a corresponding natural direction and element.

Rat

Best time of the year: mid-November to mid-December
Best hour of the day: 11.00 pm to 1.00 am.
Natural direction: north
Natural element: water
5 Feb 1924–24 Jan 1925 (Wood)
24 Jan 1936–10 Feb 1937 (Fire)
10 Feb 1948–28 Jan 1949 (Earth)
28 Jan 1960–14 Feb 1961 (Metal)
16 Feb 1972–2 Feb 1973 (Water)
2 Feb 1984–19 Feb 1985 (Wood)
19 Feb 1996–6 Feb 1997 (Fire)

Tiger

Best time of the year: mid-January to mid-February
Best hour of the day: 3.00 am.to 5.00 am.
Natural direction: east-north-east
Natural element: fire
13 Feb 1926–1 Feb 1927 (Fire)
31 Jan 1938–18 Feb 1939 (Earth)
17 Feb 1950–5 Feb 1951 (Metal)
5 Feb 1962–24 Jan 1963 (Water)
23 Jan 1974–10 Feb 1975 (Wood)
9 Feb 1986–28 Jan 1987 (Fire)
28 Jan 1998–15 Feb 1999 (Earth)

Ox

Best time of the year: mid-December to mid-January
Best hour of the day: 1.00 am to 3.00 am.
Natural direction: north-north-east
Natural element: metal
25 Jan 1925–12 Feb 1926 (Wood)
11 Feb 1937–30 Jan 1938 (Fire)
29 Jan 1949–16 Feb 1950 (Earth)
15 Feb 1961–4 Feb 1962 (Metal)
3 Feb 1973–22 Jan 1974 (Water)
20 Feb 1985–8 Feb 1986 (Wood)
7 Feb 1997–27 Jan 1998 (Fire)

Hare

Best time of the year: mid-February to mid-March
Best hour of the day: 5.00 am to 7.00 am.
Natural direction: east
Natural element: wood
2 Feb 1927–22 Jan 1928 (Fire)
19 Feb 1939–7 Feb 1940 (Earth)
6 Feb 1951–26 Jan 1952 (Metal)
25 Jan 1963–12 Feb 1964 (Water)
11 Feb 1975–30 Jan 1976 (Wood)
29 Jan 1987–16 Feb 1988 (Fire)
16 Feb 1999–4 Feb 2000 (Earth)

Dragon

Best time of the year: mid-March to mid-April
Best hour of the day: 7.00 am to 9.00 am.
Natural direction: east-south-east
Natural element: water
23 Jan 1928–9 Feb 1929 (Earth)
8 Feb 1940–26 Jan 1941 (Metal)
27 Jan 1952–13 Feb 1953 (Water)
13 Feb 1964–1 Feb 1965 (Wood)
31 Jan 1976–17 Feb 1977 (Fire)
17 Feb 1988–5 Feb 1989 (Earth)
5 Feb 2000–23 Jan 2001 (Metal)

Horse

Best time of the year: mid-May to mid-June
Best hour of the day: 11.00 am to 1.00 pm.
Natural direction: south
Natural element: fire
30 Jan 1930–16 Feb 1931 (Metal)
15 Feb 1942–4 Feb 1943 (Water)
3 Feb 1954–23 Jan 1955 (Wood)
21 Jan 1966–8 Feb 1967 (Fire)
7 Feb 1978–27 Jan 1979 (Earth)
27 Jan 1990–14 Feb 1991 (Metal)
12 Feb 2002–31 Jan 2003 (Water)

Snake

Best time of the year: mid-April to mid-May
Best hour of the day: 9.00 am to 11.00 am.
Natural direction: south-south-east
Natural element: metal
10 Feb 1929–29 Jan 1930 (Earth)
27 Jan 1941–14 Feb 1942 (Metal)
14 Feb 1953–2 Feb 1954 (Water)
2 Feb 1965–20 Jan 1966 (Wood)
18 Feb 1977–6 Feb 1978 (Fire)
6 Feb 1989–26 Jan 1990 (Earth)
24 Jan 2001–11 Feb 2002 (Metal)

Sheep (or Goat)

Best time of the year: mid-June to mid-July
Best hour of the day: 1.00 pm to 3.00 pm.
Natural direction: south-south-west
Natural element: wood
17 Feb 1931–5 Feb 1932 (Metal)
5 Feb 1943–24 Jan 1944 (Water)
24 Jan 1955–11 Feb 1956 (Wood)
9 Feb 1967–29 Jan 1968 (Fire)
28 Jan 1979–15 Feb 1980 (Earth)
15 Feb 1991–3 Feb 1992 (Metal)
1 Feb 2003–21 Jan 2004 (Water)

Monkey

Best time of the year: mid-July to mid-August
Best hour of the day: 3:00 p.m. to 5:00 p.m.
Natural direction: west-south-west
Natural element: water
6 Feb 1932–25 Jan 1933 (Water)
25 Jan 1944–12 Feb 1945 (Wood)
12 Feb 1956–30 Jan 1957 (Fire)
30 Jan 1968–16 Feb 1969 (Earth)
16 Feb 1980–4 Feb 1981 (Metal)
4 Feb 1992–22 Jan 1993 (Water)
22 Jan 2004–8 Feb 2005 (Wood)

Dog

Best time of the year: mid-September to mid-October
Best hour of the day: 7:00 p.m. to 9:00 p.m.
Natural direction: west-north-west
Natural element: fire
14 Feb 1934–3 Feb 1935 (Wood)
2 Feb 1946–21 Jan 1947 (Fire)
18 Feb 1958–7 Feb 1959 (Earth)
6 Feb 1970–26 Jan 1971 (Metal)
25 Jan 1982–12 Feb 1983 (Water)
10 Feb 1994–30 Jan 1995 (Wood)
29 Jan 2006–17 Feb 2007 (Fire)

Rooster

Best time of the year: mid-August to mid-September
Best hour of the day: 5:00 p.m. to 7:00 p.m.
Natural direction: west
Natural element: metal
26 Jan 1933–13 Feb 1934 (Water)
13 Feb 1945–1 Feb 1946 (Wood)
31 Jan 1957–17 Feb 1958 (Fire)
17 Feb 1969–5 Feb 1970 (Earth)
5 Feb 1981–24 Jan 1982 (Metal)
23 Jan 1993–9 Feb 1994 (Water)
9 Feb 2005–28 Jan 2006 (Wood)

Pig

Best time of the year: mid-October to mid-November
Best hour of the day: 9:00 p.m. to 11:00 p.m.
Natural direction: north-north-west
Natural element: wood
4 Feb 1935–23 Jan 1936 (Wood)
22 Jan 1947–9 Feb 1948 (Fire)
8 Feb 1959–27 Feb 1960 (Earth)
27 Jan 1971–15 Feb 1972 (Metal)
13 Feb 1983–1 Feb 1984 (Water)
31 Jan 1995–18 Feb 1996 (Wood)
18 Feb 2007–6 Feb 2008 (Fire)

You'll also note that for each year there is a corresponding lucky birth element too. The general rule for knowing which is your birth element depends on what number your birth year ends with as follows:

- 0: Yang Metal
- 1: Yin Metal
- 2: Yang Water
- 3: Yin Water
- 4: Yang Wood
- 5: Yin Wood
- 6: Yang Fire
- 7: Yin Fire
- 8: Yang Earth
- 9: Yin Earth.

Yang types seek to balance their energy with yin environments. Yin is dark and cool. Similarly, yin types seek to balance their energy with yang environments—light and warm.

You'll note, however, that just as 'centre' is not the natural direction for any number or sign, earth is not the natural element for any number or sign.

The elements have natural inter-relationships, as in the diagram below.

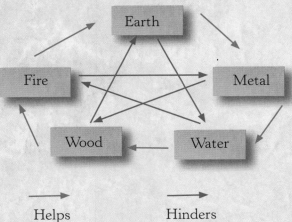

Helps →   Hinders →

For example, fire hinders metal (because it melts it), but helps earth (just as the sun warms the earth), and is in turn helped by wood (which feeds it).

So how do you use this to maximise your luck?

For best results combine your birth year data with your lucky number data and use information from both Eastern and Western traditions. For example, if you were a female born on 29 January 1960, then you are a Yang Metal Rat and your lucky colour is pink.

The best time of year for you is late summer and the best time of the day to do something risky is between 11:00 p.m. and 1:00 a.m. Your natural element of metal conflicts with your lucky lesser wood, so increase the amount of wood in your environment, particularly in the natural lucky south-west of your home or office and in the unlucky north-west.

Your lucky number is two using Eastern folklore. But using Western folklore your lucky number is also nine because you're an Aquarian, and also, because you're an Aquarian, you should carry around a garnet for luck.

Feel free to mix and match, play with and combine the various traditions, but always, always, always let intuition be your guide.

Chinese years for guidance

The animal character of a year doesn't just influence those born that year, it dominates all events that happen during the year.

Year of the Rat: (starting 7 Feb 2008 and 11 Feb 2020) A year of plenty, opportunity and good prospects. Accumulate money and make long-term investments. The wealth you accumulate this year will tide you over the leaner years. However, don't overextend yourself, as the year does not reward wild speculation or indiscriminate risk.

Year of the Ox: (26 Jan 2009 and 12 Feb 2021) A year of responsibility, a time to settle down and put your affairs in order. Work hard and the rewards you'll reap will come from tried-and-true methods. It's not the time to be experimental—be conservative. Best not to argue with the authorities during an Ox year, as the authorities will win.

Year of the Tiger: (15 Feb 2010 and 1 Feb 2022) After the plodding Year of the Ox, this is explosive, bold and brash, a year for spontaneity and sudden, radical change. The energy of the Tiger can bring new life to flagging ventures, but it's a bit of a genie in a bottle—anything without a solid foundation, be it business or relationships, could fall apart. Tiger years are filled with novelty and controversy—they can bring out the best, and the worst in us.

Year of the Rabbit: (3 Feb 2011 and 22 Jan 2023) Rabbit years are calm and peaceful, like a long visit to a health farm after the whirlwind Year of the Tiger. No one will become too anxious or concerned about anything, so it's a great year to make peace. Take it easy, you don't have to work to hard to progress. The danger is of complacency and sloth. You may put off something unpleasant for so long that it grows into a bigger problem than it might have been in the first place.

Year of the Dragon: (23 Jan 2012 and 10 Jan 2024) Another 'wake up' year. Pull out all the stops and reach for the top, or higher, with grandiose schemes. It's a year bursting at the seams with energy. Like Ox years, this is a great time to make money, as well as being auspicious for marrying, having children or starting a new business. A word of caution, though, things may look better than they really are, and don't forget others—Dragon luck abandons those who act dishonestly or disrespectfully.

Year of the Snake: (10 Feb 2013 and 29 Jan 2025) This year tends to have to deal with the fallout from the previous Dragon year. Fortunately, you find the mettle to deal with it, experiencing resourcefulness you didn't even know you had. Your calm surface may yet brew sudden radical shifts. Things that have long been incubating may hatch out. Tread lightly and don't take risks, gambling could be disastrous. These are epicurean years but they will also reward conviction and commitment to our highest ideals.

Year of the Horse: (31 Jan 2014 and 17 Feb 2026) An exhilarating year taken at full gallop with a sense of romance, whimsy and playfulness. A year of openness, when people's hearts are on their sleeves. Unfortunately, people tend to say what's on their minds, before they've engaged their diplomacy circuits. This is the best year to separate from any restraining or constrictive situation. If it isn't working in the Year of the Horse—leave!

Year of the Sheep, Ram or Goat: (19 Feb 2015 and 6 Feb 2027) Like Rabbit years, Sheep years are slow, dominated by sentimentality and nostalgia. Sheep years tend to focus on the home and hearth, family and loved ones. It's a time of creativity, but Sheep energy is a little over-sensitive, so there'll be a lot of smoothing of ruffled feathers. Focusing on relationships, negotiations of mutual expectations, boundaries and social contracts will be time well spent. With all this harmony, wars, struggles and long-standing animosities usually end.

Year of the Monkey: (8 Feb 2016 and 27 Jan 2028) A can-do year. If you've correctly used the energy of the previous year, then Monkey year is pay-off time. Business negotiations will lead to deal-making. People will be bargaining to make the most of their money. There'll be winners and losers, but Monkey energy is so playful that even if you come out second best, you'll have the good humour to pick yourself up, dust yourself off and leap once more into the fray. You'll be able to make great gains in little time if you also have fun and dance.

Year of the Rooster: (28 Jan 2017 and 13 Feb 2029) A year of dichotomies. On the one hand, you'll want to do something grand; on the other, Rooster energy can be flash-in-the-pan. Maximum effort may only yield minimum gain. There will be a lot of posturing, but little action. Simplify your life on the material plane, because you won't be able to accomplish much that is substantial. Get to know yourself better, then just go with the flow. Stay calm and centred, gain insights and make plans that you'll implement in two years' time.

Year of the Dog: (16 Feb 2018 and 3 Feb 2030) Another year of paradoxes, this brings both happiness and dissent. Loyalty tends to create strong bonds, but it also creates an 'us-and-them' mentality. However, a Dog year rewards equality, so, handled properly, it will be a year of triumph for the underdog too. Develop your morality and ethics and remain true to yourself. There will be tests, but if you do what is right, rather than what is expedient, you'll come out on top.

Year of the Pig: (5 Feb 2019 and 23 Jan 2031) Now, if you've done your homework in the last two years, welcome to the payoff. Although the Year of the Pig is prosperous for all, those who do best are those who know themselves. This is a year of generosity, in which your cup will run over. But, even though there's a lot of money around, you won't need it to feel good about yourself, because you'll have found the beat of your own drum and you'll be marching to it. However, if you've wasted the past two years, the Year of the Pig will leave you vulnerable to self-indulgence or over-indulgence.

the roll of
the dice

The roll of the dice

Gambling, even in those games that have an element of skill involved, is really all about luck, so gamblers are probably the most superstitious people that you'll meet, especially the amateurs. Professionals know how to play the odds, amateurs rely a lot more on the goddess Fortuna, Lady Luck, to be on their side. Pity that Fortuna is so fickle, but that doesn't stop gamblers from doing whatever they can to make luck turn their way.

One study showed some common superstitions among gamblers, especially those with a 'problem':
- They feel that they sometimes both need and receive spiritual help or guidance when they're gambling.
- They feel that their mood has a big effect on their winnings and that when they're feeling down they 'know' their luck will be bad.
- They often have rituals that they have to carry out when they're gambling to ensure their luck.
- They think that they have the psychic ability to predict a winner.

Will your baby bet?

If you want to know if your child will turn out to be a gambler, put out a Bible, a silver dollar and a pack of cards in front of your baby. If baby reaches for the Bible, you have a future preacher on your hands, if baby goes for the dollar, you have a banker or a financier. If the baby goes for the pack of cards, that's a pretty clear sign.

- Characteristically they feel that hunches have a big influence on their winnings and that if they have a hunch they have to follow through on it.
- They feel that people surrounding them can give out good or bad vibes, and if the vibes are bad then they need to change seats or games or they won't win.

The ideal situation then for you if you're a superstitious gambler is to:

- Find a way of getting or encouraging spiritual help.
- Cultivate your ability to feel good and positive.
- Cultivate and test rituals that will help you.
- Increase your psychic ability.
- Increase the quality and frequency of your hunches.
- Increase your sensitivity to good or bad vibes.

finding spiritual help

You might as well start at the very top and pray to the Roman goddess Fortuna. However, be aware that Fortuna comes in various guises: Fortuna Bona (Good Fortune), Fortuna Dubia (Doubtful Fortune), Fortuna Brevis (Fickle Fortune) and Fortuna Mala (Bad Fortune).

Obviously, you want as much Fortuna Bona as you can find. As few people nowadays know how to properly worship or invoke Fortuna, you won't have much competition. The goddess should be flattered by the attention.

Here are some tips:

The oak tree was sacred to Fortuna, so plant an oak tree in your garden and carry acorns with you when you gamble.

Fortuna's festival day is 11 June. Make a sacrifice to Fortuna by offering her grains and loaves of bread. Give her the good stuff, a supermarket loaf won't cut it. Simply put aside a little corner of your home, preferably in the east, put the grain and loaves on a platter kneel down and say something like: 'O Goddess Fortuna! Your humble servant offers you these fruits of the earth. Look kindly upon me.' In classical Latin, if you can. Ecclesiatical Latin won't do, as you may offend her ears with bad pronunciation.

Make a blend from the following essential oils. Again, get the good stuff—Fortuna favours the bold but she definitely looks down on cheapskates:

- vetiver to promote possibilities
- cedarwood to free your expression of inner truth
- lemon and cajuput to bring clarity and vision
- lavender angustifolia to balance new energies
- frankincense to revive intentions

Mix to taste, until every time you smell the oil you feel positive and uplifted. Apply a drop to your 'throat' chakra, in the middle of your Adam's apple.

Also wear or hold in your pocket the following stones: aquamarine, citrine, lapis lazuli, pyrite or turquoise.

Now that you've caught her attention, it's time to create the right atmosphere.

positive vibes

Fortuna is a feel-good goddess— she rewards joyful intentions and generous motivations. So it helps if you dedicate a portion of your winnings to charity, especially those involving children.

Affirmations are a good thing. You have to purify your spirit, so that there aren't any blocks in your heart to receiving the blessings of Fortuna. Incant affirmations such as: 'My happiness attracts wealth,' 'Wealth and happiness is my birthright,' 'My good fortune spreads to others,' or 'Opportunity knocks constantly.' Or make up anything that works for you. The important thing is not to have any beliefs that prevent Fortuna giving you luck.

Of course, it will help to do anything that makes you feel good, so that you and everyone around you will feel uplifted and joyous.

Wishes

It's a universal belief that when you're making a wish you should do so in silence and not reveal your wish to anyone until it comes true, or it won't at all.

Rituals and charms

There are a number of different, popular beliefs that gamblers cling to.

Many people believe that it's impossible for novice gamblers to lose on their first outing—the famous 'beginner's luck'. However, whether you're a newbie or an old hand, many believe that it's impossible to lose with borrowed money so don't lend money to an opponent.

Carrying the nail of a horny toad is lucky, as is carrying a rabbit's foot, but only if it's the left hind foot of a rabbit killed during a full moon by a cross-eyed person.

Sitting on a handkerchief is lucky. And if the local etiquette allows it, turning a chair backwards and sitting astride it is lucky.

Always stack your gambling chips neatly. Blowing or—if you can get away with it—spitting on cards or dice before you use them is lucky, as is rubbing the dice on the head of a red-headed person. Decide what your favourite card is and tap it with your right index finger for luck.

Clothing is important. If you want to play it safe then don't wear anything black and cross your fingers in the presence of the colour red. Fortuna likes neatness, so always gamble while well dressed. However, if they're on a winning streak, gamblers may wear the same clothes for days so as not to change their luck. If people at the tables are giving you funny looks or suggestively pinching their noses, explain to them that you're on a winning streak. Gamblers understand these things.

If you break a mirror while you're gambling there are two cures. You could gather the mirror pieces and throw them into a stream, taking care not to see your reflection in the pieces at any time. Alternatively, as many casinos aren't located near streams—especially in Las Vegas—a more practical cure is to break the mirror further. Grind up the pieces until no one will ever see their reflection in that mirror again.

Don't allow any dogs or even anything suggestive of dogs near a gambling table. Don't play cards on a polished table, and play conservatively if you're dealt the four of clubs or the nine of diamonds, especially in the first hand, as this is unlucky. When Wild Bill Hickok was shot in 1876 he was playing poker. In his hand were two aces and two eights—this is now called a 'dead man's hand' and is either lucky or unlucky depending on how you feel.

If you're Chinese, and especially if you're Cantonese, wearing or having the following numbers on your person in some form or another is lucky, because saying the names of the numbers out loud sounds similar to meaningful phrases:

- 18 sounds like 'definitely prosper'
- 84 sounds like 'prosper till death'
- 168 sounds like 'prosper all the way'
- 998 sounds like 'prosper for a long time'
- 1388 sounds like 'prosperity in lifetime'.

The Chinese also believe that, to encourage good luck in gambling, it's advisable for men to avoid sex and women—although in the West it's considered good luck for a male player to have a pretty woman stand behind him when he's playing. You tend to see this a lot in James Bond movies.

When gambling in China, also: avoid seeing monks or nuns before going to a casino; don't stay in hotel rooms with a four in their number; and wear red underwear when gambling. Women especially are believed more likely to win while they're having their period.

And if you're still not winning:

- Switch on all the lights at home before going out to gamble.
- Never count money during a gambling session.
- Never touch someone's shoulder when they are gambling.
- And, if you can help it, never enter a casino through its main entrance, because it's cursed.

For methods of predicting the future, like the winner of the Melbourne Cup, the Kentucky or the local Lotto game refer to the next chapter.

Always stack your gambling chips neatly for good luck.

looking into
the future

looking into the future

The world has always been filled with uncertainty, but people like to be able to plan or commit to a course of action that will actually give them results.

Many superstitions have come out of our need to read the world and understand what it's trying to tell us. For the most part, these are passive; we interpret whatever we're given. There's an assumption that everything is connected. If you can only discern the patterns of meanings, you'll gain access to hidden knowledge. It's as if a future event is like a stone dropped into pond. We're on the shore, trying to work out the size, shape, colour and weight of the stone by looking at the waves it's making.

However, for some individuals, this has never been good enough. They don't want to wait like good little boys and girls for the gods to stop messing around. They seek out procedures and techniques that empower them to look into the future, see what it holds, then take appropriate action.

This has always been a little dangerous, as gods and fellow mortals don't like mere people becoming too uppity. It's especially bad if they are representatives of an institutionalised religion that wants to keep power to itself—they often start calling you nasty names, like 'Spawn of Satan'.

However, for those who aren't put off by the Old Testament injunction that 'Thou shalt not suffer a witch to live' (*Exodus 22*:18) or by Dante's eighth circle of hell, in which fortune tellers are condemned to spend eternity with their heads screwed on backwards as a punishment for wanting to see too far forward, or for those who believe that psychic powers actually come as a blessing from a divine source, here is a small introduction to the world of prophecy, past, present and future.

As you read, bear in mind that what's most important with all of them is the state of mind of the diviner, also known as the querant. The best method for telling the future is the one with which you have the strongest affinity. Feel free to experiment and work out your own path. Make it up as you go along—that's what everyone else has ever done, but these ideas should start you off.

Building your psychic muscles

Everybody is psychic, but some of us are more psychic than others, and all methods of divination work better if you can increase your psychic ability. For example, if you believe that you can pick winning numbers or horses psychically in the first place, then it follows logically that this is a talent or skill that you can build on. You don't have to restrict yourself to using your psychic ability for winning money, because using your sixth sense in any area will help, but it might prove good motivation for developing your potential in this area.

However, it's important to note that not all psychic abilities are the same and that prescience, the ability to see the future, is different from mind-reading, creative intuition, channelling or the ability to see and talk to spirits. Divination comes in many shapes and forms.

Before you look into the future, it's important to perform a purifying ritual like sage smudging or imagining yourself surrounded by a ball of white light. This will also protect you from evil influences. For further psychic protection, put a small dot of essential oil of cloves on your forehead or on the back of your neck where the hairline ends. Do this before you do anything psychic. (Gamblers might even want to use clove oil to protect themselves from the bad vibes they may be receiving from other people).

To build up your ability at prescience, here are a few simple exercises. If you want to go the whole way, you might want to perform these exercises within a magic circle of your own invention. Simply draw a circle large enough to sit and move around in—on the ground with a stick, if you're outside on dirt, or, if indoors, on a wooden floor with chalk. Make sure the line of the circle is unbroken, because evil is sure to enter if there's even the tiniest of gaps. The practice of prognosticating while within a sacred or magic circle is called aspidomancy.

Take a die and practice predicting the number of the next roll. This is an easy way to work out how you receive psychic messages. They may come in several forms:

- **Clairvoyance:** you 'see' the number in your mind's eye.
- **Clairaudience:** you 'hear' a voice telling you the answer in you mind's ear.
- **Clairsentience:** you can 'feel' the number out, maybe in a part of your body, or maybe in some vague undefined way that still works.
- **Claircognizance:** you just 'know' the right answer.

In rare cases you may find that you're clairolfactory, and can 'smell' the number, or clairgustatory, and can 'taste' the number.

Predicting the future with dice is called astralagomancy (from the Greek word for vertebrae, because dice used to be made out of carved backbones). Here's a simple way of doing it.

Ask your question. When you feel the tug to do so, roll one die. The numbers correspond to the following answers.

- **One:** Definitely no.
- **Two:** Maybe, but probably not.
- **Three:** Maybe.
- **Four:** Maybe, but probably yes.
- **Five:** Definitely yes.
- **Six:** Roll again. You're asking the wrong question.

Make sure that the question you ask

has an answer that makes sense in terms of the potential answers that you'll get from the die rolls.

Another method uses a deck of cards. First shuffle them, then place the deck face down. Take one card out, lay it on the table face down and see if you can know what card it is. Touch the card and see if this makes any difference to the results. You might want to start with a simplified deck first, say, use only one suit, or take out all the court cards. As you improve you can build up to a full deck.

A more portable practise is to toss a coin and see if you can correctly guess heads or tails.

An even simpler method of developing your prescience is when you're waiting for a train at a railway station. If you're on a line with various types of train in use, see if you can guess what type of train is coming. At a bus stop with lots of bus lines, see if you can guess the bus number before you can see it with your physical eyes.

You can make up exercises on your own. The general principle is to find a mechanism with some element of chance, and practice divining the outcome. The key to success is to persist. Don't be discouraged if you can't guess correctly straight away. In fact, if you're constantly guessing the coin-toss incorrectly, then you're actually doing something right, because your results are actually worse than pure mathematical chance would allow. If you're wrong more than 50 per cent of the time you need to ask the spirits for psychic guidance about what you need to do to become accurate. Just ask, and the spirits will guide you.

Agalmatomancy

This involves working with statues. In ancient Greece you would walk up to a statue, whisper a question in its ear, then block your ears and walk away. The next thing you hear after you take away your hands would give you a clue to your answer.

Anthroposcopy

This involves observing people, their behaviour and physical appearance or traces. This includes hand and palm reading and the

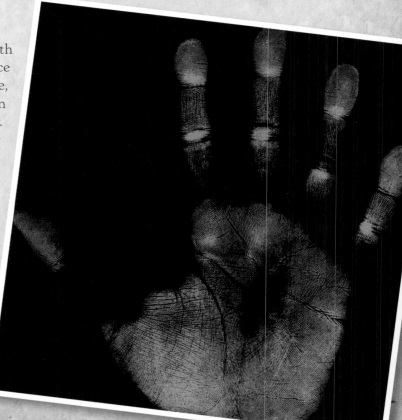

lesser-known finger and toenail reading or dactylomancy—the observation of finger movements. You may be able to read the future by walking or observing the way that others walk or reading their footprints.

The head is always a popular body part and the general methods of divination using the head and face are called physiognomy. Face reading was particularly popular in 18th and 19th-century Europe and is still common in Asia today. Another well known one involves reading skulls or the bumps on the head, which is technically known as cephalomancy or phrenology.

In South East Asia, there's a belief that a deep belly button denotes wealth; this is omphalomancy. There's also: chronomancy (the idea that 'timely' events have meaning), cledomancy (random events, chance encounters or words 'accidentally' heard) and the related transataumancy (things accidentally seen or heard), clamancy (random shouts or cries heard in crowds or at night) and my personal favourite, chresmomancy (the ravings of lunatics).

Astrology

Although these days it's used for analysing individual personalities and destiny, in ancient times astrology was only used to ascertain the destiny of nations and VIPs, like kings.

Again, astrology is a complex art that requires considerable study and you could dedicate your entire lifetime to its practice.

Cartomancy

Card reading, or cartomancy, using an ordinary playing deck or a tarot deck is an art all on its own and requires specialist knowledge. There are plenty of books available.

Drymimancy

Drymimancy is divination through liquid splashes. This would include driromancy, reading the future in the pattern of dripping blood, uromancy (urine) or scatomancy (excrement), although if you want to see the future in faeces you usually looked at animal droppings (copromancy). The Greeks refined this idea even further with stercomancy, the examination of seeds in bird droppings. And although there is no record of it there could be emetomancy (the pattern of a splash of vomit).

Extispicy

Extispicy, for example, is the practice of using animal entrails to look into the future. This usually involves killing the animal, often an ox, cow, goat, ram or sheep in a blood sacrifice to the deity of choice. The animal should be healthy and free of blemishes. Favourite organs to examine were the intestines, lungs, heart or liver, in which case the practice is called haruspicy. The practice goes back at least to 2000 BCE. It's very difficult to do haruspicy any more because not only is it messy, but a good haruspex is very hard to find nowadays.

i ching

The Chinese have used the *I Ching* (*Book of Changes*) for centuries. It's very easy to consult, the easiest method involves tossing three coins six times and coming up with a pattern called a hexagram. The hexagram has a specific number of meanings that you can use to determine the future. A good copy of the *I Ching* is easily available, but interpretation can be difficult for the novice because the *I Ching* has an unusual way of using language. Once you grow used to the terminology, it's much easier to access.

oneiromancy

Of all the methods of divination available, the one that has the most ancient origin is probably this one—divination by dreams. It requires no props, no system and no rituals. All you need is a capacity to sleep, dream, remember and interpret.

Everybody dreams—even people who say they don't actually do—they just don't remember them. The easiest way to train yourself to remember your dreams is to have a notepad and pen on your bedside table and write down whatever you remember, as soon as you wake up. You have to be quick at first, because dreams fade quickly when you're a novice oneiromancer.

Dream interpretation has a long tradition. In the *Bible*, Joseph famously received a 'get out of jail free' card and a plumb job in the Egyptian government on account of his capacity to interpret dreams. Dream dictionaries have always been popular, and it's fun to leaf through them to see if you can find an answer to what these vague, fragmented and frequently weird night visions mean. The ancient Greeks even isolated sick people in caves and encouraged them to sleep, believing that the gods would send them healing dreams.

The modern viewpoint about dream interpretation, influenced by psychoanalysis, is that dream images are so highly personal, so idiosyncratic that the best possible interpreter for your dreams is you.

Having said that though, there is the Jungian idea that there is such a thing as a collective unconscious available to all. The images in this unconscious are universal, part of the inseparable fabric of being human, and that these images go right back to the earliest awakenings of consciousness in humans—hundreds of thousands, perhaps millions of years old.

pallomancy

Divining the future by pendulum. Many people swear by this method and it's very simple.

Take any object that you can suspend by a thread. Then hold the thread between thumb and forefinger, preferably of the hand that you don't normally favour. Let the thread drop around 15 centimetres (6 inches), and hold your hand as still as possible. Seen from above, the pendulum is capable of a variety basic movements:
- up and down, vertically
- side to side, horizontally
- clockwise circles
- anticlockwise circles
- stationary trembling.

These have certain meanings that only you can decide. When you first begin to ask the pendulum, you should ask only for assistance from the highest available entities. Ask the pendulum to show you a 'yes' a 'no' and a 'maybe' for starters. With practice you become better at asking questions that make sense, your intuition improves. You may even be able to feel energy surges for particularly emphatic answers. With time, you can distinguish other movements and discover what they mean.

Pallomancy is highly personal, so the answers are tailor-made for you. It works best if you are honest with yourself and don't try to force an answer. You need to learn to 'step out of the way' and allow answers to come through. If you imagine yourself surrounded by white light while you're asking your questions you'll protect yourself from questionable psychic sources.

psephomancy

This happens when you draw ballots to determine the future. Bingo and lotto evolved from these practises. In Japan you can visit a Shinto temple, pay a fee and a priest will draw out a bamboo stick with a prediction written on it. If you have good luck, you receive the paper equivalent of the blessing. If you have bad luck, you still receive the paper equivalent, but you tie it to a tree in the temple gardens and the tree absorbs your bad luck. Modern rune casting, in as much as you can draw runes from out of a bag, can be considered a form of psephomancy

runes

These were an ancient alphabet of 24 letters used by Germanic peoples throughout northern Europe. The Roman historian Tacitus described the way the ancient Germans consulted their runes in chapter ten of his book *Germania*:

To divination and casting of lots, they pay attention beyond any other people. Their method of casting lots is a simple one: they cut a branch from a fruit-bearing tree and divide it into small pieces which they mark with certain distinctive signs and scatter at random onto a white cloth. Then, the priest of the community if the lots are consulted publicly, or the father of the family if it is done privately, after invoking the gods and with eyes raised to heaven, picks up three pieces, one at a time, and interprets them according to the signs previously marked upon them.

Runes are an easy oracle to use if you have an affinity for them, and there are a number of books and websites devoted to rune lore.

Many cultures have used letters to discover the 'hidden' meanings of things, especially sacred text. The Jewish Kabala tradition teaches that because each letter in the Hebrew alphabet corresponds with a number, every word has a numerical value and that you can gain deeper insights by understanding this. The modern practice of numerology owes a lot to this basic idea that letters equal numbers.

The ancient Chinese would burn the bones of sacrificial animals and study the cracks to see if they resembled characters in their writing systems. Scapulas (shoulder blades) were particularly popular bones for this (in scapulomancy) because they have such a large and conveniently flat surface area. The old Scottish call this practice *slineanached*. If you had a higher budget you could burn tortoiseshell (plastromancy), under the assumption that the more expensive the ingredients, the better the results.

scrying

Scrying has a long pedigree. It's cleaner than many other forms of divination, like entrail reading, but is also suitable for vegetarians. Scrying involves looking into a reflective, luminescent, transparent or translucent object, in the hope of seeing visions. It may also work by distracting the conscious mind and the physical senses, so that the sixth sense can have more freedom to engage. Favourite scrying objects include:

- Crystal (crystallomancy), such as a crystal ball (spheromancy).
- Mirrors, preferably of polished metal like brass or silver if you're a traditionalist (catoptromancy).
- Smoke, rising from a fir(fumomancy).
- Fire itself, as in a hearth fire or even a candle flame (pyromancy).
- Still water in a bowl (hydromancy) or wine in a brass bowl (catobomancy).

The medieval prophet Michel de Nostredame, better known as Nostradamus, used a form of hydromancy to gain his famous prophecies: 'Sitting alone at night in secret study; it is placed on the brass tripod. A slight flame comes out of the emptiness and makes successful that which should not be believed in vain.' The 'it' was a brass or copper bowl filled to the brim with water. Michel would gaze at the water, fall into a trance and start seeing visions.

stichomancy

All literate cultures have practiced this one, the reading of a random line or passage from a book like a dictionary. People think that it's extra significant if you use a holy book, like the *Quran*. Randomly taking a verse out of the *Bible* is known as bibliomancy,

Theomancy

This has always been popular, and involves communion with a god either directly, through ecstatic vision, or through an intermediary, like the Pythias of the Oracle of Delphi, who may have also used daphnomancy (the burning of laurel leaves). Wishing upon a star is related to the idea theomancy, from the days when the stars were gods.

Theromancy

This explores animals and their behaviour. The core belief here is that animals are closer to nature and uncorrupted—they don't have voices of higher logic or reasoning that tell them to ignore instinct. There is considerable anecdotal evidence, and an increasing body of scientific work, that suggest animals have senses and therefore access to information beyond our current range of understanding. Only recently has science discovered that pigeons actually have small 'magnets' in their heads that help them to navigate during their migrations.

The Mabila people have known about animals' skills for a long time and traditionally practise *nggam*, the art of predicting the future through the

behaviour of crabs and spiders. But you could also try skatharomancy (divination by beetle tracks) or arachnomancy (observing the behaviour of spiders).

After the animals are dead you can always practice osteomancy, reading the bones. In many cultures this involves marking the bones and casting them. Dice rolling actually started as a form of osteomancy. Alternatively you get auspicy from birds, which involves reading their entrails, and it's from this practice that we get the word 'auspice', but if you're looking at bird behaviour and what flocks are doing in the sky, that's ornithomancy.

technomancy

The modern world has now devised several forms of technomancy. Videomancy finds prophetic meaning in films, radiomancy in songs playing on the radio. The computer age has given us cybermancy, divining the future by computer oracles. There is even a website that offers you access to other websites at random, and you can play with this idea and see if there are any technosavvy gods or spirits out there who communicate through cyberspace. If it's anyone it's likely to be Saturn, or to give him his Greek name, Chronos, the god of time, whom modern astrology had linked to electronics.

One other bit of technomancy that you can do is to turn on your television set on to a channel where no station is transmitting and gaze at the snow until you see shapes, patterns and visions. Call this electromancy.

In the future we might see whole new technomacies develop and their associated 'mancys'. Imagine 'Robotomancy', foretelling the future by the movement of robots, 'nanomancy', prognostication based on the pattern or nanobots in a Petri dish or even 'hypermancy' based on the patterns you see out of a starship travelling faster than light.

A few more -mancies

As you may have noticed, the technical names for methods of foretelling the future usually end in 'mancy' from the Greek word **manteia** (prophecy). If you didn't already have enough, here are the names of a few more ways of divining the future:

Abacomancy: by patterns in dust or other powders, so there's aleuromancy (flour), halomancy (salt), amathomancy (sand). Or the remnants of fires—spodomancy (soot), ceneromancy (ashes) or even tephromancy (cremation ashes).

Aichmomancy: by sharp objects. You can look into a sword or a knife blade (macharomancy). Try also acultomancy (by the pattern of scattered needles).

Botanomancy: by plants, originally the burning of sage or figs, but could also include anthomancy (flowers), favomancy (the pattern of scattered beans), dendromancy (trees, especially sacred ones like oaks and ash) and fructomancy (fruit).

Demonomancy: by demons, if you can find the right spell of invocation, which is generally hard to do unless you're an experienced magician who has found the right spellbook.

Hagiomancy: by meditating on saints. A related idea is iconomancy (by icons) and archaeomancy (divination by sacred relics).

Hydromancy: by water, called lecanomancy if the water is in a basin. This includes cyclicomancy (swirling water in a cup), bletonomancy (by the patterns in water currents) and hydatomancy (the patterns of rainwater).

Necromancy: by speaking to the dead or even going so far as to animate a corpse, as in voodoo. For this you may or may not have to summon Satan. As always, this involves finding the right invocation.

Pyromancy: by the use of fire, either directly as in lampadomancy (looking into the flame) or by empyromancy, (by the act of burning and the effect of the fire on the burning objects). Also try carromancy (by the shape and flow of melting wax) and cerromancy (by dripping melting wax in water).

Oenomancy: by reading the drips of wine (although conceivably if you drink enough, you'll see more visions than you can handle).

Symbolomancy: by reading signs in things found on the road. Back in the days of horses, carts and dirt roads, some would see signs in the wheel ruts (trochomancy). You can still do the same thing today with tyre tracks.

Tasseomancy: by reading tea leaves and coffee grounds. This is now rare in a world of tea bags and instant coffee, but you can still look into the cup and try to see something in the stain.

witches:
superstition alive
and well

witches: superstition alive and well

Finding out about superstition can be interesting, fun and stimulating, but superstition also has its dark side. It's not all playing with candles and throwing salt over your shoulder. People are tortured and killed because of superstition and it would dishonour the memory of all those victims of fanatics whose power overwhelmed their reason if I didn't at least talk a little about the evil people have done in the name of fighting 'evil'.

I want to talk about witches.

In the year 1080 Pope Gregory VII wrote to King Harold 'the Simpleminded' of Denmark. The gist of what the Pope said to the King was that blaming bad weather, disease and other misfortunes on witches was heresy. Everything that happened was an 'Act of God'. Blaming afflictions on supposed acts of witchcraft did nothing but persecute and scapegoat innocent people—that punishing witches and sorcerers with torture and unpleasant forms of execution would do nothing but offend God and bring more of his wrath down upon mankind.

Considering the church's later history of persecution, both by Catholics and later Protestant offshoots, Gregory's statement is incredible. It seems that later generations completely ignored the proclamations of this enlightened pope and his logical and reasonable argument.

However, if anyone had remembered what the Pope Gregory had said, it wouldn't have mattered anyway. Back in the Middle Ages, women were actually the property of their fathers and later their husbands. They were usually powerless. The few women with power were aristocracy, wealthier prioresses, or, on the margins, witches. Given that women had few means of gaining power without being attached to a man, it was natural for women to resort to magic. The study of the 'old arts' was usually passed down from mother to daughter. It was common to have a midwife in the village—it was common to have a healer. She was a valued, honoured and respected person. It was a privilege to be chosen to be such a woman's understudy. They looked after the sick and the ageing—at least until the church came along. Organised religion started to say that women are evil. Twisting logic to justify their own misogyny, priests declared that their god was the healer and was male in form, so all god-mediated healing had to happen through his male servants.

Suddenly these skilled women weren't allowed to practice their art, because their skill and powers supposedly came from the Devil. If the priests failed to heal someone, it was because the victim was a sinner. If women succeeded in curing someone, they were thwarting God's plan through their pact with the Devil. Because women were mostly powerless anyway, these healers couldn't fight back and became scapegoats for everything that went wrong.

Those accused of witchcraft had little chance of escaping—less if you were a woman and none at all if you had no man to stand up for you. If you wanted to get rid of someone you could simply accuse them of being a witch. In many places, if they were found guilty, you were given their property.

So heaven help a woman if she were rich and independent. That's what happened in Salem, Massachusetts. There was a woman who became a widow but also rich with inherited land—that was bad enough—but what really clinched it for her was that she refused to wear black. She refused to follow society's expectations of her and she was *still* successful. To her fellow villagers, that meant she must have had a pact with the Devil.

Most of the hundreds of thousands killed for being witches were ordinary 'God-fearing' women, just trying to live their lives in peace. However, when their accusers used the iron maiden, thumbscrews and the rack to question these women, it's no surprise that they would admit to anything. It was the classic double bind—either way, you lose.

One of the common 'tests' for witchcraft was to throw the suspected witch into a river—a symbolic act that incorporates the idea of baptism. If the water 'accepted' the witch, she drowned. If she floated, the water was 'rejecting' her and that meant she had to be a witch and would be burned at the stake.

Salem, Massachusettes cathedral. Salem was home to the Salem Witch Trials of 1692.

The last execution of anyone connected to witchcraft in Europe occurred in Switzerland, after the trial of Anna Goldi in 1782. According to Ronald Hutton, author of an unpublished essay called *Counting the Witch Hunt*, estimates for European witch executions during the period from 1400 to 1800 are as follows:

Country	Recorded	Estimated
America	36	35–37
Austria	Unknown	1500–3000
Belgium	Unknown	250
Bohemia (modern Czech Republic)	Unknown	1000–2000
Channel Islands	66	66–80
Denmark	Unknown	1000
England	228	300–1000
Estonia	65	100
Finland	115	115
France	775	5000–6000
Germany	8188	17,324–26,000
Hungary	449	800
Iceland	22	22
Ireland	4	4–10
Italy	95	800
Latvia	Unknown	100
Luxembourg	358	355–358
Netherlands	203	203–238
Norway	280	350
Poland	Unknown	1000–5000
Portugal	7	7
Russia	10	10
Scotland	599	1100–2000
Spain	6	40–50
Sweden	Unknown	200–250
Switzerland	1039	4000–5000
Grand total	12,545	35,184–63,850

One should note that Hutton's numbers are only one estimate. Other scholars have estimated higher and lower numbers, but given the general lack of basic record keeping about such matters and problems about what's official or not official it would not be unreasonable to assume that historically and throughout the world there could be many more than two million people who have died or been killed under various pretexts of 'witchery'.

The unrecorded estimate, allowing for loss and corruption of records over time, is over 60,000, and some scholars believe the number may be much higher. Let's not even count the number of people who have died as human sacrifices to gods or the millions who have died in religiously inspired or condoned wars.

witches today

In the Introduction to this book I mentioned that some superstitions are the remnants of dead religion and half-forgotten folk beliefs. However, even if the religions that gave rise to them are dead, it doesn't mean that the superstitions themselves are. Some of them still have a lot of life in them.

If you thought all this talk about witchcraft is in the past, consider the following case. Here's a law from the Victorian books:

Section 13 of the Vagrancy Act 1958 that is entitled Fortune Telling and Pretending to Exercise Witchcraft, etc: Any person who pretends or professes to tell fortunes or uses any subtle craft means or device by palmistry or otherwise to defraud or impose on any other person or pretends to exercise or use any kind of witchcraft sorcery enchantment or conjuration or pretends from his skill or knowledge in any occult or crafty science to discover where or in what manner any goods or chattels stolen or lost may be found shall be guilty of an offence.

This law wasn't repealed until July 2005 and not before a public outcry resulting from an event that occurred in 2003.

In 2003 Olivia Watts tried unsuccessfully to run for a seat on the council of Casey,

Victoria, where witchcraft was still technically, though unconstitutionally, illegal. Later she featured in an article (about the repeal of this law) in which she was described as a witch. As a result of this, a councillor of Casey issued a press release from which I quote:

"CR Rob Wilson is concerned that a satanic cult is trying to attack or take over Casey Council. The public revelation that one the recent candidates for the City of Casey elections, Olivia Watts, formally known as Oliver [sic.] Watts, has declared herself a which [sic.] is a matter of concern for all Casey residents … The recent attacks on Casey Council have all the hallmarks of being linked to the occult and feature links between witchcraft practitioners… Cr Wilson has asked Casey's Church leaders to consider calling a Day of Prayer…"

Olivia Watts started being harassed and physically attacked. Her car and house were vandalised. She took the council and the councillor to court. The issue was finally settled eighteen months later, when Olivia Watts was paid an 'undisclosed sum as an out-of-court settlement.' In the meantime, though, Olivia Watts lost her business and her home as she struggled to pay for her legal fees.

So up until a few years ago, in Australia—a first world, mature, developed economy—a woman was still able to lose her property because of a 'witchcraft trial'.

In less developed countries, including India, the Middle East and Africa, the situation is more grave. Many men, women and children die every year, murdered by fellow countrymen who think that they are witches, for no better reason than something trivial, like having red eyes.

At this point it's impossible to tell how many eccentric or marginalised men and women have suffered and died, and will continue to suffer and die, at the hands of fanatics who have forgotten that even within their own world view that their god is supposed to be omnipotent, that no human power is greater and that no superstition has any power at all, except for the power that we give it.

❧ further reading ❧

I f you haven't found enough to keep your superstitious mind occupied, here are a few more resources to help in your research.

websites

mcclungmuseum.utk.edu/research/renotes/rn-20txt.htm

www.777.com/articles/gambling-superstitions-logic-vs-tradition

www.aclu.org/religion/schools/16295prs20001026.html

www.americangemsociety.org/birthstones.htm

www.baseball.suite101.com/article.cfm/new_york_yankees_retired_numbers

www.bellaonline.com/articles/art17412.asp

www.chinahistoryforum.com/index.php?showtopic=20025

www.cirp.org/library/disease/cancer/vanhowe2006/

www.ldolphin.org/Mast.shtml

www.findyourfate.com/gemology/superstition.htm

www.futurepointindia.com/learn/artofprediction.asp

www.gallowglass.org/jadwiga/pagan/magick_herbs.html

www.geocities.com/mikerdna/newmissal39.html

www.goddess.com.au

www.horoscope.co.uk/chinese_index.htm

www.islam-watch.org/SyedKamranMirza/Superstition.htm

www.jewelrymall.com/birthstones.html

www.jewishaz.com/jewishnews/040528/method.shtml

www.khaleejtimes.com/DisplayArticleNew.asp?xfile=data/subcontinent/2007/
   November/subcontinent_November776.xml&section=subcontinent

www.medicinenet.com/script/main/hp.asp

www.nisu.flinders.edu.au/pubs/reports/2007/injcat105.pdf

www.numerology.googlepages.com/Numerology.htm

www.oldsuperstitions.com/general.html

www.pbs.org/treasuresoftheworld/a_nav/hope_nav/main_hopfrm.html

www.sacredspacesandplaces.com/articles.htm
www.serenapowers.com/chaldean.html
www.sunnyway.com/runes/meanings.html
www.theholidayspot.com/chinese_new_year/zodiacs.htm
www.whimsy.org.uk/superstitions.html
www.woodlands-junior.kent.sch.uk/customs/ascension.htm

books

Ashley, L. and R.N. (1984), *The Complete Book of Superstition, Prophecy and Luck*, Robson Books Ltd, London.

Coombe, E. (2002), *Superstitions*, Landsdowne, Sydney.

Cooper, C. (2004), *Bizarre Superstitions*, PRC, London.

Craughwell, T.J. (2005), *Old Wives' Tales—Fact or Fiction*, Pier Nine, Murdoch Books, Sydney.

Craze, R. (1999), *Collins Gem Feng Shui*, Harper Collins, Glasgow.

Holden, L. (2000), *Encyclopedia of Taboos*, ABC–CLIO, Oxford.

Hopton, A. (1612), *A Concordance of Years*, Oxford.

Joukhador, J., Blaszczynski, A., & Maccallum, F. (2004), 'Superstitious beliefs in gambling among problem and nonproblem gamblers: Preliminary data', *Journal of Gambling Studies*, Vol. 20 (2), pp. 171–180.

Lewin, R.A. (2001), 'More on Merde', *Perspective s in Biology and Medicine*, Vol. 44 (4), pp. 594–607.

McHugh, E. (2005), *Why*, Sterling, New York.

Opie, I. and Tatem, M. (1989), *Oxford Dictionary of Superstitions*, OUP, Oxford.

Porter, T. (2007), *Tarot—The Definitive Guide*, New Holland, Sydney.

acknowledgements

Thanks to David Garland from the Pagan Awareness Network for his input on the history of witches, Alexandra Luxford for her list of Greek superstitions, Eric Hanson for his help and to my mother, Marcelle Waterkeyn for a lifetime's worth of South American superstitions and old wives' tales.

about the author

Before becoming the bestselling author of *Death Row*, *Assassination*, *Celebrity Crime* and *Where's Bin Laden?* (brilliantly illustrated by Daniel Lalic), Xavier Waterkeyn held a variety of dead-end jobs. One of them was as the manager of a psychic centre in The Rocks in Sydney, so he had ample opportunity to hobnob with clairvoyants, tarot readers, palm readers and their clients. This gave him a lot of exposure to all manner of non-conventional ideas and he built up a considerable knowledge of magical lore purely by osmosis. He remains open-minded about the subject, with a general, hard to define 'different strokes for different folks' attitude.

'Half the superstitions, new age thinking and magical traditions in the world are air-headed, made-up claptrap and mumbo-jumbo. The other half offers genuine insights into the way that the human mind functions, the way that the universe really works and reveals vast areas of unexplored human potential,' he says. 'The problem is, I still don't know which half.'

He lives in the Blue Mountains just outside of Sydney and is currently working on his next book.

index

A

actors 114–16
affirmations 246
agalmatomancy 252
agate 172–3
alcohol 44, 111
animals 116–17, 128, 138–55, 246
  Chinese birth years 235–41
anthroposcopy 252–3
aphrodisiacs 80–1, 162
appliances 88

B

babyhood 59–61
beans 101, 161
beds 88–9
birds 142, 143–4, 146, 147, 152, 153, 163
birth 54–5
birth numbers 231
birthday candles 55
birthstones 177–8
bleeding 41
blood 25, 29
bloodstones 176
boils 42, 169
bones 16
books 96
brain 17
bread 101–2
breast milk 33
brooms 89
burns 42

C

candles 96
cartomancy 253
cauls 29–30
cemeteries 76–7
cereals 103
chairs 96
Chaldean numerology grid 233
charms 246–7
Chinese birth years 235–41
Chinese New Year 212–15
chopsticks 103
Christmas 220–1
clitoris 17
clothing 89–90

clover, four-leaf 162
coffee 103
colds 43, 169
colours 63, 128–35, 231
compliments 62
consumption 43
cooking 92
coral 173
corpses 72–3, 76
cramp 43
crossroads 70–1
cutlery 90–1

D

dates 21, 29, 55, 68, 83–4, 94, 102, 109, 139, 190, 192, 202, 245
days of week 21, 27, 28, 54, 103, 116, 119, 122, 193, 231
  unlucky 222–3
death 71–3
diamonds 173–6
dice 251
doctors 116
drymimancy 253

E

ear wax 30
ears 17
Easter 215–16
eggs 103
emeralds 176
envy 62
essential oils 245
evil eye 19–20
evil spirits 198
executions 74
extispicy 253
eyes 18
  sore 48

F

faeces 30, 150
fair weather signs 188–9
fasting 103
feet 28
feng shui 119, 234
fevers 40–1, 169
fingers 22–3
fires and hearths 91–2
fish 146
fishing 116–18
fits 44–5

flowers 85, 115, 133, 162, 163, 165–6, 169 see also plants
foods
  religious practices 103–6
  magical 107
fortune telling 250–9
four-leaf clover 162
friendship 61
frogs 146–7
fruit 100–1, 160, 168, 169, 219
funerals 71–3
future, looking into 250–9

G

gambling 244–8
gemstones for healing 184–5
ghosts 198–200
gifts 61, 85
goitre 46
gold 176
graves 76–7

H

hair 20–1
Halloween 219
hands 22–3
headaches 46
heart 24–5
  animal, of 138
heliotropes 176
herbs 160–2, 163, 165, 166, 167, 169
houses where murder
  committed 201
housewarming 92
housework 92
hubris 62
hunters 120

I

I Ching 254
insects 139–40, 143, 148, 152
iron 179–80
itching 47

J

jade 180
jasper 181
joints 25
juniper 162